MEXICO

MEXICO

From Independence to Revolution
1810–1910

Edited, with commentary, by W. Dirk Raat

University of Nebraska Press
Lincoln and London

TO
C. Gregory Crampton

This work is dedicated to C. Gregory Crampton, Professor of History
Emeritus, University of Utah, where since 1945 he has taught courses
on the history of the American West and Latin America. Mentor and
friend, C. Gregory Crampton taught me Mexican history and showed
me how to love Mexico and the Greater American Southwest.

Copyright © 1982 by the University of Nebraska Press
All rights reserved
Manufactured in the United States of America

First Bison Book Printing: 1982
Most recent printing indicated by the first digit below:
4   5   6   7   8   9   10

Library of Congress Cataloging in Publication Data
Main entry under title:
Mexico, from independence to revolution, 1810–1910.

Bibliography: p.
1. Mexico—History—1810–   . I. Raat, W. Dirk (William Dirk), 1939–
F1231.5.M66   972   81–10503
ISBN 0–8032–3858–4   AACR2
ISBN 0–8032–8904–9 (pbk.)

∞

CONTENTS

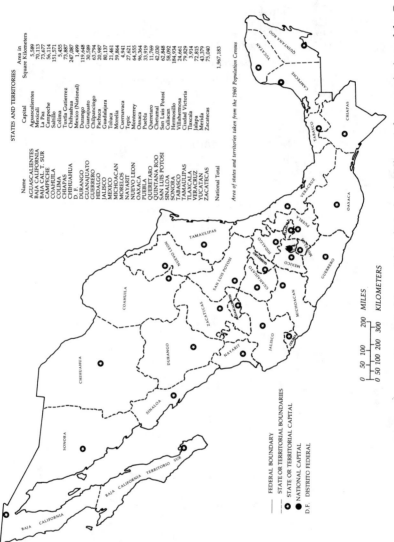

STATES AND TERRITORIES

Name	Capital	Area in Square Kilometers
AGUASCALIENTES	Aguascalientes	5,589
BAJA CALIFORNIA	Mexicali	70,113
BAJA CAL. T. SUR	La Paz	73,677
CAMPECHE	Campeche	56,114
COAHUILA	Saltillo	151,571
COLIMA	Colima	5,455
CHIAPAS	Tuxtla Gutierrez	73,887
CHIHUAHUA	Chihuahua	247,087
D. F.	Mexico (National)	1,499
DURANGO	Durango	119,648
GUANAJUATO	Guanajuato	30,589
GUERRERO	Chilpancingo	63,794
HIDALGO	Pachuca	20,987
JALISCO	Guadalajara	80,137
MEXICO	Toluca	21,461
MICHOACAN	Morelia	59,864
MORELOS	Cuernavaca	4,941
NAYARIT	Tepic	27,621
NUEVO LEON	Monterrey	64,555
OAXACA	Oaxaca	96,364
PUEBLA	Puebla	33,919
QUERETARO	Queretaro	11,769
QUINTANA ROO	Chetumal	42,030
SAN LUIS POTOSI	San Luis Potosi	62,848
SINALOA	Culiacan	58,092
SONORA	Hermosillo	184,934
TABASCO	Villahermosa	24,661
TAMAULIPAS	Ciudad Victoria	79,829
TLAXCALA	Tlaxcala	3,914
VERACRUZ	Jalapa	72,815
YUCATAN	Merida	43,379
ZACATECAS	Zacatecas	75,040
National Total		1,967,183

Area of states and territories taken from the 1960 Population Census

FEDERAL BOUNDARY

STATE OR TERRITORIAL BOUNDARIES

⊕ STATE OR TERRITORIAL CAPITAL

● NATIONAL CAPITAL

D.F. DISTRITO FEDERAL

50 100   200   *MILES*
0   100   200   300   *KILOMETERS*

Map 1. STATES AND TERRITORIES OF MEXICO. Reprinted from *Atlas of Mexico* (1970), p. 4, by permission of the Bureau of Business Research, University of Texas at Austin.

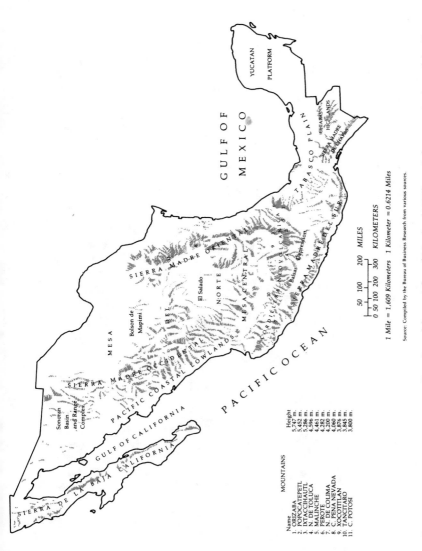

MOUNTAINS

	Name	Height
1.	ORIZABA	5,747 m.
2.	POPOCATEPETL	5,452 m.
3.	IXTACCIHUATL	5,286 m.
4.	N. DE TOLUCA	4,596 m.
5.	MALINCHE	4,461 m.
6.	PEROTE	4,282 m.
7.	N. DE COLIMA	4,200 m.
8.	C. PENA NEVADA	4,060 m.
9.	XOCOTITLAN	3,876 m.
10.	TANCITARO	3,845 m.
11.	C. POTOSI	3,800 m.

1 Mile = 1,609 Kilometers 1 Kilometer = 0.6214 Miles

Source: Compiled by the Bureau of Business Research from various sources.

Map 2. PHYSIOGRAPHY OF MEXICO. Reprinted from *Atlas of Mexico* (1970), p. 5, by permission of the Bureau of Business Research, University of Texas at Austin.

PREFACE

ALTHOUGH THE SEVENTEENTH CENTURY is usually considered the "forgotten century" in Latin American history, it would appear, from the classroom teacher's point of view, that Mexico's nineteenth century has also been neglected, at least by publishers and editors. The paucity of available materials on that period poses a special problem for instructors of introductory courses in Mexican history in which a large number of neophytes approach the blood and fire of an unfamiliar culture without the tools of the language, geography, and history of that culture. Perhaps it is the seemingly senseless anarchy of the nineteenth century which has made the subject matter unappealing, the market small, and, therefore, the publishers scarce. After all, the "ordered" mind of the Anglo expects history to follow a linear trail from the Magna Carta to the Watergate Apartments, and if it cannot always be called progress, it should at least be available in neat four-year pieces called administrations. And again, even within the context of Mexican history, how could poor, hated, misunderstood "Santy Anny" (as his Texas captors called him) hope to compete with the likes of Cortés, Montezuma, Doña Malinche, and Pancho Villa. Whatever the explanation, interpretations and documents of Mexico's Age of caudillos have never been available in English in a one-volume anthology.

The readings in this collection have been organized into four groupings representing major eras in the early national development of Mexico. These are Independence, 1810–24; the Age of Santa Anna, 1824–54; La Reforma and the French Intervention, 1855–76; and the dictatorship of don Porfirio Díaz, 1876–1910, often called the Porfiriato. The first essay in each section is an introduction designed to acquaint the student with general historical themes and problems of interpretation for the period. Each section contains primary as well as

secondary materials. Some of the primary materials consist of impor-
tant political documents like the Plan de Iguala, the Liberal Party
Manifesto of 1906, and Madero's Manifesto of 1910. Other primary
selections are contemporary accounts or descriptions of Mexico.
Examples of this second type include Santa Anna's account of the
Alamo (intentionally included to counterbalance the more prevalent
view espoused by John Wayne enthusiasts), the *Notes* of Benito
Juárez, and the descriptions of Díaz's Mexico by John Kenneth Turner,
Charles M. Flandrau, and Minister of Finance José Ives Limatour. The
latter excerpt appears here in English for the first time.

A wide range of interpretive essays have been included as well.
These are secondary works that represent both traditional and recent
scholarship. Some are considered classics by Mexicanists (scholars
who specialize in Mexican history), such as Lesley Byrd Simpson's
essay "Santa Anna's Leg" and the scholarly article by Wilbert H.
Timmons on the thought of Morelos. Recent trends in scholarship are
reflected by the regional study by William H. Beezley, the intellectual
histories by Charles A. Hale and myself, the Chicano (Mexican American) interpretation by Rodolfo Acuña on the Treaty of Guadalupe
Hidalgo, and the quantitative studies by Richard N. Sinkin and John
Coatsworth.

An important part of this volume consists of the writings of
Mexican politicians, writers, historians, and intellectuals. Nearly
one-third of all the selections were written by Mexicans. Of particular
note are those by Justo Sierra, Octavio Paz, and Daniel Cosío Villegas.
Their writings add an intellectual, philosophical, and sometimes
speculative dimension to this collection. The deeper, less tangible
meanings of Mexican history are explored by both Paz and Sierra as
they inquire into the human consequences of Independence and war
with the United States. The late Professor Cosío Villegas, grand master
of Mexican historians, provides the student with a similar adventure
in coming to terms with the Porfiriato. Whatever the truth, content,
and value of their particular interpretations, all of their writings enable the North American student to understand the perspectives and
feelings of the Mexican from the Mexican intellectual's point of view.

Although most of the selections have been published before, a
good number of them (e.g., Limantour's essay) are either not available
in an English edition or are difficult for the undergraduate student to
obtain. However, if a claim need be made for this reader, it would be

based not so much on originality as on the necessity for a reader which presents the diversity of Mexico's history and its scholarship.

Illustrating that diversity has been a major objective of this editor. Interpretations range from autobiography to political and economic history, from the history of ideas to philosophy and culture. A glimpse of the richness of Mexico's nineteenth-century history can be seen in the several historical themes contained herein: caste warfare, anticlericalism, agrarian reform, foreign intervention, caudillismo, xenophobia, Yankeephobia, economic nationalism, political and economic liberalism, *Hispanidad*, positivism, conservatism, dictatorship, revolts, revolution, social habits, *indigenismo*, education, *mestizaje*, virgin cults, fiestas, and, of course, tragedy. We call it history; we know it as drama.

Yet, along with an awareness of Mexico's unique events and the multiplicity of its history, the reader should attempt to cultivate an understanding of the underlying continuities and developments from era to era. The evolution of intellectual life is one obvious example. Liberalism, inherited from the Spanish past, was given a political and social definition by Morelos as he shaped an ideology for independence. José María Luis Mora, influenced greatly by the utilitarian philosophies of Europe, added to the political definition with his own doctrine of classical economics. This provided the next generation of liberals with an atomistic doctrine with which to attack the Church. Finally, during the days of don Porfirio, when the idea of the positive state was in vogue, liberalism took on an organic dimension that justified and promoted the corporate capitalism of the day. Other historical trends should also be noted, such as the rise of the mestizo as a New World person, the decline of Indian communities, foreign intervention, the evolution of North American influence in Mexico, the rise of caudillos from Hidalgo to Díaz, the continuous struggle between church and state, the evolution of the army, and the "development of underdevelopment," to name only a few. Mexico's history, like most history, is a blending of the unique and the general.

The inspiration for this collection has come from my dissatisfaction, as a teacher, with the limited availability of materials for the nineteenth century. It was especially irritating to me when I saw the abundance of anthologies that were available to my colleagues in United States history. Moreover, in countless conversations over coffee, from Oaxtepec to Santa Monica, I have encountered in my associates similar ideas and frustrations about the teaching of nineteenth-century Mexican history. Their number is far too large for me to mention each of them, but special thanks are due Professors John Hart, William Beezley, Marvin Bernstein, Michael Meyer, Andrés Lira, Peggy Liss, and Sheldon Liss. I also wish to thank Mary Notaro and Mary Ann Burgess for their help in typing this manuscript.

The political and topographical maps of Mexico were reproduced from Michael E. Bonine, et al., *Atlas of Mexico* (Austin: University of Texas Press, Bureau of Business Research, 1970), pp. 4–5.

NOTE ON THE EDITING

In compiling materials for this anthology I have made a concerted effort to retain the content of the original article or document. Therefore, with the exceptions of Readings 10, 14, 22, and 24, all selections have been reproduced in full or, if part of a larger work, in their original form. Editorial deletions that occur in the aforementioned readings are indicated by ellipses. Any other ellipses, such as those found in Reading 4, occur in the original. Any commentary in these notes belongs to the original author or editor and are not mine. These notes have been modified to conform to the style set forth in the University of Chicago's *A Manual of Style* (12th ed., 1969). The titles of some of the readings have been altered to meet the needs of the structure of this anthology. The original titles can be found in the source notes on the opening pages of the essays.

PART I
INDEPENDENCE, 1810–24

ONE OF THE FIRST OVERT ACTS leading to Mexico's independence came in 1808 after the French occupation of Madrid. Peninsular Spaniards (Spaniards from Spain, or *gachupines*) in Mexico, fearful of a government seizure by the creoles, staged a coup d'état that resulted in the removal of the viceroy and the imposition of the aged Pedro de Garibay, a man more in sympathy with peninsular aims. With the *gachupines* having made the first move, the politically active elements of the creole population were scattered into local groups of conspirators, without weapons or authority. From the group in the city of Queretaro there arose a leader by the name of Miguel Hidalgo, a priest from the nearby parish village of Dolores. On September 16, 1810, the cry of revolt was initiated by Hidalgo when he issued his proclamation, the Grito de Dolores to the inhabitants of that village (see Reading 2).

With the capture and execution of Hidalgo in 1811, the leadership of the movement was assumed by José María Morelos. A competent military commander and political organizer, Morelos did not succumb to the pressure of Spanish troops until 1815, when he too was captured and executed (see Reading 3). Between 1815 and 1820 the movement degenerated into sporadic guerrilla activity, with Vicente Guerrero being the most important insurgent. In 1820 conservatives in New Spain chose Agustín de Iturbide, an officer in the royalist army, to maneuver for independence. By 1821, the liberals and the conservatives agreed to join forces for independence by adhering to the Plan de Iguala (see Reading 4). When the fighting was over, Iturbide became emperor of Mexico but was forced in 1823 to abdicate to the liberals, who established a federal republican government.

Mexico's independence movement was distinctive in Latin America. Its leaders were not powerful aristocrats like Simón Bolívar or San Martín, but common curates like Hidalgo and Morelos or lowly mestizos like Guerrero. They did not have the polish of their South American counterparts, but perhaps they were more aware of the needs and problems of the poor. In any case, an important difference between the movement in Mexico and that in South America (with the possible exception of Venezuela) was the social reform and caste warfare which accompanied the political revolt for independence in Mexico. Although the initial victory went to conservative creoles, many mestizos and Indians were politicized in the process (see Readings 1 and 5). With the continuous mixing of the races *(mestizaje)* during the nineteenth century, mestizos like Porfirio Díaz would

3

emerge after the wars of La Reforma to assume positions of power in the army, the Church, and the government. Although the conditions of the Indian would worsen throughout the century, the theme of *indigenismo* was a continuous one which finally erupted in full fury with the zapatista revolt after 1910. Thus the struggle for independence set in motion those forces which eventually led to the revolution of 1910.

Mexico's nineteenth-century heritage was affected in other ways by the events of independence. In addition to winning a military victory over Spain, the creoles had to concern themselves with the problems of organizing a new political order and rebuilding a war-torn economy. Problems of nation building were made all the more difficult by the fact that Mexico was not a well-unified nation, but a loose collection of hamlets and provinces isolated from one another with no transportation or communication links between them (see Reading 1). One of the first attempts at government making came with the Chilpancingo Congress of 1813, which developed a liberal republican form of government for Mexico by 1814. Many of the ideas of the Apatzingán Constitution reflected the hopes and aspirations of Morelos, one of Mexico's first nationalist liberal thinkers (see Reading 3). However, with the restoration of Ferdinand VII to the throne of Spain in 1815, the Morelos revolt came to an end and the constitution never received a fair trial.

After 1821 the creoles argued among themselves concerning Mexico's political future. Simply stated, they divided into liberal and conservative factions, with the liberals favoring republican institutions and federalist formulas while the conservatives advocated constitutional monarchy and a centralist state. The form of government was also an economic issue, since many centralists honestly believed that only a strong national government could promote industry and commerce.

The economic problem was critical. The war had ruined the mines and the fields, and the peninsulars, who had been the main source of capital, had been forced to flee the country. Under Spanish mercantilism, industry had been limited and virtually nonexistent. Had Hidalgo achieved political power, it is possible that the liberals would have implemented a program to promote and protect infant industries (see Reading 2). As it developed, the liberals did not follow the example of Hidalgo, but chose to focus on the Church and the promotion of landholdings, thus leaving to the conservatives the program of industrialization. The conservative program, a type of neomercan-tilism, did not ultimately succeed either. Instead, Mexico exchanged Spanish colonialism for British and later American neocolonialism.

Thus by 1824 Mexico was independent in name only. The Church was a living symbol of the three-hundred-year colonial rule of Spain, and powerful hacendados still controlled the rural districts. The creoles, whether liberal or conservative, were aristocrats who argued among themselves about the form of government but were united in their opposition to the aspirations of mestizos and Indians. Neocolonialism had replaced colonialism. A weak and dependent collection of hamlets, Mexico joined an international community dominated by creditor-industrial nations. Independence was a hazardous path to follow, but the only other trail led back to Spanish colonialism.

MEXICO'S SEVERAL INDEPENDENCES

Víctor Alba

Víctor Alba, a native of Spain and citizen of Mexico, was the founder and editor of the Mexican magazine Panoramas. *He has written several articles for periodicals in Latin America, Europe, and the United States. In this selection Alba suggests that only legal independence occurred in the break with Spain and that Mexico was still socially, economically, and psychologically dependent upon its Spanish past as of 1824. Note also the themes of social revolution, indigenismo, regionalism, and anticlericalism, and how they relate to the problem of social organization.*

MANUAL ABAD Y QUEIPO (1775–1823), Bishop of Michoacán, described New Spain at the beginning of the nineteenth century as follows:

> It is composed . . . of 4 million inhabitants who may be divided into three classes: Spanish, Indian, and half-caste (Negroes and mestizos). The Spaniards comprise a tenth of the total population, and they alone hold almost all the property and wealth of the realm. The other two classes, who make up the other nine-tenths, may be subdivided into thirds: two of mixed breeds and one pure-blooded Indians. The Indians and mixed breeds take care of domestic service, agricultural labor, and ordinary offices of trade, arts, and crafts. That is, they are servants, menials, or day laborers for the first class.

The bishop went on to say that in Mexico there are no shades of difference between the two chief classes: "they are all either rich men or paupers, noblemen or villeins," and this system gives birth to

Reprinted from Víctor Alba, *The Mexicans* (New York: Frederick A. Praeger, 1967), pp. 37–48, by permission of Phaidon Press Limited and Holt, Rinehart and Winston.

"envy, thievery, poor service on the part of the latter; contempt, usury, hardheartedness on the part of the former." He concluded that an agrarian law was needed to enable the Indians, Negroes, and mestizos to acquire property which would encourage them to take an interest in the laws and government. His proposal was to give them the idle, uncultivated lands of the great landholders, and he added that they should not be burdened with tributes; that they should be permitted to hold civil office; that they should have the choice of living wherever they might wish; and that cotton and woolen mills be established.

The critical picture drawn by the bishop notwithstanding, the situation of New Spain was better at the turn of the nineteenth century than it had ever been. Perhaps for this reason, the need for reform was felt all the more keenly. Because some degree of well-being had been achieved, there was leisure for reading and taking to heart the works of the Encyclopedists, Jeremy Bentham, and Benjamin Constant, and the speeches of the new leaders of the fledgling United States.

Only very small groups were affected by the new ideas, however. When Napolean's armies were threatening Spain, New Spain was represented in the Cortes in Madrid by instructed delegates who made almost no mention of social problems. They did, however, offer a petition that "the natives and original peoples of America, Spanish and Indian alike," be granted the same rights as Spaniards in Spain, and that half the public offices be given to American appointees. Miguel Ramos Arizpe (1775–1843) went further; he asked for recognition of the Negroes as citizens with the right to positions and honors, since the Negroes and mestizos paid almost all the taxes and filled almost all the ranks in the army.

On September 16, 1810, a Creole priest in Michoacán, Miguel Hidalgo (1753–1811), proclaimed the independence of New Spain to the cries of: "Long live Mexico!" and "Death to the Gachupines!"; "Long live Ferdinand VII!"; and "Death to the Gachupines!"; "Long live Ferdinand VII!"; and "Death to bad government!" Hidalgo was not a man of doctrine, although he had read the Encyclopedists, and the Indians who followed him (four Indians were among his first followers, and others soon joined them) understood nothing of such matters. But they did understand the Guadalajara Manifesto (December 6, 1810), which proclaimed the abolition of taxes and tributes imposed on the Negroes and mestizos and ordered the emancipation of the slaves and the surrender of lands to Indians and Negroes.

Hidalgo was defeated, captured, tried by the Inquisition, sentenced to death, and executed in 1811. According to the viceroy's propaganda, he was an enemy of property, not a champion of independence. But the social conscience of the man who carried on his work, José María Morelos (1765–1815), was even stronger than his. For Morelos, who continued the struggle until his death four years later, adopted such revolutionary measures as nullifying internal tariffs, dividing up the land, burning official archives, proclaiming the abolition of slavery, and convoking a congress. The congress met in September, 1813, in Chilpancingo, near the Pacific coast, proclaimed Mexico's independence for the second time, and made Morelos head of the independent government. (Like Hidalgo, Morelos was later taken prisoner, tried, and executed.) Meanwhile, Mexican delegates to the Cortes of Cádiz (1810–12) pressed for autonomy, and conservative Spaniards in Mexico deposed their viceroy for being too liberal, replacing him with another, more reactionary one.

A man of action beneath his priestly garb and also more open to ideas than Hidalgo, Morelos drew up several plans for organizing Mexico and sketched out some political programs, or "plans." (Thus, he may have originated the Mexican custom of marking off historical periods according to the plans drawn up during them, each of which carries the name of the town where it was proclaimed.) There is no doubt that Morelos was more perceptive than the lawyers and merchants who made up the congress that ratified Mexico's first constitution on October 22, 1814. This Constitution of Apatzingán, inspired by the liberal Spanish Constitution of Cádiz (1812), did little more than to declare the regime of the craft guilds null and void and demand that property be respected always. The rebels wanted to make changes and to create a new society, but they lacked a clear idea of how to go about it or what it ought to be.

Soon the liberal spirit of Cádiz was to be shattered by Ferdinand VII, the young king whom Napoleon had forced to abdicate (along with his father, Charles IV) and had kept sequestered in Bayonne. For a time, though, it gave courage and hope to the Spanish guerrilla fighters against the French army, and, with the help of the English, the Spaniards forced the French to withdraw from the Peninsula. Meanwhile, the Spaniards in Mexico began to think of separating from Spain—that is, from the liberalism of Cádiz. They did nothing, however, for fear of advancing the cause of Morelos' liberal followers. (One Spaniard, however, Francisco Javier Mina [1789–1817], who had won fame as a guerrilla fighter against Napoleon, came to Mexico following the war in Spain to take his stand beside the rebels. Unfortunately for Mina, there were few bands of active fighters then, and he was taken prisoner and shot.)

After the restoration of Ferdinand VII, in 1814, loyalty reigned once more in Spain and Mexico, for the king was a reactionary. Mexico City, which had been faithful to the crown, was the scene of many Creole conspiracies, most of which were uncovered and crushed without difficulty. The struggle for independence went on, sporadically and diffusely, in remote regions. The army was ineffective because for some time Spain had not been able to send any soldiers to the colonies; hence, the troops were mainly Indians and mestizos, though the officers were Spaniards and Creoles.

These by and large unfocused struggles constituted a real but disguised civil war. Society was divided between liberals and conservatives. In Spain, an army mobilized to be sent to the "Indies" mutinied in 1820. One of the captains, Rafael de Riego, seized command and set up a government which lasted three years, and which restored the Cádiz Constitution of 1812. Thereupon, the reactionaries of Mexico suddenly discovered that they were great Mexican patriots and that they, too, wanted independence. What changed their minds was a suggestion sent by the Spanish king to Viceroy Juan Ruíz de Apodaca suggesting the proclamation of Mexican independence: behind this generosity, apparently, was the intention of making Mexico his own kingdom if he should fail to oust the liberals in the Spanish government. Whether or not this was true, there was a reactionary independence plot that involved the viceroy himself and a clever, cruel, and rapacious soldier named Agustín de Iturbide (1783–1824). The viceroy sent Iturbide to defeat Vicente Guerrero, the last of the rebels of 1810, who continued his resistance from a refuge in the southern mountains. Iturbide opened a parley with Guerrero; they signed a plan (the Iguala Plan) and proclaimed independence on February 24, 1821. The Iguala Plan offered guarantees to everyone— the insurgents, because they had fought for independence; the reactionaries, because their plan offered the Spanish monarchs and infantes the throne of Mexico; the Church, because it proclaimed Catholicism as the state religion. An army was assembled, called the *Trigarante* (roughly, Three-Guarantee), with that Mexican passion for injecting into the language complicated words that would later become accepted usage. A flag with three stripes—green, white, and red—was adopted. The officials sent from Spain deposed the viceroy, but many Creole officials went over to the insurgents.

A new viceroy arrived from Spain. Iturbide went to receive him at Córdoba, conferred with him, and convinced him that he should adopt the Iguala Plan. The Three-Guarantee troops occupied Mexico City. But King Ferdinand refused to ratify the Córdoba agreements. A congress was elected to decide the country's destiny. Iturbide, supported by the Spaniards, succeeded in dominating the congress, which had at first favored a republic, and had himself proclaimed Emperor Agustín I. He made many mistakes and committed many violent deeds, dissolved the congress, and finally abdicated in 1823 when the republicans mutinied. A year later he came back, was captured in the north, and executed at Tamaulipas. His nine-month empire had included Texas and California in the north and territories as far south as Nicaragua, which had voluntarily joined the empire. Later, the countries of Central America withdrew peacefully; those in the north were occupied by the United States at various times and by various means.

Mexico's independence, then, was the achievement of two opposed sectors, each working toward a different immediate objective. One side wanted to separate from a liberal Spain and continue the system without the motherland. The other side wanted separation from Spain too, but it wanted to wipe out the colony and establish a new order—especially a new political order. The Iguala Plan, the base of the transitory alliance of these contradictory elements, declared that "All the inhabitants of New Spain, without any distinction whatsoever between Europeans, Africans, or Indians, are citizens of this monarchy, with the option of choosing any employment which accords with their merits and virtues." To Iturbide, this meant that the status of the Europeans must be guaranteed; to the liberals (the ideologists of independence, the readers of Rousseau), it meant the abolition of slavery—which, in fact, was legally forbidden in 1824, after the downfall of Iturbide—and a consecration of the principle of the equality of all men before the law. In Mexico, however, this was to relegate the Indians to a position of inferiority and leave them without any special protection. Thus the plan as construed favored the *latifundio*, as we shall see later, and inadvertently nourished those things that came to a head in the Revolution of 1910. In this sense, independence carried within it the seeds of revolution to come.

Immediately after the proclamation of the republic, which came soon after Iturbide's downfall, the Mexicans split into two main wings, which were to endure, under other names perhaps, until the Revolution. These were the centralists and the federalists. The centralists of 1824 became the conservatives of a later day; the federalists became the liberals. The centralists wanted to industrialize the country, and they looked toward Europe rather than the United States, which they distrusted. For the most part, they were strong Catholics who relied on the Church and army to provide foundations for the new nation; they won support in Mexico City and the industrial and mining cities surrounding it. One author has compared them to the Hamiltonians of the young United States. If so, the Jeffersonians were the federalists and liberals, the people in the provinces who looked to the United States and distrusted Europe, especially Spain, were opposed to a powerful central government, and favored instead stronger provincial authorities. They hoped to abolish the special jurisdictions and privileges of the Church and the army, whose members were exempted from civil trial. (Priests were tried by ecclesiastical tribunals only, regardless of the civil or criminal charges against them, and the military only by courts-martial.) The liberals were against any type of corporative structure, too; they opposed the guilds, collective property, and, particularly, Church ownership of land. On principle, they were also opposed to the indigenous communes, the *ejidos*, a position that was to bring a train of complications and unfortunate consequences.

During the following quarter-century, the struggle between centralists and federalists over the organization of the state was the hub around which Mexican history revolved. The conflict between conservatives and liberals over the direction in which society ought to move was almost as crucial. Incident and drama attended the conflict: wars, uprisings, dictatorships on the one hand, and study, sacrifice, idealism, and the establishment of industries on the other. Such events seem picturesque now, but they were starkly real to those who lived through them. Here and there distinguished figures stepped forth, some of great stature, others somewhat grotesque.

Mexico was divided into many large segments. In the center was Mexico City, with an agglomeration of wealth around it. Puebla, with its textile mills founded a few years after independence; Guanajuato, Pachuca, and Taxco, with their mines. In the north was the rich Bajío region of fertile lands and dignified cities, rich in architecture and liberalism; along the Gulf, Nuevo León and Monterrey, industrious and orderly; and Veracruz, the port in which the traveler preferred not to linger for fear of the yellow fever. All of forgotten Mexico was compressed into the narrow end of the horn of plenty: the ancient Maya of Yucatán, where the Indians still lived in a state of virtual slavery, despite several rebellions combining social protest and local pride. There the middle class was separatist because it felt that the politicians in Mexico City had abandoned it. The distant coastlands of the Pacific were still in the grip of local petty chieftains. The enormous semidesert of the north was actually controlled by the missions, for Mexico had never succeeded in populating it. In later years, farmers from the eastern United States settled there. As for the virtually independent regions of Sonora, Nayarit, and Chihuahua, where some Indians lived on a subsistence level, no one bothered about them.

During that era of few roads, the geography of the country helped to shape its political institutions. Most communities, whether city or hamlet, were isolated. They had few contacts with the rest of the country; they purchased little and sold little; they were ruled by the *caciques*, the local strong men. More often than not, the *cacique* was a man who had fought for independence with Morelos or one of the lesser *caudillos*, and who kept the spirit of independence alive with the people's help, given largely because he was from their own locality.

The capital and the wealthy cities formed a world apart; they *were* the state; their leading figures were men who had fought against independence for eleven years and accepted it only to appropriate it. Mexico City dealt with the world, that world about which the provinces knew nothing. The people outside this urban enclave identified themselves with their *caciques* because he was a local fellow, and they regarded him as a bulwark against the central government, though in fact he not infrequently played into the hands of the government in order to maintain his control. But the entity that truly constituted an autarky to those who dwelt within it was the hacienda, with its enormous tracts of land, its central cluster of buildings with rampartlike walls, its chapel, its dozens, hundreds, even thousands of families dependent on it. To their owners, who sold the abundant surplus harvests in the cities or the export markets, the haciendas were a part of the market economy. But the peons had nothing to do with this rationale of the hacienda.

On the other hand, the hacienda as an institution set the tone of

Mexico's everyday culture and way of life. Even in the cities, relationships between master and servant tended to preserve its style, and the houses of the very rich were organized like the hacienda household. But on the hacienda, control was tighter. The people had to buy in the hacienda store; they were paid in scrip, and they could not leave the grounds as long as they were in debt to the store, which meant all their lives. The local community was strong and authoritative; the Mexican felt that he was a part of the community—his hacienda, his village, his small city, or his quarter of a big city. As a nation, the Mexicans remained in the hands of an exiguous minority of politicians, intellectuals, and cultured people.

From the time of independence on, the social question was the crucial one. Ultimately, all the political and religious disputes were disguises for the question of how Mexican society was to be organized. The anticlericalism of many rebels such as Fr. Servando Teresa de Mier (1765–1827) and José Joaquín Fernández de Lizardi (1776–1827), a writer and journalist, was but an outward expression of a deep social unrest. Mier constantly demanded freedom of religion and a Church poor in worldly goods. Lizardi was the first man in his country to pin the label of mortmain on the clergy's property, which he said was prejudicial to the nation's progress as long as it lay stagnant and sequestered in the power of the Church. In his opinion, the opposition of the Church to independence could be traced back not to the whim of the bishops or to simple fealty to the crown, but to the fear that the economic privileges of the clergy would vanish in an independent country.

Concern about social issues failed, however, to inspire anything much beyond a certain paternalism in these men. Fr. Servando said, in 1822, as he was addressing the congress: "The great number of feast days must be decreased, for they are extremely harmful to the poor who are forbidden on such days to do the work so necessary to their subsistence." In his outline for a constitution, Mier recognized that "no man has a right over another man, *unless he himself has granted it*. . . ." With those words, he justified the foundation of the hacienda system. In truth, no one dared to probe the problem to its depths.

With independence came a degree of interest in the Mexican economy. In 1823, several deputies proposed the establishment of two weekly university classes in economics, adding a suggestion that "the jargon of scholasticism be dispensed with." No great knowledge of economics was needed, however, to see that hunger for land was keen. Juan Francisco de Azcárate (1790–1831) drew up plans for land settlement in 1822; the following year, the congress ordered a division of the lands in Puebla; in 1827, Lorenzo de Zavala (1788–1836) distributed the land of forty villages; and in 1829, Francisco García (1786–1841), governor of Zacatecas, founded a bank that was instructed to buy land and divide it among those peasants who had none, in a perpetual leasehold. Settlement was encouraged. Practical offers were made, such as those for dividing the lands of the Isthmus of Tehuantepec, where tracts were broken up into three parts: one to be distributed among retired military men and bureaucrats; another to be sold to foreign and national capitalists; and the third to be distributed among the people without land who lived in the region. A few years later, the government offered the farmer who had received land enough credit to pay for moving, tools, and equipment, plus maintenance for a year. The law forbade the accumulation of great tracts of land by a single owner and prohibited the resale to the clergy of lands distributed under it.

During Mexico's long advance toward independence, the country passed through two clearly marked stages. At first, proponents of independence did not deny their colonial past; instead they used it as the basis of their plea for separation from Spain—then without a king, for this was at the time that Charles IV and his son Ferdinand VII had abdicated and were sequestered by Napoleon during the Peninsular War. This left the colonies without the traditional tie that bound them to the monarch's person, and the independence group considered that the absence of a ruler in Madrid nullified the pact between the motherland and the colonies. In the second stage, all things Spanish were abjured and the colonial past along with them. Fr. Servando de Mier in his memoirs accused Spain and all of Europe of feeding off America. But even as the colonials denied the past, they felt a certain nostalgia for their origins, which was sharply accentuated in those who were aware of their status as mestizos. Fr. Servando offered a twofold remedy: an "American constitution" for Mexico and the defense of the Indians. And Morelos proclaimed to the peripatetic congress of the first days of independence: "The twelfth day of August, 1521 [the day when Tenochtitlán surrendered to the Spaniards], was followed by the eighth day of September, 1813 [the day when Congress was convened]." Later he announced: "We are going to re-establish the Mexican Empire." By this he meant the Aztec empire, for the word Mexico derives from *Mexica*, the name given to the Aztecs. Patriots went so far as to propose that an emperor of Indian origin should rule them, their candidate for the throne being a descendant of Moctezuma who belonged to the Spanish aristocracy. Aztec legend was made graphic on the great shield, showing the eagle and the serpent. Thus did the liberals look back on ancient days.

The conservatives did not care for these manifestations of nostalgia; they wanted Mexico to be a continuation of the colony and its institutions. And the small sector of the people concerned with politics, who formed public opinion, favored a union of conservatives and liberals in a common effort to reject their Spanish origin.

In the public mind, then, Mexico was seen as a possibility, but the differences among the political leaders were deep and divisive. Until the Revolution of 1910, the country's political history was a record of the struggle between two concepts: one, that Mexico was still in the making; and the other, that it was whole and complete. The landowning classes, very small in number, were of the first opinion; the bureaucratic and business middle class of the second. Not infrequently, attitudes that seemed proper to one side were adopted by the other. Industrialization, for example, became an obsession with certain conservative politicians, whereas the liberals paid little heed to it. Conversely, a good many cultured landowners dedicated their leisure to study of pre-Cortesian antiquities, while many middle-class intellectuals studied economics. (Throughout the eighteenth century in Spanish America, a scientific movement had been warmly encouraged by Charles III for the purpose of learning more about the geography, botany, topography, and natural resources of the viceroyalties. And many distinguished men of science were studying the Americas when the struggle for independence interrupted their activities.)

Consequently, most of the politicians who emerged with independence were forced to improvise, for their only training had been under the viceroys, where politics did not exist, but only the administration. The influence of the French *Encyclopédie*, Thomas Paine, and the institutions and debates in Philadelphia and Paris lingered vividly in the memory. But each gleaning had to be sifted through a great mass of people with deep religious convictions. Lorenzo de Zavala, a Mexican historian and bold adventurer in politics, described this situation confronting the first politicians in independent Mexico:

There is a constant clash between the doctrines professed, the institutions adopted, the principles being established and the abuses already sanctified, the customs that prevail, and the semifeudal rights that are respected; between national sovereignty, equality of political rights, freedom of the press, popular government and the intervention of armed forces, privileged status, religious intolerance, and the owners of immense territories.

The Iguala Plan, the alliance between the colonialist soldier Iturbide and the rebels who believed they could resuscitate Cuauhtémoc, consecrated Mexico's formal independence. Iturbide's fall established its political independence. But a long road stretched ahead, which had to be traveled before economic and social independence could be reached, until the country could enjoy its wealth, and the voice of the masses could be heard.

THE PARISH PRIEST, MIGUEL HIDALGO

Hugh M. Hamill, Jr.

Hugh Hamill, a professor of Latin American history at the University of Connecticut, specializes in the history of eighteenth- and early nineteenth-century New Spain, and is author and editor of works on psychological warfare and dictatorship in Latin America. In this excerpt from his book The Hidalgo Revolt, *Hamill shows how Hidalgo fostered and promoted the development of several infant industries in the village of Dolores. Hidalgo's program of industrialization was his way of promoting self-reliance and was a modest move away from dependence on Spanish mercantilism. An obvious question that emerges from Hamill's essay is whether a dilettante like Hidalgo (or any dilettante for that matter) could ever be an effective commander and revolutionary.*

In August, 1803, Miguel Hidalgo y Costilla brought his entourage, which included two of his illegitimate daughters, his younger brother, his cousin, and two half sisters, to the town of Dolores southeast of San Felipe in the Bajío. Dolores was a desirable parish. It produced revenues amounting to between eight and nine thousand pesos annually. The town was located on the edge of a fertile plain to the east of the Sierra de Guanajuato. Its population was more than 15,000 when Hidalgo arrived. Baron Humboldt, who was in the vicinity examining the mines of Guanajuato in August and September of 1803, listed Dolores first among the healthy towns of New Spain. He reported that the death-to-birth ratio was 100:253. The naturalist compared this to the Kingdom's average of 100:183 and to that of the United States, 100:201.

The parish of Dolores was a definite improvement for Hidalgo. The larger population and the rich ecclesiastical fees must have appealed to the newly arrived priest. Hidalgo does not seem to have had further serious financial problems, although his "poor economy" and spirit of generosity were immediately apparent. Finding his brother's house not to his liking and noticing that the Dolores Ayuntamiento had no building for its offices, he donated the structure to the regidores. This politic move pleased the town council, but it forced Hidalgo to buy another house with his own money.

Miguel Hidalgo had observed his fiftieth birthday shortly before he came to Dolores. The best description of him after 1803 was provided by a personal acquaintance, Lucas Alamán. "He was of medium height, round shouldered, of dark complexion and lively green eyes, his head drooping slightly over his chest, rather bald and white-haired, as if he were already past sixty, yet vigorous, although neither active nor quick in his movements; of few words in ordinary conversation, yet animated in arguments like a collegian when he was in the heat of any dispute. Conservative in his dress, he wore only what the priests of small villages were accustomed to wear. (This costume was a raglan of black cloth with a round hat and large walking stick, and a suit of knee breeches, waistcoat and jacket of a type of wool which comes from China and is called prunella.)"

Once established in his new parish, Hidalgo commenced a life of intense activity. His official responsibilities were heavy at first, but as he increased the scope of secular activities he gradually delegated parish affairs to the ecclesiastics subordinate to him. Finally he received permission from the new bishop of Michoacán, Marcos de Moriana y Zafrilla, to turn over the religious tasks of the parish to one of his vicars, Francisco Iglesias. That Hidalgo continued, however, to supervise the parish is indicated by his report on the conditions of the congregation of Dolores in 1809. He also retained the respect of the diocesan officials for his scholarly judgment. In 1804 the secretary of the bishopric asked Hidalgo to examine the *Bachiller* José María Centeno to see if he was equipped to become a preacher and confessor. Hidalgo questioned Centeno in ethics and Latin and "found him well informed." Despite equal division of his share of the church revenues with Iglesias, Hidalgo received a sufficient amount of money to carry out his own enterprises. He lost interest in the distant hacienda of

Xaripeo. The property was rented to one Luis Gonzaga Correa, so that Hidalgo might be free from the responsibility which it had entailed.

The life Hidalgo led in Dolores was similar to that he had enjoyed in San Felipe. Tertulias, dances, games, and excursions to the countryside with music at every possible occasion were all part of his routine, although there were some differences. In San Felipe, Hidalgo had devoted himself to humanistic studies and sought to share this learning among his friends and parishioners. However, these endeavors were somewhat overshadowed by a search for diversion and frivolous amusement. In Dolores, there was an alteration of his intellectual focus and degree of seriousness. Lighthearted entertainment continued, but inroads in the gay festivities occurred.

The groups which gathered for discussion of important events and ideas revealed a significant shift in their composition and in the topics which were introduced. The people who came to Hidalgo's house for the tertulias might with more reason than in San Felipe have caused his establishment to be called "Francia Chiquita." As we have observed, the parish house in San Felipe Torresmochas was called that because of "the equality with which everyone was treated." In Dolores this lack of discrimination was accentuated—more poor Indians and castes gathered in Hidalgo's drawing room with the Spanish and criollo citizens of the town. This may be explained by the practical matters which the curate chose to bring to his friends' attention.

Current events and literary topics were frequently debated, but Hidalgo's orientation grew more scientific as time passed. He was not so interested in literary cultural enlightenment, and was more concerned with the development of social consciousness and economic awareness.

During the seven years in Dolores, Hidalgo dedicated himself to a program of industrialization. Even by 1810 when the machinations of the Querétaro conspiracy were receiving the bulk of his attention, he did not neglect his many enterprises. It is noteworthy that *after* giving the Grito, as he was about to lead his earliest followers out of Dolores to begin his campaign, Hidalgo gave orders to the workers remaining in the pottery plant, silkworm department, and apiary to continue their labors in his absence.

Hidalgo's interest in industries was designed to bring greater economic self-sufficiency to the region of Dolores. He probably believed that the traditional Spanish policies of mercantilism, coupled with Bourbon vacillation about encouraging colonial industries, kept

New Spain a raw-material- and bullion-producing colony and a market for peninsular exports. Because the colonists were frequently prohibited or discouraged from the production of many commodities, it was difficult to improve the national economy and promote greater material self-reliance. The preeminence of the mining industry, an inefficient agricultural system, and the government monopolies did not stimulate the most healthy economic life. Hidalgo was by no means alone in his endeavor to encourage native industry. Such high ranking officials of Church and State as Abad y Queipo and Viceroy Revillagigedo, both of whom were peninsulares, took an active interest in the amelioration of the colonial economy. Their attempts at improvement, however, were frequently ignored or rejected by royal orders. Nevertheless, as has been noted, the relative economic prosperity of the Bajío in which Dolores was located was high compared to other New Spanish regions. However inspired Hidalgo's industrialization program might have been, the regional demand for agricultural and manufactured goods had long been high because of the rich mines in Guanajuato. Dolores was within the ten-league supporting radius of that city.

By study and experiment Hidalgo acquired enough theoretical and practical knowledge to direct the activities of a number of artisans. Many of the gatherings at his house took the form of a night school. In order to carry out his projects, he constructed a rudimentary factory on a lot roughly 200 feet square which belonged to the Church. This was called the *alfarería*, or "pottery works." There were rooms opening onto the large enclosed patio, however, which were used for purposes other than ceramics. Outside the town, on the nearby hacienda of La Erre, Hidalgo planted a large grove of mulberry trees for the nourishment of silkworms. Eighty-four of these trees were still growing in the middle of the nineteenth century.

Hidalgo was willing to underwrite the various infant industries at their inception. He planned to sell the articles and goods which he and his laborers produced, once they had developed satisfactory techniques. This marketing scheme was carried out. Wares from Dolores were sold at fairs and in markets throughout the Bajío.

The manufacture of pottery was the most successful and extensive of his undertakings. The alfarería was well equipped to transform unrefined clay into beautifully decorated bowls, cups, and plates. Alamán spoke in glowing terms of the earthenware from Dolores and described it as being in great demand and more attractive than the

Talavera pottery of Puebla. Hidalgo, as the master craftsman, is described by one of his potters, Pedro José Sotelo. Sotelo, who later fought for Hidalgo's cause, told of the director's experiments with metals and glass to create new colors and types. Hidalgo also fashioned new ceramic designs both on the wheel and in the molds.

Another important activity initiated by the curate was tanning. A collateral descendant of Don Miguel, Sr. Luis Hidalgo, a sculptor in wax living today in Mexico City, told me that the lucrative shoe industry of León, in the State of Guanajuato, traces its origins to the leather curing process developed in Dolores during the first decade of the nineteenth century. Father Hidalgo also established workshops for carpentry, harness making, blacksmithing, and weaving wool. He purchased bees from Havana from which he developed such a surplus of wax- and honey-producing hives by 1808 that he sent a number of them to Correa to care for at Xaripeo.

Hidalgo encouraged two agricultural products which were frowned upon by the royal government: wine and olive oil. The protection of peninsular industries and preservation of their colonial markets determined the restrictions on the American cultivation of vineyards and olive groves. In 1802 following a number of exceptions to this policy, a decree was issued which forbade the establishment of vineyards in the future. Any petition by a citizen to make wine was to be presented to local crown officials. If it was proven that the production of wine was needed in that particular area because of an inadequate supply from Spain, then the merits of the case were to be sent to Madrid for final approval. Hidalgo made a trip to Mexico City to request viceregal sanction for the development of his small vineyard and olive grove. In this enterprise he was supported by his brother Manuel, who had become a lawyer in the Audiencia. The details of his expedition have been but vaguely reported by all authorities, yet it is evident that he received no official support or encouragement. The government, however, was lax in its supervision of the Dolores industries. Although the olive grove was not developed, Hidalgo did continue to produce grapes and make them into wine. Alexander von Humboldt reported that, even though wine could hardly be included in the territorial riches of New Spain, there were some vineyards, including those "near Dolores." One day in January, 1810, Hidalgo, the Intendant Riaño, and Abad y Queipo were dining together in Guanajuato. Hidalgo is reported to have invited these two friends to come to Dolores at harvest time in September so that they could observe the grape-pressing process for his wine industry. The offer was accepted by the two men, but events intervened which brought Hidalgo to call instead on Riaño in a less friendly fashion.

Mention has already been made of the mulberry trees which Hidalgo planted. He apparently tried to establish both the production of raw silk and its manufacture into vendible cloth. This phase of his activities did not receive the same attention as the pottery factory, however. There is no indication that finished silk material played a part in the expanding commerce of Dolores. That some cloth was made is certain, for Hidalgo is known to have given a silk robe to the wife of his brother Manuel and to have made a cassock for himself out of the same material. The sericulture project is nonetheless important, for it reflects one of the few active attempts to revive the widespread silk production of the sixteenth century.

The Second Conde de Revillagigedo as Viceroy of New Spain (1789–94) attempted to stimulate the culture of raw silk as part of his plan to reinvigorate the colonial economy. He reasoned that if a large amount of the yarn could be produced in Mexico it would provide occupation for thousands and would fill the Spanish weavers' demand which peninsular silk raisers were unable to supply. Therefore, in 1790 Revillagigedo began to promote the cultivation of mulberry trees and silkworms. Support from the Throne was slow in coming, however, and despite the encouragement which the Viceroy received from private citizens no one was eager to commit himself financially to an enterprise uncertain of royal sanction. The plans languished amid governmental red tape. All Revillagigedo was able to accomplish was the publication of an instruction booklet on the cultivation of mulberry trees and the care of worms. Silk production was almost nonexistent at the time, and publication of the treatise—more literary than scientific—was scarcely adequate stimulation. A man in Querétaro complained to Revillagigedo in 1794 about the apathetic royal attitude toward the business. He said that one José Ignacio Rincón had been able to accumulate over 100,000 of the insects in his house as a hobby. Experienced technicians and financial support were necessary, however, to transform this result of "natural curiosity" into the appreciable production of silk yarn.

When the first approval by the Crown of the re-establishment of sericulture in New Spain finally arrived in 1796, it was too late. In spite of Viceroy Branciforte's endeavor to carry out his predecessor's projects, what enthusiasm there once was had waned. The colonial government, committed to promotion by publication of instructions alone, was unable to solicit widespread public investment in trees and worms. The written instruction, even though widely circulated, made no impression on the illiterate Indians. Rather, skilled sericulturists were needed who might demonstrate the techniques and stimulate production by example.

The manual which Revillagigedo sponsored came to Hidalgo's attention. The *Instruction concerning the cultivation of mulberry trees and raising of silkworms* . . . unfortunately devoted 106 of its 132 articles to the planting, pruning, and tending of mulberry groves. (So thorough was the treatment of mulberries that there is one section entitled "How to preserve them from the teeth of cattle.") The silkworm, on the other hand, receives scant attention in ten short articles.

Hidalgo was the type of literate and energetic individual who might have carried out the hopes of Viceroys Revillagigedo and Branciforte. The skill he demonstrated in the pottery works at Dolores could have been used to teach many of his poorer parishioners the intricacies of sericulture. That his efforts were not far-reaching may be due to the inadequate treatment of the silkworm in the *Instrucción*. . . . A more probable explanation of Hidalgo's failure to create a thriving industry was advanced by Abad y Queipo. This was a certain carelessness and lack of organization which Hidalgo demonstrated in this and other enterprises. Abad himself was extremely interested in the silk industry and was busily engaged in planting mulberry trees by the thousands just before the Revolt. Nourishing silkworms was considered a delicate undertaking which required considerable knowledge and patient selection of leaves. According to Alamán, who heard it from the bishop-elect himself, Abad y Queipo once asked his friend Hidalgo what method he had adopted for picking and feeding the mulberry leaves to the silkworms. Hidalgo surprised the prelate by saying that he followed no method whatsoever, but simply tossed any of the leaves which came from the trees to the worms and let them eat whatever they wished.

At Dolores Miguel Hidalgo's orientation was almost entirely secular. He began his day, it is true, by saying Mass. The rest of his daily routine found him with his industrial ventures and his reading. Quite obviously Hidalgo never felt the spiritual call associated with devout and dedicated clergymen. He had not even assumed the full duties of a parish priest until he was almost forty. The basic vow of chastity was apparently never given any consideration. It seems that the priesthood was a sinecure for Hidalgo. For an American criollo he had achieved unusual success as a teacher and college administrator. Only as a priest could he have won high position in the episcopal college of San Nicolás. Later, when he was no longer connected with the administration, his clerical rank provided him with a good annual income. As he grew older, he moved to richer and richer parishes. As long as he performed the minimum duties expected of him, the Church hierarchy had no complaint. He seems to have had no difficulty delegating most of the responsibilities of the church in Dolores. The prestige of his post and his priestly garb were doubtless useful to him in his travels and put him on easy footing with men of importance. During the early part of the Revolt, the fact that he was a representative of the Almighty had a favorable effect in attracting Indians and castes to the insurgent army.

The Dolores industrial experiments were, in part, an outlet for Hidalgo's energies and ambitions that did not find fulfillment in ecclesiastical exercises or the pursuit of pleasure. They were also the result of a sincere concern for the poor people of his parish. Boyhood companionship with the Indians of Corralejo and Tejupilco, the influence of the historian Clavigero's study of pre-Cortesian culture, and the peasants welcomed to the tertulias of "Francia Chiquita"—all testified to Hidalgo's abiding interest in the Indians and castes. The attempts at Dolores to improve their economic welfare, haphazard as they may have been, suggest Hidalgo's real preoccupation with the problems of social inequality and miserable living conditions.

Hidalgo's activities in Dolores were, then, extremely diversified. Pottery, silk growing and weaving, beekeeping, olive oil production, tanning, harness making, smithing, spinning and weaving wool, carpentry, and wine making engaged his attention. Hidalgo stimulated so many industries that it is not surprising that he gave uneven guidance to them. He had an original mind which sought new problems and interests. The enthusiasm he had once shown for theology, philosophy, and the arts became channeled into subjects of a more practical nature. Although he had the ability to reflect and cogitate, he was also impetuous. He became enthusiastic about one project after another. He devoted all his energies to the promotion of idea after idea, but the responsibilities following yesterday's inspiration were frequently neglected in the exhilaration of today's pursuit. What he lacked was a sense of sober organization, long-range planning, and deep submersion into the intricacies and contradictions of any one field. In all the multiple social and intellectual activities of his life, with the exception of theology, Hidalgo was a dilettante. (Perhaps the failure to make a success of his silk industry reflected the same weakness which forced his resignation from San Nicolás.) His notorious financial problems indicated an unwillingness to attend to details, and his generous distribution of houses to needy cabildos showed a disinclination to worry about matters in the future. It will be seen that his boldness and quickness to make decisions stood Hidalgo in good stead as a neophyte general. But his inability to organize a project with great care and deliberation, and his failure to see the implications of his actions, were weaknesses which helped to determine the nature of the Revolt.

THE POLITICAL AND
SOCIAL IDEAS OF MORELOS

Wilbert H. Timmons

*Wilbert H. Timmons, who teaches Latin American history at the University of
Texas at El Paso, is the author of* Morelos of Mexico *and articles on Morelos and the
secret society known as* Los Guadalupes. *This essay, originally entitled "The
Political and Social Ideas of José María Morelos, 1810–1814," was reproduced from*
Essays in Mexican History. *In this essay Timmons traces Morelos's nationalistic
ideas of 1811 to his more mature political thought of 1814. Note how Timmons as a
critical historian deals with his sources in terms of authenticity and credibility (an
activity referred to as external and internal criticism in historiography).*

THE GRITO DE DOLORES, which initiated the long struggle for Mexican
independence, was proclaimed by Miguel Hidalgo in 1810 in the name
of Ferdinand VII, the captive monarch of Spain, as a creole protest
against Spanish officialdom and economic domination. Vaguely conceived, prematurely begun, and poorly organized, the Hidalgo revolt,
though envisaging an autonomous creole kingdom, rapidly evolved
into an Indian rebellion and then degenerated into a race war that
exalted murder, pillage, and plunder. After enjoying some initial
successes, the movement all but collapsed with the capture and
execution of its leader in 1811, and seemingly would have been
stamped out completely within a short time had it not been rescued by
another parish priest-turned-military commander, José María
Morelos, a mestizo.

Reprinted from Wilbert H. Timmons, "The Political and Social Ideas of José María
Morelos, 1810–1814," in *Essays in Mexican History,* ed. Thomas Cotner and Carlos
Castañeda, pp. 72–89, by permission of The University of Texas Press. Copyright © 1958
by the Institute of Latin American Studies, The University of Texas.

Morelos, whose name is frequently cited to designate the so-called second phase of the independence movement, was one of the most remarkable figures in Mexican history. Though lacking Hidalgo's polish and intellectual attainments, Morelos excelled as a military leader and organizer, and as a statesman of great ability and vision, for not only did he provide the revolutionary effort with a much more effective leadership, but he also set forth a clearer conception of its aims. At all times during his spectacular public career his thoughts and actions were motivated by the noblest purposes and highest ideals; and his political and social program, which featured a bold and sensitive nationalism, was a reflection of his deep appreciation and understanding of the aspirations of the Mexican people. He made such a significant contribution to the ideology of the era, that when independence was achieved in 1821 on terms which fell short of what Morelos fought for, his program remained a goal for the Mexican future.

The primary inspiration in the shaping of Morelos' ideas in the earlier stage of the independence movement was its initiator, Miguel Hidalgo. Their relationship began in 1790 at San Nicolás College in Valladolid when for about a year and a half Morelos was enrolled as a student while Hidalgo was the rector. Although there is but little reason to believe that a particularly close association developed at the time, it seems logical to assume that the rector's broad learning and scholarly accomplishments had a profound effect on the impressionable student, and that in all probability the name of Hidalgo might have become one that the young Morelos would not soon forget. At any rate, both left the college in 1792, Hidalgo to take charge of a parish, Morelos to continue his studies elsewhere in preparation for an ecclesiastical career.[1] Apparently, it was the last contact between the two until after the Grito de Dolores in 1810.

Morelos' decision to join the revolution rested basically on an accumulation of grievances against Spanish officials, distrust of Europeans generally, and an acute awareness of the injustices of the Spanish colonial system; but it was the Cura of Dolores, Miguel Hidalgo, who transformed Morelos' resentment into action.[2] He first heard of the Grito de Dolores in early October, 1810, but apparently thought nothing of it until he was ordered to publish in his curacy the ban of excommunication of Hidalgo and his followers. No doubt the name struck a responsive note, for Morelos later declared that the ban against his former rector compelled him to go in search of Hidalgo to obtain more information about it and the movement which he was leading.[3] Morelos therefore left his curacy in pursuit of Hidalgo, overtook him in Valladolid, and accompanied him to Indaparapeo, where the two men held an interview on October 20. Hidalgo declared that he could not understand the meaning of the edict of excommunication inasmuch as Spain was in the hands of the French, and the *peninsulares* in Mexico City were on the point of surrendering the kingdom of New Spain to them, killing the Americans and confiscating their property. Furthermore, Hidalgo explained, according to Morelos, that since the Spanish king was captive in France, the viceroyalty of New Spain was doomed unless all Americans united in its defense, for the rule of the *gachupines* (the Spanish) in Mexico, in conspiracy with the French, might be just as distasteful as French rule in the Peninsula. Morelos replied that he had heard lawyers maintain that a kingdom might be governed by its own inhabitants in case its king was absent; he concluded that he found himself in agreement with Hidalgo's arguments, and therefore he decided to join the revolution because, as Cura Hidalgo, who had been his rector, said, "the cause was just."[4]

For at least a year after Morelos received a commission to spread the revolution southward, his ideas continued to reflect those of Hidalgo. Like his former rector, he viewed the revolt as a movement in defense of king, country, and religion; and though it is possible that he disliked the allegiance to Ferdinand and personally would have preferred repudiating the king altogether, he consented to the use of the king's name in the interest of co-ordinating the aims of the revolution, and publicly declared that the rights of the king should be protected.[5] Yet Morelos condemned the Seville junta, the regency, and the Spanish Cortes as illegitimate creations dominated by Europeans who squandered the money the Americans had contributed to fight the French, and who enacted legislation designed to win favor and support rather than to relieve the oppressed condition of the king's subjects.[6]

The problem of reconciling religion with the revolution might have been a delicate one for a priest, for so closely interwoven were church-state relations that heresy was barely distinguishable from treason. But Morelos, styling himself "an American cura," insisted that he had no quarrel with religion, that the conflict had not been motivated by controversy over dogma or doctrine, and that on the contrary he was fighting in defense of religion in order to protect the purity of the faith against gachupine and French tyranny.[7] No doubt he was bitterly disappointed when Manuel Ignacio Campillo of Puebla, the only creole bishop in New Spain at that time, denounced the rebellion and warned Morelos that he would "ascend an ignominious scaffold."[8] But the insurgent chief refused to compromise or retreat. "Would to God," he replied, "that Your Excellency might take up the pen to defend this war in favor of the Americans. You would undoubtedly find greater justification for it than was the case of the Anglo-Americans or the people of Israel. The justice of our cause is *per se nota.*"[9]

Like Hidalgo, Morelos viewed the revolution as a mighty social upheaval dedicated to the destruction of the power of the gachupines, "the enemies of all mankind," who for three centuries had robbed and enslaved the native population, stifled economic development, squandered the wealth of the kingdom, and violated the sacred beliefs of the people. He insisted that since Spain had fallen to the French, the gachupines in the capital, under the direction of Viceroy Xavier Venegas, were plotting with Napoleon's agents to maintain their control of New Spain.[10] Morelos therefore called for a strong and united effort among the various native-born groups, the elimination of social distinctions within their ranks, and the establishment of a new system "by which all inhabitants except gachupines [would] no longer be designated as Indians, mulattoes, or castes, but all [would be] known as Americans."[11] This bold declaration, set in a strong nationalistic mold, is one of Morelos' most original and basic social concepts.

To the creoles who would support the revolution, Morelos gave his blessing and pledged not only that their property would be protected, but that political power and administrative responsibilities would be placed in their hands.[12] In behalf of the mestizos and Indians, he decreed that slavery, castes, and personal tribute were to be abolished, that debts owed to Europeans were to be repudiated, and that the Indians were to retain the income derived from the lands they worked. Furthermore, Morelos, like his predecessor Hidalgo, to insure Indian support, invoked the name of the Virgin of Guadalupe, the Indians' patron saint, as a rallying cry of the revolution.[13]

So long as Hidalgo was the acknowledged leader of the insurrection, he very largely determined its ideology; but with his passing, new ideas, objectives, and emphases began to emerge, with the result that revolutionary thought entered a new phase in 1812, particularly as the influence of Morelos became more pronounced. With the capture

of Hidalgo in March, 1811, leadership of that aspect of the movement
fell to Ignacio López Rayón, a creole lawyer who had served Hidalgo as
his personal secretary and as secretary of state in the revolutionary
government. He urged the consolidation of authority in a national
junta on the model of the one in the Peninsula, which would govern
New Spain in the name of Ferdinand VII, protect the faith, and
prevent the country from falling into the hands of the French. Various
insurgent chiefs were invited to co-operate with Rayón's plan, and
Morelos promptly replied that he would, but that since he would be
unable to serve as a member, he was designating José Sixto Verduzco
to represent him. Morelos' concluding remark may have come as
something of a surprise to Rayón: "It would be inadvisable to have
more than three members on the junta, because it is not easy to
develop a *republic* with the rule of many."[14]

Subsequently, a junta of three members under the presidency of
Rayón was established at Zitácuaro; and when Morelos significantly
objected to the continued use of the king's name, the junta replied that
it was planning independence but that the allegiance to Ferdinand
was being maintained for reasons of expediency to attract wavering
creoles and others who might be reluctant to rebel against the king.[15]
Morelos then assured them of his support, and though he rejected an
appointment as the junta's fourth member, he voiced his determination to uphold its authority.[16]

In order to give the insurgent government an aspect of legality,
and to regain some prestige for himself after it was so badly shattered
when the viceroy's forces assaulted Zitácuaro Rayón prepared, early
in 1812, a constitution which reflected to a considerable degree the
ideas of Hidalgo. It sought the establishment of an autonomous kingdom, with sovereignty, which emanated from the people, to be exercised in a national junta of five members in the name of Ferdinand VII;
but for the duration of the current conflict, one captain general of the
four in the kingdom (three of them were the junta members; Morelos
was the fourth) was to be chosen by the others to be generalissimo and
was to govern with absolute powers.[17] There does not seem to be
much doubt that Rayón in his efforts to legalize the junta and repair
the damage to his own prestige sought the establishment of a disguised dictatorship for himself.

Rayón's plan of government was submitted to Morelos, who
raised objections on two major points and made a number of sugges-

tions on less important matters. Beginning by asserting that "the mask of independence must be removed now that the fate of Our Ferdinand VII is common knowledge," Morelos insisted that the use of the name of the monarch should be terminated inasmuch as any reference to it was "hypothetical." "There is no reason," he said, "for deceiving the people by doing one thing while pretending something else, that is to say, to fight for independence while supposing that it could be accomplished through Ferdinand VII." Morelos also pointed out that the generalissimo should be chosen on a broader basis and should hold office for life.[18]

Rayón's constitution was never put into effect. For one thing, his influence and prestige during 1812 came to be overshadowed by that of Morelos, whose brilliant military victories attracted considerable attention and support, and whose revolutionary aims stopped nothing short of complete independence from Spain. Apparently by the end of 1811 Morelos had found the justification for such a course, when he declared: "Now there is no Spain because the French control it; there is no Ferdinand VII because either it was his desire to go to France (and in that case we are not obligated to recognize him as king), or he was carried away by force, and now he does not exist. Even though he be living, it is lawful for a conquered kingdom to be reconquered, and for an obedient kingdom to repudiate a king when his laws become oppressive."[19] Furthermore, the liberal constitution of 1812, which had been drafted meanwhile by the Spanish Cortes and proclaimed in effect by Viceroy Venegas, eclipsed Rayón's plan and rendered it obsolete. A typical charter of the era of the French Revolution, the Spanish constitution of 1812 contained numerous provisions designed to curb autocratic power and to guarantee personal rights; but since the document left New Spain in the status of a dependency, Morelos denounced it. "The Cortes of Cadiz," he exclaimed, "has asserted more than once that the Americans were equal to the Europeans, and to appease us they pretend to treat us as brothers; but if they had proceeded with sincerity and good faith, it would follow that at the same time they declared their independence, they should have declared ours; and they should have allowed us to establish our own government as they were allowed to establish theirs."[20]

The Spanish constitution of 1812 had been in effect in New Spain only a short time when writers and editors sympathetic with the insurrection began to take advantage of the grant of freedom of the press to denounce the viceregal government; moreover, those whose views were known to favor independence began winning all the elective offices in the new system of representation. Before the end of 1812, Viceroy Venegas therefore felt constrained to suspend the constitution, an act which the insurgents were quick to condemn as the ultimate in deceit and treachery. They now had sufficient evidence, Morelos asserted, of the duplicity of Spaniards. "They call elections," he exclaimed, "to reveal the electors; they grant the license to print in order to seize the writers."[21] Although Viceroy Félix Calleja permitted a few elections to be held in the early months of 1813, the Spanish constitution of 1812 had practically become a dead letter by that time.

As the nationalism of Morelos' thought became more intense during 1812 and guided his political objectives in the direction of independence, so also did it confirm and strengthen his basic social and religious concepts during that period. He continued to insist that the insurrection, far from being an attack on the sacred faith, was on the contrary a struggle in its behalf; and he warned the Oaxacans that the viceregal government was abusing their Christianity and seeking to make them believe that the rebellion was a religious affair, when actually it was only an unjust determination of the Spanish to maintain their tyranny forever.[22] He encouraged a greater use of the name of the Indians' patron saint, the Virgin of Guadalupe, and directed by decree that a special mass be celebrated in her honor on the twelfth day of each month.[23] Finally, Morelos declared invalid the bans and censures of Bishop Antonio Bergosa y Jordán of Oaxaca against rebel priests and ordered that they be ignored. "We have heard with sadness and regret the censures of the Oaxaca chapter," he said, "but our consciences will remain clear and quiet so long as the defenders and adulators of Spain do not prove that the Mexican insurrection is unjust. Upon the truth or falsity of that proposition depends the validity or nullity of the censures imposed by our bishops."[24]

Again in 1813 Morelos demanded that the Europeans must be excluded from the government, and that the "very beautiful conglomeration of social gradations"—Indian, mulatto, and mestizo—must be abolished, "for all native-born were to be designated Americans," a name "by which we can distinguish ourselves from the Europeans and from the Africans and Asiatics, who inhabit other parts of the world." He insisted that virtue was the only factor which should determine distinctions among men and their usefulness to state and church; he therefore again called for the abolition of slavery and the tribute, the repudiation of debts owed to Europeans, and the restoration of the lands to native-born owners. "All should work in that occupation," he concluded, "which will render a person most useful to the *nation*. By the sweat of our brows we must work so that all of us will have bread. The women should busy themselves in their own honest labors; the priests must take care of souls; the laborers must be employed in agriculture, and the artisans in industry; the remaining men should devote themselves to the army or to the government."[25]

Morelos, in the meantime, had accepted the appointment as a fourth member of Rayón's junta, and since he was desirous of obtaining that body's approval of his political and social ideas, he urged the selection of a fifth member, insisting that a citizen from the province of Oaxaca be named. But Rayón quickly countered with a candidate of his own, thus producing a stalemate, increasing the distrust between the two chiefs, and evoking the charge that Morelos was a despot.[26] To make matters worse, Rayón and his associates began to quarrel among themselves and had to be severely reprimanded by Morelos, who reminded them of the damage they were doing to the insurgent cause. "I will sacrifice myself to obey the Supreme Junta," he wrote, "but I cannot give my support to any one individual in it for the purpose of destroying the others; the result would be the destruction of the entire governmental system. Furthermore, I will never accept a tyrannical government—that is, a monarchy, even though I should be chosen sovereign. It is essential that we rule ourselves by a published constitution so that the provinces will understand that all the rest has been a great mistake."[27]

Although José Murguía, in early 1813, was chosen as a fifth member of the junta by an assembly in Oaxaca, as Morelos had requested, his suggestion that the membership of that body be increased to seven or nine failed to materialize.[28] So intense was Morelos' disgust with the bickering and quarrelsome junta, and so great his desire to establish an effective revolutionary government that would be able to deal with the difficult tasks ahead, that he decided to convoke a new national congress of provincial representatives to meet in Chilpancingo in September. It would replace Rayón's junta as the provisional government, but instead of maintaining the connection with the Spanish monarchy, it would proceed to declare independence and to prepare a republican constitution.

On June 28, 1813, Morelos issued the decree convoking a national congress of deputies chosen by the provinces, to meet in Chilpancingo on September 8 for the purpose of forming the new government.[29] Although he acknowledged Hidalgo as the inspiration for calling such an assembly, considerable credit for translating the idea into action undoubtedly belonged to Carlos María Bustamante, insurgent historian and journalist, who had demonstrated and publicized so effectively the necessity for a new government.[30] Ignacio Rayón, as might be expected, voiced his disapproval of these proceedings, calling them "illegal and immature," but to no avail.[31]

Shortly after his arrival in Chilpancingo, Morelos presented two important documents—the first, his *Reglamento*, or Form of Government, in fifty-nine articles, dated September 11, 1813; and the second, "his Sentiments of the Nation, or Guiding Principles," in twenty-three articles, dated September 14. The two documents together amounted practically to a constitution, and should be regarded in that light.

Making use of the principle of division of powers in the Reglamento, Morelos declared that the executive should be exercised by a generalissimo, elected for life from a list of insurgent generals by a plurality of votes of the army officers holding the rank of colonel or above. His numerous powers included the right to initiate legislation, and to decide what measures could be considered by the legislature. The legislative power was to be vested in a congress, composed of *propietarios* chosen by the provinces and *suplentes* named by Morelos himself for those provinces under royalist control. Members were to serve four-year terms and receive an annual salary. There was to be a president and a vice-president, rotated among the members each four months, and two secretaries, appointed by Morelos for four years. Any member of congress would be permitted to propose projects for consideration, such matters to become law with majority approval. For the time being, the judiciary was to remain in existing tribunals, but as soon as practicable two courts were to be established for handling civil and ecclesiastical cases respectively. Provision was made also for a junta of five elected members to review cases of disloyalty to state or church. Finally, the document called for a declaration of independence without reference to any monarch.[32] The Reglamento was read to those deputies who had assembled in Chilpancingo on

September 13 by Juan Nepumuceno Rosains, acting as Morelos' secretary.

On the following day Rosains read the names of those who were to compose the congress. It appears that Morelos' original intention was for that body to be made up of representatives elected by the provinces, for two of them who were already in Chilpancingo had been selected in that way; but because the arrival of the deputies from the other provinces did not meet with his expectations, he decided to proceed with the formation of the congress without further delay by choosing the other deputies himself. It meant that the provinces would have representation, though not elected representation of their own choice. In the class of propietarios were the members of the Supreme Junta—Ignacio Rayón, José Sixto Verduzco, and José María Liceaga, for Guadalajara, Michoacán, and Guanajuato, respectively— as well as the two elected deputies, José Murguía for Oaxaca, and José Manuel Herrera for Tecpán. Appointed as suplentes were Carlos María Bustamante for Mexico, José María Cos for Vera Cruz, and Andrés Quintana Roo for Puebla.

The charge has been made that since Morelos named all the members himself, with the exception of the two who were elected from Oaxaca and Tecpán, which he controlled, the opportunity to introduce representative government was ruthlessly cast aside by a powerseeking and ambitious military chief for his own purposes at the very time he could have furthered Mexico's political development. That the Congress was Morelos' own creature is undeniable, but his actions must be measured against the backdrop of existing conditions in the country, when even a limited application of democracy could so easily have degenerated into anarchy and chaos. On the contrary, perhaps Morelos should be commended for sponsoring the use of the elective process to the extent that he did. Moreover, it is rather remarkable that Morelos chose to bestow membership on Rayón and his associates, in view of their pettiness and quibbling in the past; but in spite of his gesture toward reconciliation, they continued to insist that the new body was only an extension of the older one.

With the naming of the members completed, Rosains read the "Sentiments of the Nation," a set of principles by which the Congress was to be guided in its labors. After stating that "America is free and independent of Spain and any other nation, government, or monarchy," the document declared that "the Catholic religion shall be the only religion without the toleration of any other, that its ministers shall be supported by the *diezmos* and the first fruits, that the people shall not be compelled to pay any obligation other than devotional contributions and gifts, and that dogma shall be sustained by the church hierarchy." After affirming his belief in popular sovereignty and the principle of separation of powers, Morelos gave expression to his growing nationalist sentiments by declaring that offices should be held exclusively by Americans, that no foreigners should be admitted except artisans who could teach their crafts, that no foreign merchants should be allowed to go into the interior, and that no foreign troops should be permitted on national soil.

Reforms of a social and humanitarian nature included demands for the abolition of torture, slavery, and class distinctions, as well as for legislation in the interest of stimulating patriotism and devotion to duty, curbing poverty and destitution, improving living conditions, and eliminating ignorance and violence. Property must be respected, he insisted, and the home should be considered a shrine. Morelos believed that the war could be financed by import duties, a tax on rents, and careful administration of goods confiscated from the Europeans; he therefore called for the abolition of monopolies, the *alcabala*, and the tribute. Lastly, December 12 was to be celebrated in honor of the Virgin of Guadalupe, and September 16 in commemoration of the beginning of the independence movement.[33]

Did Morelos view the revolution as a struggle of proletarian against proprietor and therefore recommend to the Congress of Chilpancingo policies with a socialist slant, as the distinguished historian Lucas Alamán has charged? The basis for such a contention is an undated document usually referred to as *Medidas políticas*, written by Morelos, published for the first time by Alamán, including the following provisions:

1. All properties of the rich, the nobles, and the high officials, whether creoles or gachupines, will be subject to confiscation, half going to the poor, and half to the insurgent army.

2. The same will apply to church property.

3. Royalist buildings will be burned, and their tobacco crops, mines, and sugar plantations destroyed.

4. All haciendas greater than two leagues will be broken up into smaller plots.[34]

Alamán, however, probably without realizing, used and published an incomplete, abbreviated copy which contained so many omissions and deletions from the true original as to cause serious distortion both in content and meaning.[35] As a result, Mexican writers of every conceivable shade of opinion have used the incomplete Alamán document to support his particular point of view, with the conservatives just as vociferous in their denunciations of Morelos for his socialist tendencies as the radicals have been in their praise for his progressivism.

Close scrutiny of the complete *Medidas políticas*, however, indicates that it was written late in 1812, several months before Morelos had even thought of convoking a congress, and that instead of being a socio-economic program to be presented for congressional consideration, it was a political and military expedient that sought the complete destruction of the viceregal system in New Spain. It should be regarded as a last-ditch and desperate effort to render as useless as possible the means and resources by which the royalists waged war; it was an uncompromising application of the "scorched-earth" technique in a war that remained primarily guerrilla in character from beginning to end. Morelos therefore recommended the seizure of royalist revenues and resources not because he desired to redistribute them to the poor, but because he wanted to deprive the government of using them; and he proposed the division of the haciendas not because he championed agrarian reform, but because he felt that smaller plots would be easier to care for, and would therefore yield more, to the benefit of the revolutionary effort. It will be recalled that Morelos, in the "Sentiments of the Nation," declared that the home was a shrine, and that private property, except that which belonged to the Europeans, should be protected.

The formal opening of the Congress was celebrated with an address delivered by Morelos, but written and sent from Oaxaca by Carlos Bustamante, declaring in part:

> Our enemies have been obliged to reveal to us certain important truths. . . . They are: that sovereignty resides basically in the people, but is transmitted to monarchs; that by their absence, death, or captivity, it devolves once again on the people; that they are free to reorganize their political institutions in any way agreeable to them; and that no people have the right to subjugate another. You, who govern this august assembly, accept the most solemn pledge that we shall die or save this nation. . . . We are going to re-establish the mexican empire and improve the government; we are going to be the spectacle of the cultured nations that will respect us; finally, we are going to be free and independent.[36]

After Verduzco was elected president of the Congress, and Quintana Roo vice-president, it proceeded with the election of the generalissimo, who was to exercise the executive power. That Morelos should receive the unanimous approval of the army officers of the rank of colonel and above and the subsequent approval of Congress came as no great surprise; but being ever sensitive to the charge that he was seeking a military dictatorship, he hesitated, accepting the position only after he had convinced the Congress that he considered the office a responsibility rather than a reward, and after he had rejected the title of "Highness," which the office carried, in favor of the more modest one, "The Servant of the Nation." He thereupon took an oath "to defend at the cost of his life the Catholic religion, the purity of the Most Holy Mary, the rights of the American nation, and to discharge to the best of his ability the office which the nation had conferred on him."[37] Rosains took an oath as secretary to the executive, and the session closed with a solemn Te Deum.

Although a few members such as Ignacio Rayón were slow to arrive in Chilpancingo, it began to appear toward the end of October that the presence of all would soon be forthcoming; the Congress therefore prepared to open for regular business by fixing the hours for meeting and declaring that any individual should feel free to attend the sessions or submit petitions for the consideration of the members.[38] Early in November they took up the proposals outlined in the "Sentiments of the Nation," and decided to discuss first a declaration of independence from Spain. Morelos sounded the battle-cry, exclaiming, "we are free by the grace of God, and we are independent of the arrogance and tyranny of Spain";[39] and Congress followed a few days later on November 6 with its approval of Mexico's first declaration of independence. Its language, written by Carlos Bustamante, is as follows:

The Congress of Anáhuac, legally installed in the city of Chilpancingo of America Septentrional by its provinces, solemnly declares in the presence of God, judge and moderator of dominions, and author of society who creates those dominions and removes them according to the unalterable designs of His disposition, that under the present circumstances in Europe, it has recovered the exercise of its usurped sovereignty; that in view of this [Spain] remains defeated forever and ever, and therefore the dependence on the Spanish throne should be dissolved . . .[40]

After drafting a decree to enlist the support of the Mexican people for independence, the Congress busied itself with the confirmation of

Morelos' social reforms. Thus all race and caste distinctions were swept away in favor of the equalizing term of "American"; the tribute was abolished; the alcabala was reduced; debts owed to Europeans were repudiated; all slaves were liberated; and finally, the Society of Jesus was restored for educating youths in doctrine, and for propagating the faith.[41]

Morelos' work at Chilpancingo marked the high point of his statesmanship, and was important for several reasons: a greater concentration of authority, unity, and political stability was achieved than at any time since the Grito de Dolores; revolutionary objectives were clarified and more specifically defined; and the foundations of the Mexican nation were laid, for with the adoption of the Morelos program by the Congress, there resulted national independence from Spain, a new national government, a new social system based on national rather than class lines, a national army, currency, flag, seal, and symbols, and a religious faith which was universal in scope but national in emphasis.

But if Chilpancingo represented Morelos' political career at its height, it also was a turning point which signified the beginning of his decline. With the defeat of the French and the subsequent liberation of Spain in 1814, royalism and reaction returned to the Peninsula, and troops which formerly had to be used against the French could be released for duty overseas in suppressing the rebellions throughout the Spanish domains. The result was that revolutionary fortunes in Mexico and elsewhere sank to a new low in 1814. Viceroy Félix Calleja, who had the aggressiveness, determination, and ability that his predecessor Venegas lacked, had not been idle in 1813 as Morelos and his army wasted precious time besieging Acapulco. Valladolid and Puruarán, fought late in 1813, were insurgent disasters of such magnitude that the Congress was put to flight, to become from that time on a wandering, itinerant body. It increased its membership to sixteen, and assumed the executive power, which Morelos without protest relinquished in disgrace; and though he was designated deputy from Nuevo León, it was a token appointment that did little to disguise the hard, blunt fact that his star had fallen.

By that time many of the congressional leaders had come to the conclusion that the drafting of a written constitution was an absolute necessity. Not only would it establish a more legal government, lend dignity and prestige to the cause, and facilitate relations with foreign powers, but it might also help to repair damage to the revolutionary movement and revitalize its efforts. Congress therefore announced on June 15, 1814, that a constitution would be forthcoming,[42] Morelos' only comment being that he was not in any position to raise any objections since he had been taught from childhood that "when the master speaks, the servant must keep quiet."[43] About that time, Morelos and the other members retired to Apatzingán, where after four months of labor Mexico's first constitution was completed. It was signed by eleven members of the Congress, including Morelos, and proclaimed on October 22, 1814.

The Constitution of Apatzingán, which set forth a centralized republican form of government in two hundred and forty-two articles, was the product of a vast and varied number of sources, including Spanish colonial law, eighteenth-century French philosophy, the French constitutions of 1791 and 1795, and the Spanish constitution of 1812.[44] Contrary to general impression, Morelos' direct influence on the drafting of the document was slight, perhaps even negligible; only in a negative sense, judging from the fear of militarism and dictatorship evident in the constitution, did Morelos exert influence. On the whole, the framers who attended the meetings were not men of great accomplishment or experience; Carlos Bustamante, Ignacio Rayón, and Andrés Quintana Roo, though absent from the sessions, contributed their views and may have played a greater role in the drafting than any of the other members.[45]

The Constitution of Apatzingán was drawn up in two main parts—Principles, comprising six chapters; and Form of Government, involving twenty-two. It featured popular sovereignty, separation of powers, an article defining the rights and duties of citizens, and one declaring the Roman Catholic to be the sole religion. The legislative power was to be exercised by a congress of delegates elected in an indirect system by Mexico's seventeen provinces. Its power included the appointment of the three-man executive, the judges, generals, and diplomatic representatives, together with the right to issue decrees, and enact tax measures. The executive was to consist of three individuals named by the congress, none of whom would be allowed to exercise military command. Within the judicial system there was to be a *residencia* tribunal of seven members which could try officials in each of the three branches of government.[46]

Morelos never liked the constitution, termed it "impracticable," and declared later that although he did not have time to think about it, he decided to sign it because he believed it the best that could be drafted under the circumstances that existed late in 1814.[47] The document was placed in effect with the Congress composed of about the same personnel as before, and with Morelos, Liceaga, and Cos selected to make up the plural executive; but the Constitution of Apatzingán never received a fair trial, inasmuch as the Congress, hounded by royalist armies during 1815, flitted from place to place without ever finding an opportunity to function.

Finally, it became necessary late in 1815 to transfer the Congress eastward to Tehuacán, not only to escape the menacing forces of Agustín Iturbide, but also to place the insurgent government closer to the eastern seaports where the expected forthcoming assistance from the United States might be received more easily. Morelos was entrusted with the command of the congressional escort, and he was serving in this capacity in November, 1815, when he was captured by a royalist party, though the members of Congress succeeded in effecting their escape. Carried to Mexico City under heavy guard, Morelos was tried for heresy and treason, convicted, and executed by a firing squad. His death was a shocking loss to the revolutionary movement, to be sure, but in actuality it came as an anticlimax after the insurgent disasters of 1814.

Morelos' leadership stands out even more conspicuously when projected against the period of chaos and uncertainty that followed his death. Mexican independence remained an elusive matter for another five years, when finally in 1821 it was accomplished in conjunction with a conservative reaction in Mexico that opposed a liberal uprising in Spain. As a result, the Morelos program was only partially achieved, but the fires of Mexican nationalism that Morelos had lighted and kindled could not be extinguished, and his promises to the Mexican people became their great hope for the future, the goal toward which they have strived and worked from that day to the present.

Emperor Maximilian was one who understood Morelos' place in Mexican history, and on September 30, 1865, in commemoration of the one hundredth anniversary of Morelos' birth, the Emperor paid him the following tribute:

> We celebrate today the memory of a man who was born in obscurity from the lowest ranks of the people, and who occupies today one of the highest and most illustrious places in the glorious history of our country. A representative of the mixed races, . . . he has written his name in golden letters on the pages of immortality. How has he done it? With two

qualities which are virtues of a true citizen: patriotism, and the courage of an indomitable conviction.

He desired the independence of his country; he desired it with the consciousness of the justice of his cause; and God, who helps always those who have faith in their mission, had endowed him with the special qualities of a great leader. We have seen the humble son of the people triumph on the battlefield; we saw him, a poor curate, govern the provinces under his command in the difficult moments of their painful regeneration; we saw him die shedding his blood like a martyr for freedom and independence; but this man will live forever, and the triumph of his principles is the basis of our nationality.[48]

NOTES

1. Nicolás Rangel, ed., "Miguel Hidalgo y Costilla, 1753–1811," *Boletín del Archivo General de la Nación*, 1 (September–October 1930): 29; Julián Bonavit, *Fragmentos de la historia del Colegio Primitivo Nacional de San Nicolás de Hidalgo* (Morelia, Mexico: Talleres de la Escuela industrial militar "Porfirio Díaz," 1910), pp. 48–50.

2. Morelos' revolutionary activities prior to the Grito were of an extremely limited nature and were of no particular significance. He knew of the Valladolid conspiracy of 1809 but took no part in it. That he was connected with the Querétaro activities of 1810 that involved Hidalgo and others continues to be rather widely accepted in Mexican historical writing, though the documentary basis for this thesis was declared a forgery almost fifty years ago by the distinguished Hidalgo scholar, José M. de la Fuente. See his "Un Autógrafo de Hidalgo," *Boletín de la Sociedad de Geografía y Estadística* 3 (1908): 41–53.

3. Declaration of Morelos, Mexico City, 1815, in *Morelos: documentos inéditos y poco conocidos*, ed. Luis Castillo Ledón, 3 vols. (Mexico: Secretaría de Educación Pública, 1927), 2:331–32. The Declaration of Morelos is the testimony he gave before the civil and ecclesiastical authorities in 1815 after his capture; it is a complete narrative of his life and career, recorded by a secretary in the third person. Although it contains a number of inaccuracies and factual errors, it constitutes one of the most valuable sources of information not only for Morelos but for the era in which he lived. Hereafter it will be cited as Declaration of Morelos, *Morelos: documentos*.

4. Ibid., 2:331–32; 3:27, 30–31.

5. Proclamation of Morelos, "Treason of the Europeans Revealed," undated (1811?), *Morelos: documentos*, 1:129, 131, 138.

6. Ibid., pp. 132–33.

7. Proclamation of Morelos, "Copy of a Paper which an American cura sends to his Fellow-citizens," undated (1811?), MS, José María Morelos Papers, 1795–1815, University of Texas Archives, Austin, Texas.

8. Bishop Manuel Campillo to Morelos, 14 November 1811, in *Colección de documentos para la historia de la guerra de independencia de México de 1808 a*

1821, ed. Juan E. Hernández y Dávalos, 6 vols. (Mexico City: J. M. Sandoval, 1877–82), 3:402. Hereafter cited as Hernández y Dávalos, *Documentos*.

9. Morelos to Bishop Manuel Campillo, 24 November 1811, ibid., p. 486.

10. Proclamation of Morelos, "Treason of the Europeans Revealed," undated (1811?), *Morelos: documentos*, 1:128–38.

11. Proclamation of Morelos, Aguacatillo, 17 November 1810, ibid., p. 123.

12. Proclamation of Morelos, "To the Creoles who join the Gachupines," undated (1811?), ibid., pp. 138–39; see also Decree of Morelos, Tecpán, 13 October 1811, Hernández y Dávalos, *Documentos*, 3:402.

13. Proclamation of Morelos, Aguacatillo, 17 November 1810, *Morelos: documentos*, 1:123.

14. Morelos to Rayón, 13 August 1811, ibid., pp. 126–27. The italics are mine. José Sixto Verduzco had been ordained a priest in December 1797, at the same time as Morelos.

15. The Supreme National Junta to Morelos, Zitácuaro, 4 September 1811, Hernández y Dávalos, *Documentos*, 1:874.

16. Morelos to [Rayón?], 23 October 1811, ibid., 3:405.

17. Constitution of Ignacio Rayón, 1812, ibid., 6:200–202.

18. Morelos to Rayón, 2 November 1812, ibid., p. 205; idem to idem, 7 November 1812, ibid., 4:662.

19. Proclamation of Morelos, "To the Creoles who join the Gachupines," (undated, 1811?), *Morelos: documentos*, 1:139.

20. Proclamation of Morelos, "Manifesto to the Inhabitants of Oaxaca," undated (late 1812?), ibid., p. 150.

21. Morelos to Rayón, 15 January 1813, Hernández y Dávalos, *Documentos*, 4:818.

22. Proclamation of Morelos, Oaxaca, 23 December 1812, *Morelos: documentos*, 1:149–50.

23. Proclamation of Morelos, Ometepec, 11 March 1813, ibid., pp. 154–55.

24. Quoted in Mariano Cuevas, *Historia de la iglesia*, 5 vols. (Mexico: vols. 1–3, Antigua Imprenta de Murguía; vols. 4–5, Imprenta Teresita, 1923–32, 5:88–89.

25. Proclamation of Morelos, Oaxaca, 29 January 1813, *Morelos: documentos*, 1:156–57. The italics are mine.

26. Morelos to Rayón, 16 December 1812, Hernández y Dávalos, *Documentos*, 4:690; idem to idem, 31 December 1812, ibid., pp. 760–61; Rayón to Morelos, 16 January 1813, ibid., p. 820.

27. Morelos to Rayón, 29 March 1813, in Antonio Peñafiel, *Ciudades coloniales y capitales de la República Mexicana—Estado de Morelos*, 5 vols. (Mexico: Secretaría de Fomento, 1908–14), 2:117; idem to idem, 31 March 1813, Hernández y Dávalos, *Documentos*, 5:5–6.

28. Morelos to José María Liceaga, 29 March 1813, ibid.

29. Proclamation of Morelos, Acapulco, 28 June 1813, ibid., p. 133.

30. Carlos Bustamante to Morelos, 26 May 1813, ibid., pp. 50–51; see also Alberto María Carreño, "Los primeros pasos hacia la democracia y la inde-

pendecia mexicana (1810–1813)," *Memorias de la Academia Mexicana de la Historia* 3 (January–March 1944): 41–91.

31. Diary of Ignacio Rayón, 5, 11, and 24 July in Ignacio Rayón, *Apuntes para la biografía del Exmo. Sr. Lic. Ignacio Lopéz Rayón* (Mexico 1856), no page numbers.

32. Regalmento of Morelos, Chilpancingo, 11 September 1813, *Morelos: documentos*, 2:165–72.

33. The Sentiments of the Nation, Chilpancingo, 14 September 1813, ibid., pp. 175–77.

34. Lucas Alamán, *Historia de Méjico desde los primeros movimientos que prepararon su independencia en el año de 1808 hasta la época presente*, 5 vols. (Mexico: J. M. Lara, 1849–52), 3:559, 575, and apps., pp. 69–70.

35. Alamán used and published the document which had been printed by a certain Juan Martineña in an incomplete form. Whether Martineña or someone before him made the deletions is not clear; at any rate, the complete document was one of those copied by the royalist secretary, Patricio Humana, in October 1814, and may be found in the Archivo General de la Nación, Sección de Historia, vol. 116. So far as the author has been able to determine, the complete Humana document has been published only in two places—one is in Hernández y Dávalos, *Documentos*, 6:219–21; and the other is in a paperback edition published for popular consumption, entitled *Documentos de la guerra de independencia*, pp. 60–64. All other sources give the abbreviated document which Alamán used, and which Hernández y Dávalos published twice.

36. Discourse of Morelos, Chilpancingo, 14 September 1813, *Morelos: documentos*, 2:177–81. Lucas Alamán *(Historia de Méjico* 3:560) asserts that the following statement was written by Bustamante in the original draft, but was deleted by Morelos: "We are going to prepare the seat which should be occupied by our unfortunate prince, Ferdinand VII, in view of his return from captivity."

37. Session of the Congress, Chilpancingo, 15 September 1813, *Morelos: documentos*, 2:181–88.

38. Decree of Congress, Chilpancingo, 25 October 1813, ibid., p. 193.

39. Proclamation of Morelos, Tlacosautitlán, 2 November 1813, ibid., p. 191.

40. Declaration of Independence, Chilpancingo, 6 November, 1813, Hernández y Dávalos, *Documentos*, 5:214.

41. Alamán, *Historia de Méjico*, 3:571–72; Mariano Cuevas, *Historia de la nación mexicana* (Mexico: Talleres tipográficos model, 1940), pp. 441–42.

42. Manifesto of the Congress, Tiripitío, 15 June 1814, Hernández y Dávalos, *Documentos*, 5:543–44.

43. Morelos to the Congress, 15 June (?) 1814, ibid., p. 544.

44. Manifesto of the Congress, Apatzingán, 23 October 1814, ibid., pp. 721–22.

45. Pedro de Alba and Nicolás Rangel, eds., *Primer centenario de la constitución de 1824* (Mexico: Talleres gráficos "Soria," 1924), pp. 24–27.

46. The Constitution of Apatzingán, 22 October 1814, Hernández y Dávalos, *Documentos*, 5:703–20.

47. Declaration of Morelos, Mexico City, 1815, *Morelos: documentos,* 3:30.
48. Quoted in Alfonso Teja Zabre, *Morelos* (Buenos Aires: Espana-Calpe Argentina, 1946), p. 208.

PLAN DE IGUALA

Agustín de Iturbide

Ironic as history is, the work begun by Hidalgo and Morelos was completed by the conservative officer Agustín de Iturbide, on February 24, 1821, when he issued a plan of independence from Iguala in the southern province of Guerrero. The plan, agreed to by liberals and conservatives alike, was a masterpiece of politics and wisdom. The ideas of independence and of preserving Roman Catholicism appealed to all factions. Article 12 was of special importance since its ambiguous language seemed to declare social equality for mestizos and Indians while guaranteeing existing property relations for creoles and Spaniards.

It is of interest that the plan was issued from Guerrero, one of the more revolutionary provinces in the history of modern Mexico. This was the province where Morelos operated and the site of the Chilpancingo Congress of 1813. It was also in the mountains of this state, along the banks of the Mescala River, that Vicente Guerrero led his ragged, half-starved insurgents during the guerrilla phase of the war for independence. Later, during the Era of Reform, Juan Álvarez would fight Maximilian from here.

AMERICANS, and I include not only those born in America, but also Europeans, Africans, and Asians who reside in America, please hear me. . . . For three hundred years North America has been under the tutelage of the most Catholic and pious, heroic and magnanimous of nations. Spain raised it and made it prosper, creating these rich cities, these beautiful towns, these extensive provinces and realms which will come to occupy an important place in the history of the world. The population and culture of North America have grown, and its natural abundance from the soil, its mineral wealth, and its advantages of

Reprinted by permission from Joseph S. Tulchin, *Problems in Latin American History: The Modern Period* (New York: Harper & Row, 1973), pp. 115–17. Translated from Lucas Alamán, *Historia de Méjico* vol. 5 (Mexico, 1852), app., pp. 8–11, by Charles A. Hale.

climate are well known. Also known are the disadvantages of North America's great distance from the mother country; in reality the branch is now equal to the trunk. It is the universal opinion that there should be complete independence from Spain and all other nations. This is what Europeans think, as well as Americans of every origin.

The very cry that resounded in the town of Dolores in 1810 and which caused such unfortunate disorder, debauchery, and other evils in our fair land, impressed upon people's minds that the general union of Europeans and Americans, Indians and Castes [*indios e indígenas*], is the only solid base on which our common happiness can rest. Can there be any doubt after the horrible experience of so many disasters, that anyone would fail to join the union to achieve such great things? European Spaniards: your country is America because you live in it. In it you have your beloved wives, your fond children, your haciendas, commerce, and possessions. Americans: who among you can say that he is not of Spanish descent? Behold the gentle tie that binds us. Add the other bonds of friendship, of mutual interests, of education, of language, and of similarity of feelings, and you will see that these bonds are so close and so powerful, that all men united in one opinion and one voice will of necessity promote the common welfare of the realm.

The moment has come for you to declare your uniformity of sentiment, and for our union to be the powerful hand that emancipates America without need of outside aid. At the head of a valiant and resolute army, I have declared the independence of North America. She is now free; she is now her own master; she no longer recognizes or depends on Spain, nor on any nation. Let all hail her as independent and let the hearts which uphold this serene expression be valiant and united with the troops that have resolved to die before quitting such a heroic enterprise.

The army is moved only by the desire to preserve the purity of the holy religion that we profess and to promote the common good. The solid bases on which its resolution is founded are as follows:

1. The Roman Catholic Apostolic religion, without toleration of any other.
2. The absolute independence of this kingdom.
3. Monarchical government, tempered by a constitution that is congenial with the country.
4. Ferdinand VII, and if necessary those of his dynasty or of another now reigning, shall be the emperor, so that we may have a ready

monarch and thus prevent pernicious acts of ambition.

5. There shall be a junta, pending the meeting of a Cortes to put this plan into effect.

6. This junta shall call itself the Governing Junta and shall be made up of members already proposed to the Viceroy.

7. It shall govern by virtue of the oath it has given to the King, until he appears in Mexico to receive it personally, at which time all previous commandments shall be suspended.

8. If Ferdinand VII decides not to come to Mexico, the Junta or the Regency shall govern in the name of the nation, until it is determined who should be the crowned head.

9. This government shall be upheld by the Army of the Three Guarantees. . . .

10. All its inhabitants, with no distinctions between them save their merit and virtue, are citizens qualified to choose any occupation whatever.

11. Their persons and properties shall be respected and protected.

12. The property and privileges of the secular and regular clergy shall be preserved.

13. All government departments and all public employees shall remain as they are today. The only employees who shall be removed are those who oppose this plan, and they shall be replaced by those who are most outstanding for their steadfastness, virtue, and merit. . . .

Americans: Here you have the establishment and creation of a new empire. You have the oath sworn by the Army of the Three Guarantees, transmitted to you by him who has the honor of addressing you. You have the objective for which he is urging your collaboration. He asks of you only that which you should ask and desire for yourselves: union, fraternity, order, internal peace, abhorrence of and vigilance against any turbulence. . . . Having no enemies to combat, let us trust in the God of Armies who is also the God of Peace, that making up this combined force of Europeans and Americans, of dissidents and royalists, we serve as mere defenders, simple spectators of the great work that I have sketched for you today, to be finished and perfected by the founding fathers. . . . In your outburst of jubilation, proclaim: Long live the sacred religion that we profess! Long live North America, independent of all nations on the globe! Long live union, maker of the common happiness!

THE MEANING OF
MEXICAN INDEPENDENCE

Octavio Paz

Octavio Paz, born in Mexico City in 1914 and educated at the National University of Mexico, is one of the major poets, writers, and essayists of our time. This selection was taken from his The Labyrinth of Solitude, *which has become a modern classic of critical interpretation. In addition, Paz has written* A la orilla del mundo *and* The Other Mexico: Critique of the Pyramid. *Paz, a career diplomat in the service of the Mexican Ministry of Foreign Affairs, resigned in 1968 as Mexican ambassador to India in protest against the massacre of Mexican students in the plaza of Tlatelolco on October 2, 1968. Note how in this excerpt Paz compares the Mexican experience with that of Spain and the United States, and how, for Paz, the true meaning of independence can only come about through a struggle by the people of Mexico against the "constitutional lie."*

THE REFORMS undertaken by the Bourbon dynasty, especially by Charles III (1759–1788), improved the economy and made business operations more efficient, but they accentuated the centralization of administrative functions and changed New Spain into a true colony, that is, into a territory subject to systematic exploitation and strictly controlled by the center of power. The absolutism of the Austrian house was of a different nature; the colonies were kingdoms possessing a certain autonomy, and the Empire resembled a solar system. New Spain, at least at the beginning, revolved around the Crown like a minor planet, but it shone with its own light, as did the other possessions and kingdoms. The Bourbons transformed New Spain from a vassal kingdom to a mere overseas territory. The creation of the

From Octavio Paz, *The Labyrinth of Solitude*, pp. 117–24. Reprinted by permission of Grove Press, Inc. Copyright © 1961 by Grove Press, Inc.

Intendencias, the impulse given to scientific investigation, the development of humanism, the construction of monumental public
works, even the good government of various Viceroys, were not
enough to reanimate colonial society. The colony, like the metropolis
itself, was now only a form, an empty body. From the end of the
seventeenth century the ties that united Madrid with her possessions
had ceased to be the harmonious ties that bind together a living
organism. The Empire survived due to the perfection and complexity
of its structure, its physical grandeur and its inertia. Due, also, to the
quarrels that divided its rivals. The reforms of Charles III show to what
extent mere political action is insufficient if it is not preceded by a
transformation of the very structure of society and by an examination
of the assumptions on which it is based.

The eighteenth century prepared the way for the Independence
movement. In fact, the science and philosophy of the epoch (in the
scholastic reforms of men like Francisco Javier Clavijero or in the
thought and action of others like Benito Díaz de Gamarra and Antonio
Alzate) were the necessary intellectual antecedents of the *Grito de
Dolores*. But it is forgotten that Independence came when nothing
except inertia joined us to Spain: that terrible inertia of the dying
person who raises his hand and claws at the air, as if to hold on to life
for another moment. But life deserts him, in a last, violent convulsion.
New Spain, insofar as it was a universal creation, insofar as it was a
living order and not a mask, died when faith no longer nourished it.
Sor Juana, incapable of resolving the conflict between her intellectual
curiosity and the religious principles of her epoch in a creative and
organic way, renounced life and died an exemplary death. In a less
exemplary manner colonial society dragged itself through another
century, defending itself with a sterile tenacity.

Independence offers us the same ambiguous image as the Conquest. The accomplishments of Hernán Cortés were preceded by a
political synthesis that had been realized by the Catholic Kings in
Spain and had been at least initiated by the Aztecs in Mesoamerica.
Independence was likewise a phenomenon with a dual significance:
the dismembering of the corpse of imperialism and the birth of a
number of new nations. The Conquest and Independence seem like
moments of flux and reflux in a great historical wave that gathered in
the fifteenth century, flooded over America, attained a brief but
splendid equilibrium in the sixteenth and seventeenth centuries, and
finally receded after collapsing into a thousand fragments.

The philosopher José Gaos justifies this metaphor when he divides modern Hispanic thinking into two parts: that of the peninsula itself, which consists of one long meditation on Spanish decadence, and that of Spanish America, which is less a meditation than a petition in favor of Independence and a search for our true destiny. Spanish thought turns to the past and its own self, in order to investigate the causes of its decadence, or to isolate, among so much that is dead, the still-living elements that give meaning and reality to the fact—strangest of all, perhaps—of being Spanish. In contrast, Spanish American thought begins as a justification of Independence but transforms itself almost immediately into a project: America is not so much a tradition to be carried on as it is a future to be realized. This project and the idea of utopia are inseparable in Spanish-American thinking from the end of the eighteenth century to our own times. Elegy and criticism belong to the peninsula, and are represented by Unamuno, the elegiac poet, and Ortega y Gasset, the philosophical critic, among others.

This dualism is even more perceptible in the South American countries. The personalities of their leaders were less adulterated and their opposition to the Spanish tradition was more radical. Aristocrats, intellectuals and cosmopolitan travelers were not only familiar with the new ideas but also took an active part in the new movements and societies. Miranda participated in the French Revolution and fought at Valmy. Bello lived in London. Bolívar spent his apprentice years in the kind of atmosphere that produces heroes and princes; he was educated from early childhood to liberate and to govern. Our own Independence movement was less brilliant, less rich in ideas and phrases, more rigidly determined by local circumstances. Our leaders—humble priests and obscure captains—did not have a clear conception of what they were attempting to do. On the other hand, they had a greater sense of reality and were better able to hear the coded messages that the people were murmuring to them.

These differences influenced the later history of our countries. The Independence movement in South America began with a continent-wide victory: San Martín liberated half the continent, Bolívar the other half. They created great states and confederations. They thought that emancipation from Spain would not bring about the dismemberment of the Hispanic world. In a short while, however, reality shattered all their projects. The process of disintegration in the Spanish Empire proved stronger than Bolívar's clairvoyance.

In sum, two opposing tendencies struggled within the Independence movement: one, of European origin, liberal and utopian, conceived of Spanish America as a single whole, an assembly of free nations; the other, more traditional, broke the ties with the metropolis only to speed up the fragmentation of the Empire.

Spanish American Independence, like the whole history of our peoples, is difficult to interpret because, once again, ideas disguise reality instead of clarifying or expressing it. The groups and classes that brought about Independence in South America belonged to the native feudal aristocracy. They were descendants of the Spanish colonists, in a situation of inferiority to peninsula Spaniards. The metropolis, carrying out a protectionist policy, hindered the free commerce of the colonies and restricted their economic and social development with administrative and political checks. At the same time, it closed the way to the *criollos* who desired, justly enough, to enter into higher offices and the direction of the state. Thus the struggle for Independence tended to free the *criollos* from the mummified bureaucracy of the peninsula, though actually there was no proposal to change the social structure of the colonies. It is true that the programs and language of the Independence leaders resembled those of the revolutionaries of the epoch, and no doubt they were sincere. That language was "modern," an echo of the French Revolution and, above all, of the ideas behind the North American War of Independence. But in North America those ideas were expressed by groups who proposed a basic transformation of the country in accordance with a new political philosophy. What is more, they did not intend to exchange one state of affairs for another, but instead—and the difference is radical—to create a new nation. In effect, the United States is a novelty in the history of the nineteenth century, a society that grew and expanded naturally. Among ourselves, on the other hand, the ruling classes consolidated themselves, once Independence was achieved, as heirs of the old Spanish order. They broke with Spain but they proved incapable of creating a modern society. It could not have been otherwise, because the groups that headed the Independence movement did not represent new social forces, merely a prolongation of the feudal system. The newness of the new Spanish American nations is deceptive; in reality they were decadent or static societies, fragments and survivals of a shattered whole.

The division of the Spanish Empire into a multitude of republics was carried out by native oligarchies, which favored and even speeded up the process of disintegration. We should also remember the determining influence of many of the revolutionary leaders. Some of them—more fortunate in this than the conquistadors, their historical counterparts—succeeded in taking over the state as if it were medieval booty. The image of the "Spanish American dictator" appeared, in embryo, in that of the "liberator." Thus the new republics were created by the political and military necessities of the moment, not as an expression of a real historical need. "National traits" were formed later, and in many cases they were simply the result of the nationalistic preachments of the various governments. Even now, a century and a half later, no one can explain satisfactorily the "national" differences between Argentinians and Uruguayans, Peruvians and Ecuadorians, Guatemalans and Mexicans. And nothing except the persistence of local oligarchies, supported by North American imperialism, can explain the existence of nine republics in Central America and the Antilles.

Nor is this all. Every one of the new nations, on the day after Independence, had a more or less—almost always less rather than more—liberal and democratic constitution. In Europe and the United States these principles corresponded to historical reality, for they were an expression of the rise of the bourgeoisie, a consequence of the Industrial Revolution and the destruction of the old regime. In Spanish America they merely served as modern trappings for the survivals of the colonial system. This liberal, democratic ideology, far from expressing our concrete historical situation, disguised it, and the political lie established itself almost constitutionally. The moral damage it has caused is incalculable; it has affected profound areas of our existence. We move about in this lie with complete naturalness. For over a hundred years we have suffered from regimes that have been at the service of feudal oligarchies but have utilized the language of freedom. The situation has continued to our own day. Hence the struggle against the official, constitutional lie must be the first step in any serious attempt at reform. This seems to be the import of current Latin-American movements whose common objective is to realize at last the ideals of Independence; that is, to transform our countries into truly modern societies, not mere façades for demagogues and tourists. In this struggle the people must confront not only their old Spanish heritage—the Church, the army and the oligarchy—but also the dictator, the boss, with his mouth full of legal and patriotic formulas, and allied now with a power very different from Spanish imperialism: the vast interests of foreign capitalism.

Almost all of the foregoing is applicable to Mexico, with some decisive exceptions. In the first place, our Revolution of Independence was not characterized by those pretensions of universality that were both the vision and the blindness of Bolívar. Also, the insurgents vacillated between Independence (Morelos) and modern forms of autonomy (Hidalgo). The war began as a protest against the abuses of the metropolis and the Spanish bureaucracy, but it was also, and primarily, a protest against the great native landholders. It was not a rebellion of the local aristocracy against the metropolis but of the people against the former. Therefore the revolutionaries gave greater importance to certain social reforms than to Independence itself: Hidalgo proclaimed the abolition of slavery and Morelos broke up the great estates. The Revolution of Independence was a class war, and its nature cannot be understood correctly unless we recognize the fact that unlike what happened in South America, it was an agrarian revolt in gestation. This is why the army (with its *criollos* like Iturbide), the Church and the great landowners supported the Spanish crown, and these were the forces that defeated Hidalgo, Morelos and Javier Mina. A little later, when the insurgent movement had almost been destroyed, the unexpected occurred: the liberals seized power, transformed the absolute monarchy into a constitutional monarchy, and threatened the privileges of the Church and the aristocracy. A sudden change of allegiance took place: the high clergy, the great landowners, the bureaucracy and the *criollo* military leaders, confronted with this new danger, sought an alliance with the remainder of the insurgents and consummated the Independence. It was a veritable act of prestidigitation: the political separation from the metropolis was brought about in order to defeat the classes that had fought for Independence. The Viceroyalty of New Spain became the Mexican Empire. Iturbide, the former royalist general, became Agustín I. A little later he was overthrown by a rebellion. The era of pronunciamentos had begun.

PART II
THE AGE OF
SANTA ANNA, 1824–54

IN 1823, AT THE AGE OF TWENTY-NINE, Antonio López de Santa Anna (who had recently been passed over for promotion) declared the Plan de San Luis Potosí. The success of this pronunciamiento led to the abdication of Iturbide, the formation of a provisional government, and the eventual establishment of a liberal government under the federalist Constitution of 1824. It was also in 1823 that Stephen F. Austin received his grant to colonize in Texas, thus opening that Mexican province to immigration from the United States. These events, reflecting both domestic and foreign themes in the early modern history of Mexico, were symptomatic of more general conditions that characterized Mexico's age of caudillos from 1824 to 1854.

Santa Anna, the caudillo who predominated during this period, is treated negatively by American and Mexican historians alike. Lesley Byrd Simpson speaks of him as an actor who was vain and incompetent. He coined the term *santanismo* to refer to the corruption, opportunism, cruelty, and other satanic features of Santa Anna's brand of caudillo rule (see Reading 6). On the Mexican side, historian Justo Sierra uses words like *ineptitude, petulance,* and *vain pretense* to describe the character of General Santa Anna (see Reading 10). Yet even these writers speak of his bravery, his energy, his ability as an organizer, and his disdain for death. Moreover, a critical reading of Santa Anna's own testimony reflects these qualities and abilities (see Reading 7).

Santa Anna—maker and unmaker of presidents and dictators, in and out of office eleven times himself, the hero of the battles and wars of Tampico, Zacatecas, the Alamo, the French Pastry War, and Buena Vista—was to many Mexicans a living embodiment of Mexico's nationalistic hopes and fears. In an age of anarchy, his personalistic rule provided a necessary political continuity. With Spanish, French, and North American invaders on all sides, he was the defender of Mexico and an expression of Mexico's realistic fears of the foreigner (see Reading 8). In a way he was Mexico, and just as he defeated himself before general Winfield Scott outside of Mexico City, so did Mexico defeat herself in that war through disunity, mistakes, and disobedience. Whatever the verdict of history, there can be no doubting the role of Santa Anna as a living symbol with which Mexicans could identify. Thus, as Justo Sierra notes, after the defeat of 1836 and the loss of Texas "Mexico raged at Santa Anna as a lover rages at an unfaithful mistress, with whom he is still in love."

57

Without a doubt the most tragic event of the era was the war with the United States over the annexation of Texas. Beginning in 1846, it was concluded with the Treaty of Guadalupe Hidalgo in 1848. For many Americans it was simply another act of providence made manifest, and a profitable one at that. For Mexicans, who have not relegated the conflict to the past, the war left them a beaten, defeated people, bereft of nearly half of their territory. This war, along with other aggressive and imperialistic adventures by the United States against Mexico, has led to the "Colossus of the North" syndrome—a kind of collective inferiority complex combined with hatred of the gringo. And, as Chicano and Mexican-American citizens of the American Southwest can testify, not all of these feelings belong to only those Mexicans on the Mexican side of the border. For the war brought the United States not only additional territory, but also a colony of Mexicans who had been citizens of those conquered and ceded lands: parts or all of the present states of California, Arizona, New Mexico, Nevada, Utah, and Colorado. The legal status and cultural identity of these Mexican Americans is also a heritage of the war with Mexico (see Reading 9).

Yet, even in that age of warfare, pronunciamientos, tumultos, and caudillismo, creole and sometimes mestizo aristocrats were attempting to organize a new society and state. And while the ideas and programs of those politicians and intellectuals were diverse, they can be generally divided into two opposing camps of liberals and conservatives. The leading theoretician of the time was José María Luis Mora, who was an adviser in the cabinet of the radical anticlerical administration of Gómez Farías (1832–34). Mora argued for individual property rights, believing that only the personal and direct interests of the individual can make capital and landed property productive. For these reasons he attacked the corporate tribunals and *fueros* (corporate rights) of the army and the Church. For Mora, corporate power was an obstacle to national growth and economic liberty. In government, Mora advocated a limited form of democracy based upon the federalist principle of shared or divided authority between the central and provincial governments.

Other important liberals include Lorenzo de Zavala, the first vice-president of Texas, who actively sought to realize his federalist principles in conjunction with Sam Houston and other Tejanos; Manuel Crescencio Rejón, who wrote parts of the federalist Constitution of 1824 and was a strong advocate of freedom of the press; and Ignacio

Ramírez, who contributed to the anticlerical and educational parts of the laws of the Reform (see Reading 11). As will be noted, many of these liberal ideas were later incorporated into the Constitution of 1857.

As for the conservatives, their most important spokesman was the historian, statesman, entrepreneur, and *pensador* Lucas Alamán (see Reading 12). He participated in the national administrations of Bustamante (1830) and Santa Anna, at one time serving as minister of foreign relations. As a historian he is best known for his *Historia de Méjico*, which is a conservative, proclerical account of Mexico's history. Conservatives like Alamán tended to be sympathetic to the Spanish past, especially its monarchy and Church, and promoted the idea of corporate wealth in mining, commerce, and industry. Reflecting the vested interests of the hacendados, the Church, and the army, the conservatives were successful in initiating the centralist Constitution of 1836. But by 1854 they had begun to decline in the face of the liberal revolution of Ayutla that sent Santa Anna into his fourth and last exile. The conservative's dream of a strong central government, supported by the Church, and promoting and protecting industrial interests, was defeated by a combination of anticlerical forces within Mexico and foreign (mainly British and North American) free traders outside of Mexico. That defeat came in the bloody three-year war of La Reforma (1858–61) when Santa Anna's antics were finally replaced by the political reforms of Benito Juárez.

SANTA ANNA'S LEG

Lesley Byrd Simpson

Lesley Byrd Simpson is Professor Emeritus of Spanish at the University of California at Berkeley. This essay, takes its title from the escapade of the Pastry War of 1838 in which Santa Anna lost his leg doing battle with the French. Professor Simpson is also the author of The Encomienda in New Spain *and has translated several works, including* Cortes: The Life of the Conqueror by His Secretary *and* Two Novels of Mexico *by Mariano Azuela. A careful reading of this selection should give the reader a feeling for the drama of the era as well as an understanding of the personality of Santa Anna.*

IT IS NOT EASY to follow the thread of reason through the generation following the Independence of Mexico. The loosely cemented strata of colonial society had split apart in the cataclysm of 1810–1821, and their mending is still an uncertain and remote aspiration. The various strata, broadly speaking, may be labeled: conservative (the upper clergy, and the landed and moneyed elements generally); liberal (anticlerical, anti-Spanish, democratic, at least in theory); military (the growing officer caste, mostly Creole, usually running with the conservatives, but likely to favor the winner); and the forgotten Indians, who supplied most of the cannon fodder. It was the beginning of the age of *caudillos*. A caudillo is a military chieftain, like Iturbide, Santa Anna, or Juan Perón (or like a thousand others who will occur to the reader), ruling by force, whatever the pretext. All Spanish America fell into the hands of caudillos a hundred-odd years ago. Most of the "republics," in fact, are still in their hands.

When the old authoritarian system of Spain collapsed, it left no

---

From Lesley Byrd Simpson, *Many Mexicos*, 4th ed., 1969, pp. 230–55. Reprinted by permission of the University of California Press.

body of citizens, in the Peninsula or in America, trained to assume the responsibility of government. If a situation came up in the old régime it was the autocrat's business to meet it. Those outside the bureaucratic hierarchy were supposed to obey and ask no questions. Autocracy was irresponsible and it tended to foster irresponsibility. The so-called ruling class of New Spain was not a ruling class in the sense that it could take over the machinery of government and run it, say, as the upper and middle classes of England did. The wealthy and privileged of New Spain were as irresponsible as the Indians they despised, and, when their wealth and privileges were threatened, they acted like spoiled children and threw things around. It was this recklessness and frivolity that made it impossible to set up a working government after Independence, and that same element continued to overthrow every government that in any way menaced its privileges and comfort. It was a lawless society; it had destroyed law. So it fell an easy prey to the first uniformed brigand who had the power to enforce his will. There were, unfortunately, a great many uniformed and unemployed brigands left over from the late wars, and one had to make the doubtful choice of the least threatening of them.

The more respectable Creoles, as a rule, avoided politics. The type of self-made general with whom they would have to associate filled them with disgust, and they were content to live apart, paying blackmail and extortion, while the country was bled white by its military parasites. (I am referring, of course, to those like Iturbide and Santa Anna, for there were noble exceptions, like the magnanimous Nicolás Bravo, who achieved deserved fame *by refusing to kill his prisoners.*) There is no other explanation for the toleration of *santanismo* (Santa Anna-ism). With a modicum of civic spirit the numerous Creoles could have shaken off their incubus; but the comfortable habits of generations were more precious, and, anyway, a great many of them were in uniform themselves. Life in the capital continued to be as gay and reckless and frivolous as if the massacre at the Alhóndiga had never taken place: cockfights and bullfights and the eternal round of flirting and parading on the boulevards—the amusements of a class that had no useful thing to do.

There were honorable exceptions among them also: men who fought on the conservative or liberal side for a new and finer country, men like Lucas Alamán, Miguel Ramos Arispe, and Valentín Gómez Farías, but the exceptions were too few to alter the picture materially. While Santa Anna's unpaid army was fighting to keep Texas in the

Republic, there was little indication in the capital that Mexico was facing the gravest crisis in her history. That was the generals' business, and what the better people thought of the generals may be gathered from the fact that no great opprobrium attached to Santa Anna for his disgraceful defeat at San Jacinto and his more than disgraceful explanation of it. Generals were expected to lie and steal and betray one another, and sell out to the highest bidder—in a word, santanismo. And santanismo existed because those who might have prevented it did not make the effort. Perhaps the deadliest heritage of Spanish autocracy was the psychology that kept the Creole class in a state of resentful aloofness.

Meanwhile, Mexico lay prostrate, and her body was fought over by uniformed bandits in and out of the government, and by the foreigners who thought to inherit the wealth of the Indies, now that Spain was out of the way. The misery of Mexico under her gay exterior can be imagined, but Creole society carried on. A new upper class appeared, the military, parvenu and jealous of its position, the men overdecorated, the women overdressed. Fanny Calderón was shocked by their vulgarity.

"18th [of January, 1840]," she wrote in her incomparable *Life in Mexico*, "for the last few days our rooms have been filled with visitors, and my eyes are scarcely yet accustomed to the display of diamonds, pearls, silks, satins, blondes, and velvets, in which the ladies have paid their first visits of etiquette . . . The Señora B——a, the wife of a general, extremely rich, and who has the handsomest house in Mexico. Dress of purple velvet, embroidered all over with flowers of white silk; white satin shoes and *bas à jours;* a deep flounce of Mechlin appearing below the velvet dress, which was short. A mantilla of black blonde, fastened by three diamond aigrettes. Diamond earrings of extraordinary size. A diamond necklace of immense value, and beautifully set. A necklace of pear pearls, valued at twenty thousand dollars. A diamond sévigné. A gold chain going three times round the neck, and touching the knees. On every finger two diamond rings, like little watches. . . ."

The political life of the time has the elusive quality of a masque. We read the lines, and they seem to mean something, but they are confusingly remote from the action. The best actor and leading man of the masque was Antonio López de Santa Anna, the incredible Santa Anna, whose first public appearance of importance was at the overthrow of Iturbide. Santa Anna had an uncanny stage sense and could time his entrances and exits to a second. He also knew when to stay in the wings.

Iturbide's fall had left the national affairs in a terrible muddle, and Congress hastily patched up a provisional government, the *Poder Ejecutivo*, which was put into the hands of three tried insurgent generals, Guadalupe Victoria, Nicolás Bravo, and Pedro Negrete. Generals had inherited the "principle of authority." These three men had proved their worth on the battlefield, but civil government was a mystery to them, so they were given a cabinet to administer the various services. The man chosen for the key position, Minister of State, was the young man whom we first met at the Alhóndiga in 1810, Don Lucas Alamán.

Alamán was a Creole aristocrat who had somehow escaped the sloth that too frequently paralyzed the members of his class. He had been educated as a mining engineer, first at the School of Mines in Mexico City, later in France and Germany. He had visited England in the spring of 1815 and there saw the light, for in England's industry, her conservative and (relatively) responsible aristocracy, her opulence, and, above all, her orderliness, he discovered the qualities that his own country needed. There could be no Alhóndiga massacre in England. Alamán's admiration for England and English institutions was to guide him in all the plans he conceived for the rehabilitation of Mexico. Order became Alamán's god; to achieve order he allied himself with those who had destroyed order, and with the man who was to destroy Mexico, Antonio López de Santa Anna.

Alamán had served as Minister of State under Iturbide, and his youth (he was thirty), energy, knowledge, and integrity make him the one bright spot in that fantastic adventure. In his philosophy he was a benevolent despot of the eighteenth century, born out of his time. He despised and dreaded the half-baked Jacobinism of the liberals and did his utmost to create a strong centralized government. He had a clear vision of the growing might of the United States, and opposed Manifest Destiny at every turn. At that time we were looking at the Isthmus of Tehuantepec as a possible corridor to the Pacific, but Alamán blocked us with a plan to colonize it. To remedy Mexico's thin population and its lack of capital (most of which had gone with the Spaniards), Alamán proposed the admission of skilled foreign mechanics and foreign capital under strict supervision—one of Morelos' ten points. Above all he insisted on a strong government for the protection of capital and industry. He was bitterly opposed by the radicals in Congress and by the men who wanted a weak government for purposes of their own. For a year he was attacked as a monarchist, priest-lover, autocrat, hispanophile, crypto-gachupín, and a number of less pleasant things. It all came to a head in a tumulto and pronunciamiento led by General José María Lobato in January, 1824, and Alamán was forced to resign.

At the opposite pole from Alamán stood the liberal leaders, Miguel Ramos Arispe and Valentín Gómez Farías, whose political creed was a rationalization of *death to the gachupines*. Under their inspiration the liberal Congress wrote the first Constitution of Mexico, that of 1824, a naïve document incorporating a good many features of the Constitution of the United States. Their prescription for the government of Mexico was complete decentralization, a federation of semiautonomous states. The federalists did everything they could to weaken the executive. They even made our early mistake of having the two highest offices go to the competing candidates for the presidency, a mistake that was to cause endless confusion and bloodshed in the years to come.

The federal system was probably the worst that could have been adopted in the circumstances. It was based on the fallacy that the old Spanish administrative districts were independent entities, each with a culture and destiny of its own. Throughout Spanish America, indeed, the endemic anarchy of the first half-century of independence is chargeable largely to that assumption. The liberal authors of the Constitution of 1824 took it for granted that everything in the Spanish system was bad and that the only thing to do was to throw it all out and make a fresh start. They ignored the immense weight of three centuries of habit, and they chose to ignore also the fact that the old system, with all its faults, was a tried and working system, while the new Constitution erected a weak and unfamiliar government in a country ravaged by civil war and overrun by bandits; riveted upon it the tyranny of provincial caciques; allowed for no effective check on the Church or the army, which by that time was a privileged caste, infinitely more rapacious than anything seen in colonial times; and it imposed an uncomprehended democratic ideology upon a people who had known nothing but rule from above for a very long time. In short, the federal system was an invitation to anarchy.

With all its pretensions of democracy, the Constitution of 1824 was another "plan," imposed by the radicals in Congress, with the backing of foreign agents and provincial satraps. But there it was, and nineteen more or less independent republics were created, each with the fatal power of accepting the Constitution or ignoring it—a tradition that still persists, making the state governments of Mexico something of a puzzle to outsiders, although of late years the strong Revolutionary Party (PRI) has successfully suppressed the tendency of local caciques to shake off control from Mexico City.

The first president chosen under the new Constitution was the amiable and patriotic insurgent general, Guadalupe Victoria, who had been Santa Anna's figurehead in the "Plan de Casa Mata." The vice president and choice of the minority was one of Morelos' former generals, the decent and civilized Nicolás Bravo. But always generals! The government was a hodgepodge selected from all factions. The hated but indispensable aristocrat, Lucas Alamán, was again called to head the Ministry of State, and, through innocence or patriotism, he worked for the crazy-quilt government as if he thought it stable or desirable. He negotiated with George Canning for the recognition of Mexican independence, and signed a commercial treaty with England at the same time. He continued to oppose Manifest Destiny and became the thorn in the flesh of our meddling minister, Joel Poinsett. He refused to open the Santa Fe Trail to American commerce until we should conclude a commerical treaty with Mexico, while at the same time he discreetly put obstacles in the way of that treaty. His "perfidy" (according to Poinsett) led him to oppose the admission of American settlers into Texas. The radicals and Poinsett's "York Rite" Masons labeled Alamán antiprogressive, Anglophile, undemocratic, despotic; they accused him of high crimes, misdemeanors, and treason; and they brought about his second fall in September, 1825. Alamán's defeat was a triumph for the centrifugal forces of Mexico and, as Poinsett wrote to Secretary of State Henry Clay, it was also a victory for the United States over England.

President Guadalupe Victoria lasted out his full term of four years—a phenomenon that was not to be repeated for a long time. His administration was threatened only once, in December, 1827, by the vice president, General Bravo, now the hope of the conservatives, whose "plan" demanded the suppression of secret societies (the Masons) and the expulsion of Joel Poinsett, and, of course, the creation of a strong central government. Bravo was unsuccessful and had to flee the country. The exile traffic was to strain the scanty capacity of the Vera Cruz road for many years.

In the election of 1828 the radical "York Rite" party, supported by

Poinsett, backed the old Indian insurgent, General Vicente Guerrero, against the "Scottish Rite" conservative candidate, General Manuel Gómez Pedraza, a former officer in the royal army. (The reader should not let himself be confused by the Masonic labels. The lodges only in the loosest sense represented opposing philosophies, but were hardly more than pressure groups supporting this or that candidate according to their interests.) Pedraza won the election by the close margin of ten to nine (each state having one vote), and Guerrero was persuaded to "pronounce."

For four years Santa Anna, like Br'er Fox, had lain low, but now his nose told him that the wind was blowing liberal, and so from his lair in Vera Cruz he "pronounced" Guerrero president. Santa Anna was arbiter of Mexico.

One of the incidents of the Victoria administration was the first of a series of expulsions of the Spaniards who had remained in Mexico under Iturbide's "Three Guarantees." The expulsion was a reprisal against Spain for refusing to recognize Mexican independence. At the same time it was a triumph for the patriots who were carrying on their ancient feud with the gachupines. It was also a triumph for Joel Poinsett and those foreigners who aimed to replace the Spaniards as the exploiters of the country's resources. But for Mexico it was a disaster, for the Spaniards were the middle class of Mexico. Many of them had Mexican wives, and their children were Mexican. They ran the shops and the small factories; they managed the haciendas; they owned a substantial part of the vanishing capital of the country, and they took it with them. A second expulsion in 1829 was a reprisal against the silly attempt of Ferdinand VII to reconquer Mexico by landing a small expeditionary force at Tampico, under the command of General Isidro Barradas.

What! With Santa Anna in Vera Cruz! President Guerrero gave the leading man his cue, and Santa Anna led a division against the sick and starving Spanish troops, who had already been defeated by the heat and the mosquitoes. A short but violent action ensued, and the fatherland was saved by Santa Anna.

It was high time, because Guerrero, having been given dictatorial powers to meet the Spanish invasion, was suddenly discovered to be trampling under foot the most sacred heritage of the fatherland. He was accused of being a Jacobin, an atheist, a Mason, a destroyer of religion, and the rest—the usual outcry of the centralists. Vice President Anastasio Bustamante "pronounced," evidently without consulting Santa Anna, who countered with one of his famous Napoleonic proclamations: "I shall stubbornly oppose those who, on any pretext whatever, would temerariously hurl from the presidential chair the Illustrious General, Citizen Vicente Guerrero, and they will succeed in doing so only over my dead body, when I shall have perished defending the Chief Magistrate of the Nation!"

Santa Anna's nose had failed him. The conservatives were strong. More pronunciamientos. Soon the whole country, except for a few diehard liberals under General Juan Alvarez, had accepted Bustamante. Santa Anna made the best of it and retired to Manga de Clavo, his hacienda in Vera Cruz. Congress legitimized Bustamante, who occupied the uneasy seat of the presidency for the first time, on January 1, 1830. At his back "he had the good will of the clergy, the applause of the well to do, the effective support of the army, the clericalism of the Senate, and the indecision of the Chamber of Deputies."

The wheel had made a complete revolution back to despotism. For three years Bustamante's conservative party ruled Mexico through terror, imprisonment, and assassination, all in the name of law and order and the protection of property. Lucas Alamán was again Minister of State. The foulest blot of the Bustamante administration was the murder of Guerrero. That old insurgent had joined forces with Juan Alvarez in his ancient stamping ground in the south. Defeated at Chilpancingo by General Bravo, he retired to Acapulco and took refuge on the Italian brigatine *Colombo*, commanded by his friend Francisco Picaluga, who sold him to the government for 50,000 pesos in gold.[1] That Alamán should allow himself to be a party to this sordid affair shows how even a man of his principles could be deluded by jesuitical reasoning. He must have order! And Vicente Guerrero, one of the finest old stalwarts of Independence, faced a firing squad in Cuilapa, Michoacán, February 14, 1831.

The country went wild with rage and grief; that is, the "mob" did. The *yorkinos* made capital of that and the natural reaction against Bustamante's despotism. The uproar was so loud that the sensitive nose of Santa Anna informed him (after three years) that the will of the people was being flouted, and he "pronounced" in favor of General Gómez Pedraza, a *moderado*. A chorus of pronunciamientos notified the conservatives that the game was up, and Pedraza was installed as provisional president on January 3, 1833. The new Congress showed its gratitude to Santa Anna by voting him the titles of "Liberator of the

Republic" and "Conqueror of the Spaniards," and, on March 30, 1833, elected him president. The radical Valentín Gómez Farías was elected vice president. But Santa Anna, who detested the dull routine of government, pleaded ill health and left the Poder Ejecutivo to Gómez Farías.

The liberal leader was fifty-two years old at the time. He had studied medicine and political science, and was a tremendous anti-clerical. Under his lash Congress indicated the ministers of the ousted Bustamante government and was especially ferocious against Lucas Alamán, who was obliged to go into hiding to avoid arrest and worse. Congress worked hard for forty-five days. Its program was a complete liberal house cleaning. It worked in the knowledge that its time was short. It meant to put in a whole liberal program, regardless. The liberals attacked the Spaniards who had escaped the expulsion; they secularized the missions of California; they encouraged emigration to California by exempting the colonists from tithes; they decreed the seizure of the Cortés estate; and they limited the jurisdiction of the military and ecclesiastical tribunals to the army and the clergy, for those courts had long been a refuge of privileged laymen.

The conservatives were panic-stricken and sounded the alarm. The uproar grew. A certain Colonel Ignacio Escalada "pronounced" in Michoacán. His "plan": "The garrison protests that it will sustain with all its strength the Holy Religion of Jesus Christ and the immunities and privileges of the clergy and the army, which are threatened by the usurping authorities." It proclaimed "the Illustrious Conqueror of the Spaniards, General Don Antonio López de Santa Anna, Protector of the Cause and Supreme Chief of the Nation."

Santa Anna heard his country's call. His return from Manga de Clavo was the occasion for a popular demonstration. More pronunciamientos demanded that he be named dictator. Santa Anna was puzzled. After twenty days in power he left the stew to cook a while longer and went back to Manga de Clavo. The liberal Congress also made a bid for the support of the Illustrious Conqueror of the Spaniards by putting him in command of the government forces. But Santa Anna's actions were ambiguous. He allowed himself to be "taken prisoner" by the conservative General Mariano Arista, until he should consent to become "Supreme Dictator and Redeemer of Mexico." Gómez Farías managed by some miracle to put down the insurgents in the capital and generally showed more strength than Santa Anna had expected. So Santa Anna "escaped" from his captors and appeared before Congress, swearing "to defend the Constitution till death," and vowing that his hatred of tyranny was "eternal." Congress simply did not believe him. Meanwhile, the insurgents laid siege to Puebla, and Santa Anna met the challenge in his best style: "We march to bring aid to the brave sons of Puebla who . . . are defending their sacred walls with a valor worthy of being perpetuated in the annals of our history!"

While the two armies sparred harmlessly at Puebla, Santa Anna had one of his frequent strokes of luck. The capital was invaded by the cholera. The superstitious populace was told that the plague was a sign of divine wrath against the impiety of Gómez Farías and the liberals. On the very day that Congress proved its atheism by abolishing tithes throughout the Republic and by secularizing the university, Santa Anna returned to Mexico City, announcing that he had suppressed the revolt. The government was delighted. It declared the clergy subject to civil action for using the pulpit for propaganda against the government and it exiled Bishop Labastida y Dávalos. Then it reached the height of madness: It cashiered all the officers who had taken part in the rebellion!

Pronunciamientos. Santa Anna was invited by the army chiefs to cut loose from the liberal rabble. Their slogan: *Religión y Fueros!*— meaning, the clergy and the army above the law. It was still too early for Santa Anna to decide, and he had to retire to Manga de Clavo because his health had been broken in the service of the fatherland.

Meanwhile, the liberal Congress went on destroying religion and the army. The country was in danger! And who do you suppose came forward to sacrifice himself for the fatherland? Right!

In April, 1834, the garrison of Cuernavaca "pronounced" for Santa Anna. Its "plan" called for the dissolution of the liberal Congress, the expulsion of Gómez Farías, the suppression of the militia (liberal), the protection of religion, and the rest. Provincial caciques "pronounced" in unison, all except the cacique of Zacatecas, which Santa Anna took and sacked. In the capital: Te Deums and solemn Masses of thanksgiving. Religion was saved. Santa Anna, paladin of the Cross. Gómez Farías in flight to New Orleans. From a newspaper of the day: "Yesterday the execrable Gómez Farías at last left this capital crushed under the weight of the just imprecations of a whole city . . . and his terrible and lawless deeds. . . . Like a comet of ill omen, Gómez Farías brought cholera and misery, immorality and tyranny, espionage and treachery, ignorance and sacrilege, the exaltation of criminals and the abasement of honest men, the triumph of the filthy rabble and the crushing of the select, the terror and mourning of families, proscription, tears, and death in a thousand most horrible forms. . . ." A fair sample of the long litany of vituperation which has been leveled at every liberal leader from José María Morelos to Lázaro Cárdenas.

Santa Anna now felt strong enough to dispense with his mask. For eight months he reigned as absolute dictator, with soldiers and martial law. He dissolved Congress; he discharged all government employees suspected of liberal leanings; he put his own men into all national and state offices. When he had the situation well in hand, and the liberal house cleaning of Gómez Farías had been completely undone, he called a new hand-picked Congress in December, 1834. But it turned out to be so incredibly reactionary that even Santa Anna was frightened at the thoroughness of his job. The conservative Congress meant to settle once and for all the nonsense of popular sovereignty. It ignored the Constitution of 1824 and set up a new "principle of authority" in the shape of a Poder Conservador, a supreme executive responsible to no one, not even to its creators. It was the *Fuehrer-Prinzip* in all its purity. And Br'er Fox, he lay low. He knew his people.

In spite of Alamán's warnings, Texas had been allowed to fill up with Yankee immigrants, rude men who despised the "greasers" and who had some reasonable complaints about Mexican notions of justice and administration. The inevitable happened, and Sam Houston and his Texans, supported, incidentally, by liberal Mexicans, "pronounced" for the restoration of the Constitution of 1824 and against the dictatorship of Santa Anna. The Liberator of the Republic and the Conqueror of the Spaniards was not one to let slip this opportunity of saving the fatherland in true Napoleonic style, and he unsheathed his unconquerable blade, which, as he put it in his inimitable prose, "was the first to descend upon the necks of the rash enemies of the fatherland!"

Santa Anna established his headquarters at San Luis Potosí, where he set about creating an army out of several thousand green recruits rounded up by his press gangs. He had energy, and he had a colossal nerve. There was not a cent in the war chest. His men had nothing to eat for days at a time. Using his authority as president, Santa Anna borrowed money from the *agiotistas* (a new class of bloodsuckers who financed the bankrupt government at three and four per cent a month); he manufactured munitions; he requisitioned horses, oxen, and carts; he drilled his men into the semblance of an army; and in the dead of winter he set out across the desert on the six-hundred mile march to San Antonio.

It was a frightful ordeal. Men and animals died from cold and hunger, drowning, exposure, and disease. Santa Anna, however, was above all that. Human life meant little when the fatherland was in danger. And then he had to keep ahead of the revolution that was threatening to break out at home from one day to the next. Six weeks of marching brought him to San Antonio and the old Franciscan mission of the Alamo, where the Texans had imprudently fortified themselves.

On March 6, 1836, the Alamo was surrounded—Bill Travis and his hundred and fifty against Santa Anna's thousands of half-starved recruits. An hour's fierce fighting, brave men against brave men. Numbers and fire power won, and Santa Anna continued the savage tradition of the wars of independence by shooting his prisoners. And, just to prove to the Texans that he was serious, he ordered General José Urrea, over Urrea's protest, to shoot the garrison of Goliad. Santa Anna was to learn that *death to the gringos* also worked both ways.

At San Antonio the news of the expected revolution overtook him, and he had to decide between saving the fatherland by going back to Mexico, and saving it by completing the conquest of Texas. He chose the second alternative as offering the greater glory. He divided his army into three divisions, which overran the country, spreading terror and desolation. Santa Anna himself acted the great conqueror. He issued orders and counterorders in such profusion that his troops marched until they dropped from exhaustion. He resembled Stephen Leacock's general, who mounted his horse and rode off in all directions. He led his division on a forced march of *forty miles* in one day and descended upon Harrisburg, the capital, which he took without firing a shot. Santa Anna was invincible and the Texans were cowards.

And then came the climax, or tragic ending. Santa Anna met Sam Houston's Texans at San Jacinto and with unparalleled frivolity encamped on a rise a short distance from the enemy. The day was warmish and the Conqueror was tired. He did not even bother to post sentries. He was awakened from his siesta by a yell that was to haunt him for the rest of his life: *"Remember the Alamo!"* Sam Houston's revenge was complete. He lost three men killed and eighteen wounded. Santa Anna lost his whole army: 400 dead, 200 wounded, and 730 prisoners. In fifteen minutes!

Santa Anna escaped on horseback. He disguised himself in some cast-off clothing that he found in a hut, but was captured and betrayed by the salutes of his own men. The Texans were for shooting him on the spot, but Sam Houston was too humane or too canny to allow it, and Santa Anna, with the pistols of scowling Texans nervously twitching, dictated the orders that freed Texas of Mexican troops.

Sam Houston started his fallen enemy off for Mexico, according to agreement, but at Galveston a crowd of new men insisted on shooting "Santy Anny." They were argued out of the notion, and the Liberator again escaped death by a hair's breadth. The Texans then sent him to Washington to have a talk with Andrew Jackson, who got nothing out of him but a lot of meaningless protestations, and Santa Anna was back in Mexico in the spring of 1837, just a year after the Alamo and San Jacinto.

In some unexplained manner Santa Anna in that year had undergone a complete metamorphosis. The traitor who had lost San Jacinto and Texas was now, at least in the minds of his admirers, the hero who had saved the honor of the fatherland at the Alamo. They put on a great display of fireworks when he landed at Vera Cruz. Concerts, speeches, poems to the savior of the fatherland. And wouldn't he consider resuming the presidency? But Br'er Fox knew better than to rush things. He could afford to wait. He retired to Manga de Clavo and dictated his version of the war in Texas—a version in which he won all the victories and his subordinates suffered all the defeats.

During the past few years a number of claims had been filed by French citizens against the Mexican government, one by a M. Remontel, who had a pastry shop in Tacubaya. It seems that some army officers had invaded his shop one night, locked him in a back room, and devoured all his pastries. They knew how to insult a Frenchman. The indignant proprietor claimed 800 pesos in damages. It was the smallest item in the huge bill for 600,000 pesos presented by Louis Philippe's minister, but it gave its name to the famous "Pastry War" that ensued. The Mexican government ignored the claims, and, on April 16, 1838, the port of Vera Cruz was blockaded by a French fleet.

Six months of tiresome haggling having come to nothing, Admiral Baudin opened fire on the decrepit old fortress of San Juan de Ulúa on November 27. From his retirement at Manga de Clavo Santa Anna heard the distant cannonading. What! A war going on and he had not been informed! He shouted for his famous white horse and galloped off toward Vera Cruz, arriving during the negotiations for surrender. Treason! He borrowed a skiff and had himself rowed out to the fortress, where he tried to persuade the commandant to blow the place up rather than surrender. But the capitulation had already been signed, and Santa Anna raged back to Manga de Clavo. He may have had a hand in President Bustamante's refusal to accept the terms, and orders came that Santa Anna was to take the field against the French. San Jacinto was forgotten.

Santa Anna against the King of France! A good match. But the bored Admiral Baudin refused to fight. Indeed, if it had not been for the Prince de Joinville, there would probably have been no war at all. The Prince, however, was cut out of the same Byronic cloth as Santa Anna, and thirsted for glory. France, *la douce France*, had been insulted, and only blood could wipe out the stain. *Revanche!* So Baudin prepared a landing party, and Santa Anna was awakened by shouting and firing in the streets. In his underclothing, with his unconquerable blade tucked under his arm, the hero escaped, leaving General Arista to hold the French. Once outside, Santa Anna was his old self. Orders flew, and soon a detachment of Mexican troops was exchanging shots with the prince de Joinville's marines from behind a barricade. French honor was appeased after several hours, and the Prince withdrew to his ships. Victory! Santa Anna mounted his white horse. Charge! At that moment the god of luck took him by the hand and led him into the path of a French cannonball. His left leg was shattered below the knee. Never would the fatherland be allowed to forget Santa Anna's leg.

The death that the hero expected momentarily resembled that of a romantic opera star, who manages to sing lustily while his life blood flows in a red torrent. On his carefully arranged deathbed the wounded hero lay, while strong men wept unashamed, but his agony did not prevent his dictating a fifteen-page last message to his beloved fellow citizens, which ended: "I also beg the government of the fatherland to bury me in these same sand dunes, so that my companions in arms may know that this is the battle line I have marked out for them to hold."

The death scene was what is known in Hollywood as a "wow." Santa Anna might well have said: "Mexico is worth a leg!" The pitiful stump of Santa Anna's leg was to be paraded with such effect that revolutions and more revolutions would have to be fought, thousands upon thousands of Indian boys would have to die, and half the territory of the nation would have to be sacrificed, before that leg could be paid for. Santa Anna loved his wound with pathological intensity. He never tired of talking about it. He affected invalidism, and a romantic pallor ennobled his features. Fanny Calderón was impressed.

"In a little while entered General Santa Anna himself; a gentlemanly, good-looking, quietly-dressed, rather melancholy-looking person, with one leg, apparently somewhat of an invalid, and to us the most interesting person in the group. He has a sallow complexion, fine dark eyes, soft and penetrating, and an interesting expression of face. Knowing nothing of his past history, one would have said a philosopher, living in dignified retirement—one who had tried the world and found that all was vanity—one who had suffered ingratitude, and who, if he were ever persuaded to emerge from his retreat, would only do so, Cincinnatus-like, to benefit his country. . . . It was only now and then that the expression of his eyes was startling, especially when he spoke of his leg, which is cut off below the knee. He speaks of it frequently."

Santa Anna had two great loves: himself and his fighting cocks. Next came the gaming table, where his gambler's vanity made him coolly risk large sums on the flip of a card with the same unconcern with which he staked men's lives and his country's destiny. And now his leg, which became almost as dear to him as his fighting cocks.

By 1839 unhappy Mexico had become so inured to "plans" and pronunciamientos that they no longer caused a ripple of excitement. The capital fell a prey to its ancient plague of tumultos, with mobs yelling for this or that general, or against this or that action of the government, or just yelling. Banditry had become a semirespectable profession, and gallant highwaymen who apologized to their female victims were not unknown. In the north, Santa Anna's old companions, Generals Urrea and Mejía, upon whom he had laid the blame for the loss of Texas, "pronounced." The Poder Conservador was frightened. Would the mutilated Liberator accept the presidency?

The death scene at Vera Cruz had had the touch of genius, but it was only a rehearsal as compared with the Return of Cincinnatus. Slowly and painfully the carriage of the great man bumped over the stones of the neglected Vera Cruz road. At every stop: triumphal arches, bands, bunting, rockets, speeches, poems, and military parades, while the pallid hero lay limp and unsmiling, ackowledging the ovations with a wave of his languid hand, his empty trouser leg mutely reminding the fatherland of his sacrifice. Who so small now as to remember San Jacinto?

The grateful Poder Conservador voted him the new title of *Be-*

nemérito de la Patria (Well-Deserving of the Fatherland) and made him president for the fifth time. Why he should wish to rule is a mystery for the psychologists to solve. The treasury was exhausted, as usual, and a rebel army was descending upon the capital. Never mind. He would rule with or without money, by terror, confiscation, and oppression. Mejía took Vera Cruz and marched on Puebla. Santa Anna's order to his generals: "The firing squad for all captured officers!" Mejía's last speech: "Santa Anna is doing to me what I should have done to him, only he is shooting me three hours after my capture, while I should have shot him in three minutes!"

The fatherland had been saved again, and Santa Anna began to put on unmistakable airs of royalty. But he was bored. The eternal financial crisis was a bore. The "plans" and pronunciamientos that continued to pop were a bore. He was homesick for his cockpit at Manga de Clavo. "Ill health" compelled his retirement, and General Nicolás Bravo was left to face the music.

Hell itself broke loose as soon as the dictator was out of earshot. The *puros* (that is, the extreme Jacobin liberals), with the veteran Valentín Gómez Farías again at their head, sought to restore the Constitution of 1824, and General Urrea, who had escaped Santa Anna's firing squad the year before, was on hand to make the indispensable pronunciamiento, on July 15, 1840. For twelve days the forces of Bravo and Urrea were locked in a bloody embrace in the streets of the capital and the unfortunate citizens were cut down by cannon fire, while they had to listen to the proclamations that Gómez Farías and Bustamante hurled at each other. Meanwhile, no word came from Manga de Clavo. How was Santa Anna to know which side was representing the true interests of the fatherland? Stalemate. An arrangement was made between forces, Gómez Farías again trudged off into exile, and the liberals went back to their holes.

General Anastasio Bustamante was again president, by the grace of Santa Anna and the Poder Conservador. But Bustamante was unlucky in his efforts to get money, and General Gabriel Valencia "pronounced." This time Santa Anna's nose did not fail him, and he warned President Bustamante to hearken "to the penetrating cry of a generous people." Bustamante did not hearken closely enough, so Santa Anna himself "pronounced." His forces moved rapidly from Vera Cruz to Puebla, and from Puebla to Tacubaya. More fighting in the streets, twenty-eight days of it, while dead soldiers rotted in the gutters.

The capital, long inured to pronunciamientos and barracks revolutions, regarded this one with hopeless resignation. Fanny Calderón, who was in the midst of it, saw it as a kind of fiesta, with comic overtones. "September 2, 1841. Mexico looks as if it had got a general holiday. Shops shut up, and all business is at a stand. The people, with the utmost apathy, are collected in groups, talking quietly; the officers are galloping about; generals, in a somewhat partycolored dress, with large gray hats, striped pantaloons, old coats, and generals' belts, fine horses, and crimson-colored velvet saddles. The shopkeepers in the square have been removing their goods and money. An occasional shot is heard, and sometimes a volley, succeeded by a dead silence. The archbishop shows his reverend face now and then upon the opposite balcony of his palace, looks out a while, and then retires. The chief effect, so far, is universal idleness in man and beast—the soldiers and their quadrupeds excepted."

General Bustamante was at his wits' end to outplay the Benemérito de la Patria. Suddenly inspired, he did a back somersault and himself "pronounced" for the liberals and the Constitution of 1824! General Juan Almonte, commanding a division of government troops, had a reasonable doubt of Bustamante's sincerity and "pronounced" on his own account for the same Constitution. This was patently an absurdity, so a military junta from the three forces met and reached an agreement, whereby President Bustamante followed Gómez Farías into exile. But that left the presidency vacant. And who do you think was chosen? Right again!

By this time Santa Anna had thrown off all pretense of ruling by law. There was no law but his caprice. He must have soldiers and more soldiers. His personal bodyguard was made up of twelve hundred men in gorgeous uniforms. Money? The country had demanded a dictator; now it could pay for him. Santa Anna "borrowed" money, hundreds of thousands of pesos, until the country was picked as clean as the bones of a dead Indian boy in Texas. It is only fair to add that the money was not all wasted. Santa Anna's vanity needed monuments with his name on them. A new theater was built; a new market; the city streets were paved—all this in the capital, of course. Dictators have their uses. If there had been any railroads in Mexico the trains would undoubtedly have run on time, or nearly so.

The year 1842 marked the apogee of the glorious dictatorship. Mexico City enjoyed a continual fiesta: holidays to celebrate Santa Anna's birthday, Independence, and what not; parades of the guard;

drums and bugles and salvos of artillery; solemn Masses at the cathedral. "His Serene Highness," as Santa Anna was now addressed, had to be amused.

On September 27, 1842, occurred the greatest and most solemn celebration of the year. The corpse of Santa Anna's leg was dug up at Manga de Clavo and brought to the city. His Serene Highness's bodyguard, the cavalry, the artillery, the infantry, and the cadets from the military academy at Chapultepec, all dressed for parade, escorted the urn containing the grisly relic across the city to the magnificent centotaph that had been erected for it in the cemetery of Santa Paula. Ministers and the diplomatic corps attended, hat in hand. Speeches, poems, salvos. A graceful acknowledgement by the Liberator himself, who solemnized the occasion by wearing a new cork leg, which may still be viewed by the skeptical in the National Museum.

The bill came very high: taxes and more taxes; a twenty per cent duty on imports; a "voluntary" contribution by all the householders of the capital; bottomless depression. Santa Anna, bored by the complaints, retired again to Manga de Clavo and his cockpit, leaving General Bravo to carry on. But Bravo could not cope with the roar of hatred that went up on all sides, and the hero was hastily recalled. The seventh return of Cincinnatus.

The country fell a prey to cynicism and boredom; boredom and a deepening hatred for the little man with the cork leg; hatred of his ceaseless extortions; boredom with his emptiness and vanity. But no boredom exceeded that of His Serene Highness, who seized the first opportunity to retire to the fine new estate of El Encero which a grateful country had given him.

General Valentín Canalizo, who had been left to run the show, satisfied no one. How could he? Another weary cycle of pronunciamientos, and Cincinnatus was sent for again. The eighth return.

Texas, whose independence Mexico refused to recognize, wished to enter the Union. The United States government pressed for the settlement of old claims. By 1844 war threatened. But Santa Anna the patriot would shed every drop of his blood before he would relinquish a foot of the sacred soil of the fatherland. If the gringos wanted war, he would show them. He ordered a levy of 30,000 new troops, and his press gangs rounded up droves of uncomprehending Indian boys. The defense program was to be financed by a forced loan of four million pesos, source unrevealed.

The black despair of the country and the hatred of the government made themselves known in the only way possible: General Mariano Paredes "pronounced" in Jalisco. Santa Anna marched west to meet him, but no sooner had he left the capital than a furious tumulto broke out. The statue of the Benemérito de la Patria was torn from its pedestal, the shiny new cenotaph in the cemetery of Santa Paula was violated, and the Leg was destroyed. The garrison of Mexico City "pronounced." Santa Anna was caught between two fires. That in the city was the more threatening, and he hastened back to put it out. But his troops were fed up and began to desert. By squads, by companies, by regiments, they deserted, while small arms, cannon, and equipment filled the ditches. Within a short week the army of Santa Anna was nothing but a memory. With his cook and two adjutants he fled to the mountains of Vera Cruz, where he was recognized by a party of Indians and captured. At the fortress of El Perote a military tribunal tried to find an excuse to shoot him. He was saved by his stump and limped off into exile. Universal relief. Only one general did him the honor of "pronouncing" in protest, while the clergy and the rich sang Te Deums for their and their goods' delivery.

On March 1, 1845, the United States announced the admission of Texas into the Union. Minister Almonte demanded his passports. The Mexican government promptly declared war on us. War? Surely no country in history was ever less prepared to fight. The army: 20,000 men on the rolls, and *24,000 officers*. The treasury was empty. The despair of the people flamed up in hatred against the criminal stupidity of their rulers. General Paredes "pronounced" again. Half a dozen generals in various parts of the country "pronounced." The war could take care of itself. General Paredes marched on the capital. General Valencia prepared to defend it. There was really little sense in their fighting each other, so they made an arrangement by which Paredes became president and dictator. Paredes to the country: "I am resolved to make my ideas triumph or perish in the attempt. I am determined to punish no one for his past misdeeds, but I shall shoot anyone who opposes me, be he archbishop, general, minister, or anyone else!" His prose was not up to Santa Anna's.

The garrison of the capital could not stomach the pretensions of Paredes, and "pronounced." The country was without a leader. The country was in danger. Yes, Santa Anna was back from his exile, uninvited. He was received with distrust, but received. The smart Yankees had let him through the blockade at Vera Cruz, and Santa Anna retired to El Encero to await the inevitable call. The factions in the capital were bidding for his support. The liberals looked stronger. The liberals won it. Valentín Gómez Farías, also back from exile and again at the head of his puros, begged Santa Anna not to offend his people by withholding his presence from them. And Santa Anna, now a liberal democrat, clad in decent civvies, was driven in an ordinary hack through the silent streets of the capital to the palace, where he was persuaded to accept the presidency. In the treasury were exactly 1,839 pesos with which to finance the war with the "Colossus of the North."

Whatever his shortcomings, Santa Anna was an incomparable organizer. He announced a new levy and beat together an army of 18,000 men, without money. Gómez Farías, now vice president, moved heaven and earth to raise funds. He slapped a sequestration order on the property of the clergy for four million pesos, none of which got to Santa Anna in time. The generalísimo could not wait. The fatherland really was in danger. Santa Anna drove his starving and freezing troops three hundred miles from San Louis Potosí to Buena Vista to meet Zachary Taylor. On the way he lost 4,000 men from desertion, hunger, and disease. It was an army of desperate and fainting men that faced General Taylor on February 22, 1846. The excellent American artillery, firing from well-prepared positions, chopped through the Mexican ranks, but they came on, taking position after position at the point of the bayonet. They fought magnificently; they fought until they drove Taylor's men to the last ditch; they fought until they dropped from hunger and fatigue. A heavy storm stopped the battle, and Santa Anna retired under cover of darkness. His men could take no more. He had lost 1,500 in killed and wounded. If the American troops had not been fought to a standstill, they could have annihilated their exhausted enemy. As it was, Taylor allowed Santa Anna to withdraw unmolested.

The Retreat from Moscow. The army that entered San Luis Potosí seventeen days later was an army of barefoot skeletons. The news of the defeat was received in Mexico City with the usual pronunciamientos against the government. Deadlock between Gómez Farías and the rebels. The Great Arbiter hastened to the scene. He was the only one who could decide the conflict, *because he was the only one without convictions.* And, of course, he reassumed the presidency.

The army of Winfield Scott landed at Vera Cruz. It would be pointless to repeat the story of Scott's mad invasion of Mexico. He had about 10,000 men. Mexico City alone could have raised a force of several times that many, if it had wished to do so. But the Mexicans were defeated in advance by hatreds, jealousies, poverty, despair, indifference, and apathy. Why fight? What could be worse than the degradation they had already suffered? Many of the "decent people" even welcomed the American invasion as a relief from the intolerable military anarchy. Santa Anna was to prove them correct.

Mexico City was not properly defended. Why? Because Santa Anna refused to share the glory with General Gabriel Valencia, commander of the northern division. There is no other explanation for the easy American victory. The Americans were heavily outnumbered; their line of supplies was three hundred miles long and thinly held; they had no reserves and no way to get any. With the spirit he had shown against Taylor at Buena Vista, Santa Anna should have crushed Scott. Instead, when everything was set for the battle and Valencia was in a strong position, Santa Anna ordered him to retire. Valencia exploded with frustration and fury; he cursed Santa Anna for a coward and refused to obey. Whereupon Santa Anna withdrew his own troops and left Valencia to be cut to pieces. Santa Anna himself marched out of the city with his fresh army without firing a shot, abandoning the scanty defenders of the Castle of Chapultepec to certain destruction, including the boys of the military academy, the famous *Niños Héroes*. He marched past the convent of Churubusco, which was held by a regiment of Irish deserters from Scott's army— misguided men who thought they were fighting for the Church against the Protestants. (Fifty of them were tried later and hanged for desertion, much to Scott's distress.)

The rest is in the textbooks: the Treaty of Guadalupe Hidalgo, by which we took half the territory of Mexico and thereby fulfilled Manifest Destiny; Mexico dismembered and helpless, and condemned for all time to dependence upon us.

The paranoiac Santa Anna led his troops off intact, while he proclaimed, declaimed, and heaped abuse upon the "betrayers of the fatherland." His disgusted army melted away, as it had done once before. By the time it reached Puebla there was only a handful left, and His Serene Highness deserted in his turn and fled to Tehuacán. A band of wild Texans followed close behind and came within an ace of capturing him. "Remember the Alamo, Santy Anny?" The fugitive tried to take refuge in Oaxaca, but the governor refused him permission. The governor was a Zapotec Indian named Benito Juárez. So Santa Anna decided that the enemy was safer than his own people, and surrendered to Major Kenly at El Perote.

Benemérito de la Patria! What a price for a leg!

Santa Anna, actor to the last, entertained his captors with a banquet at El Encero, dictated an eloquent farewell message to an ungrateful fatherland, and exiled himself to Venezuela, April 6, 1848.

The immense disaster that he and his kind had brought upon Mexico had the immediate effect that the reader has already anticipated: pronunciamientos by all parties and caudillos, denouncing the betrayal of the fatherland, denouncing Santa Anna, and denouncing each other. Death to the monarchists! Death to the liberals! Death to the santanistas! Death!

The provisional government gave way to a "moderate" government under General José Joaquín Herrera, who, with his successor, General Mariano Arista, performed miracles to meet the financial crisis. The fifteen million dollars of conscience money we paid Mexico after the war was soon gone. The moderates suffered the fate of their kind and pleased no one. And then General Arista committed the unpardonable sin: *He reduced the army!*

Pronunciamientos in Guadalajara. Arista resigned. The new provisional president, Juan Bautista Ceballos, dissolved Congress by force and made an arrangement with the rebels. Confusion. The army and the conservatives decided it was time for a strong hand. Their "plan": Religion and property, and the rest, *under the perpetual dictatorship of Antonio López de Santa Anna!* He had not even been consulted.

The conservatives were not without powerful arguments in favor of a dictatorship. The Constitution of 1824 had amply proved the unsuitability of a weak federal system. The disaster of 1848 had destroyed the last vestige of national unity. Mexico had become many Mexicos in fact. The municipal district of Cuernavaca seceded from the state of Mexico, and the district of Yautepec seceded from Cuernavaca. Mexico split into cells, and the cells into more cells, each with its cacique making and interpreting laws, and collecting taxes and import duties as he pleased. Justice was bought and sold at the lowest prices in history. A British agent, one Mr. Falconner, got wholesale rates when he bought thirty-five members of the national legislature for 60,00 pesos. Commerce was at a standstill. The police of the capital gathered up the bodies of those who died of hunger. The soldiers quartered in Mexico City conducted themselves like an invading army, and looted and murdered at will. The situation was intolerable, and men of all persuasions began to look wistfully back on the days of Santa Anna. The conservatives, led by Lucas Alamán, saw no help for Mexico but a monarch, failing which, the best substitute they could think of was the old dictator, whom they hoped to control. They were to sink still lower in the dark years to come.

Santa Anna, now sixty, was brought back from Venezuela and, for the eleventh and last time, limped into office, in April, 1853. The dying Alamán, worshiping order to the last, consented, on his own terms, to head the government of the man he despised and needed. Alamán to Santa Anna: "In your hands, General, lies the happiness of the fatherland." He had no illusions about the man he meant to use merely as a stopgap for a monarchy. But the old aristocrat, probably the only disinterested figure among the conservatives, was past leading any party. He finished his tragic and monumental *Historia de México* and died, June 2, 1853, a month after taking office.

Without the brain and energy of Alamán to restrain them, the conservatives went the whole way back to Oriental despotism. Santa Anna was made Perpetual Dictator and was dressed up to look like royalty. The liberals were suppressed or driven into exile. Benito Juárez made cigarettes for a living in New Orleans. A number of liberals joined old General Juan Alvarez in the south and invited Santa Anna to come and get them. The Perpetual Dictator now had the best military machine he had ever commanded, but somehow it lacked punch. His campaigns were fiascos. The liberals had no army to speak of, but they refused to be crushed. On the contrary, their movement gained strength daily. The dictator was up against a thing he could not control or understand: a war of ideas, a revolt against the whole stupid, suffocating, backward-looking notion that the destiny of a people can forever be directed by a handful of willful men with guns.

Santa Anna reverted to type and went in for lavish and expensive display: uniforms, brass buttons, fancy coaches, and suchlike folderol. Money ran low, and he sold the Mesilla of Arizona to the United States for ten million dollars, with which he was able to buy the loyalty of the generals for another year or so. But the liberal movement would not down. Provincial caciques joined it one after another, until the dictator began to feel besieged. Worst of all, he was beset by his ancient affliction, boredom. The lick-spittle sycophants, the silly titles, the nauseating adulation, the endless round of meaningless functions would have turned the stomach of a hardier man. He discovered that he was hardly more than a prisoner in the hands of the gang that had brought him back from his comfortable hacienda and his fighting cocks in Venezuela. He became acid and irritable. He was lonely in his imitation royalty, and in his loneliness takes on dignity for the first time in his life. The great actor had made one too many last appearances. Then, one day in August, 1855, with a touch of his old audacity, Santa Anna ordered his coach and galloped off to Vera Cruz and exile, and off the stage of Mexico.

Seventeen years later the old man was allowed to hobble back to the fatherland he had served so ill. He spent his last four years in solitude, and died forgotten, on June 21, 1876.

NOTE

1. The reader will be pleased to learn that Picaluga, the Judas of the tragedy, was executed as a bandit in Genoa, in 1836.

THE ALAMO

Antonio López de Santa Anna

In 1837 Santa Anna published a manifesto to his fellow citizens relative to his operations during the Texas campaign, including his capture in May of that year. In this excerpt Santa Anna describes his preparations, the march, and the battles at Béxar and the Alamo. His account also illustrates the tremendous problems of logistics for a campaign of this kind, including the large number of troops involved, the long distances to be marched, and the problems of transportation, supply, intelligence, and communication. The financing of this kind of expedition was also a major concern for a weak country like Mexico.

Santa Anna argues that much of the bloodshed of the Alamo could have been avoided if his earlier orders had been followed (a rationalization on his part?) or if the "courageous" [Santa Ann's word] defenders of the Alamo had accepted his terms of surrender. It is interesting to note how Santa Anna describes the North American "conquerors" and how he particularly disliked the Mexican traitors who fought with the Texans (for example, men like Lorenzo de Zavala, the first vice-president of Texas).

I WENT TO Mexico, therefore, in November, 1835, to take charge of a war from which I could have been excused, for the fundamental law of the country offered me a decorous excuse that my broken health made all the more honorable. Nevertheless, aware of the adverse circumstances I have expressed, I still desired to try to serve my country. In a few days I gathered six thousand men, clothed and equipped. At the cost of immense sacrifices, rising above obstacles that seemed insuperable, this force set out from San Luis towards the end of December, 1835. The difficulties arising from the need of securing food supplies

Reprinted from Carlos E. Castañeda, trans., *The Mexican Side of the Texas Revolution* (Washington, D.C.: Documentary Publications, 1971), pp. 10–17, by permission of the publishers.

sufficient for the army while crossing four hundred leagues of desert lands, and those attendant upon its conveyance, as well as the transportation of other equipment, arms, munitions, etc., were all difficulties that, though not pressing at the time of organization, were, nevertheless, of the utmost importance, particularly since the cost of transportation was extremely high in that long stretch. Hospitals had to be located and protected; a great number of rivers had to be crossed without bridge equipment, without even a single boat; the coast had to be watched and the ports kept open to receive provisions and to prevent the enemy from receiving reenforcements or from retreating—all of this with only one serviceable war vessel—and lastly, we had to raise a reserve force to come to our help in case of a reverse, a frequent occurrence in war, when, in order to complete the number of those deemed necessary for the campaign, we had had to use raw recruits.

When a general is given command of an army and everything that is necessary is furnished to him and placed at his disposal, he should be held strictly responsible if he departs from the established rules of war. The government has said, and with truth, that all the resources at its command were placed at my disposal in this campaign, but these being so few, could it have given me many? Could they have been sufficient to carry on a war according to usage when all those resources which are necessary for such an undertaking were practically lacking? . The army under my command consisted of only six thousand men when it left Saltillo[1] and of these at least half were raw recruits from San Luis, Querétaro and other departments, hastily enlisted to fill the ragged companies. The people of Nuevo León and Coahuila, at the instigation of their worthy and patriotic governors, donated food supplies to the army. These, added to those that were brought, made a considerable amount that in a country so vast, where all transportation is done on mule back, was extremely embarrassing to me, although indispensable for our needs. In order to transport it, I made use of extremely heavy ox-carts, a means of transportation never used by armies but which because of the lack of the necessary equipment, and in spite of the most active efforts made to secure it, I was obliged to use. Our needs had been foreseen and that was all that could be done, for to meet them all was an impossibility. The great problem I had to solve was to reconquer Texas and to accomplish this in the shortest time possible, at whatever cost, in order that the revolutionary activities of the interior should not recall that small army before it had fulfilled its honorable mission. A long campaign would have undoubtedly consumed our resources and we would have been unable to renew them. If the only four favorable months of the year were not taken advantage of, the army, in the midst of the hardships of a campaign, would perish of hunger and of the effects of the climate, upon those who composed the army under my command, who were accustomed to a more temperate climate. In order that the soldier by means of repeated marches and frequent battles should forget the immense distance which separated him from his family and home comforts; in order that his courage might not fail; and, in short, to maintain the morale which an army obtains from its activity and operations, it was of the utmost importance to prevent the enemy from strengthening its position or receiving the reenforcements that the papers from the North asserted were very numerous. In a word, the government had said to me that it left everything to my genius, and this flattering remark became an embarrassing truth, making it necessary in this campaign to move with all diligence to avoid the many difficulties that delay in action would undoubtedly bring about. This realization established the norm for all my operations and I always tried earnestly to shorten them. Had we been favored by victory to the last, this policy would have shown a surprised world our occupation, in sixty days, of a territory more than four hundred leagues in extent and defended by the enemy.

Béxar was held by the enemy and it was necessary to open the door to our future operations by taking it. It would have been easy enough to have surprised it, because those occupying it did not have the faintest news of the march of our army. I entrusted, therefore, the operation to one of our generals, who with a detachment of cavalry, part of the dragoons mounted on infantry officers' horses, should have fallen on Béxar in the early morning of February 23, 1836. My orders were concise and definite. I was most surprised, therefore, to find the said general a quarter of a league from Béxar at ten o'clock of that day, awaiting new orders. This, perhaps, was the result of inevitable circumstances; and, although the city was captured, the surprise that I had ordered to be carried out would have saved the time consumed and the blood shed later in the taking of the Alamo.

Having taken Béxar and the proceeds of the small booty having been sold by the commissary department to meet its immediate needs, all of which I communicated to the government, the enemy fortified itself in the Alamo, overlooking the city. A siege of a few days would have caused its surrender, but it was not fit that the entire army should be detained before an irregular fortification hardly worthy of the name. Neither could its capture be dispensed with, for bad as it was, it was well equipped with artillery, had a double wall, and defenders who, it must be admitted, were very courageous and caused much damage to Béxar. Lastly, to leave a part of the army to lay siege to it, the rest continuing on its march, was to leave our retreat, in case of a reverse, if not entirely cut off, at least exposed, and to be unable to help those who were besieging it, who could be reenforced only from the main body of the advancing army. This would leave to the enemy a rallying point, although it might be only for a few days. An assault would infuse our soldiers with that enthusiasm of the first triumph that would make them superior in the future to those of the enemy. It was not my judgment alone that moved me to decide upon it, but the general opinion expressed in a council of war, made up of generals, that I called even though the discussions which such councils give rise to have not always seeemed to me appropriate. Before undertaking the assault and after the reply given to Travis who commanded the enemy fortification, I still wanted to try a generous measure, characteristic of Mexican kindness, and I offered life to the defendants who would surrender their arms and retire under oath not to take them up again against Mexico. Colonel Don Juan Nepomuceno Almonte, through whom this generous offer was made, transmitted to me their reply which stated that they would let us know if they accepted and if not, they would renew the fire at a given hour. They decided on the latter course and their decision irrevocably sealed their fate.[2]

On the night of the fifth of March, four columns having been made ready for the assault under the command of their respective officers, they moved forward in the best order and with the greatest silence, but the imprudent huzzas of one of them awakened the sleeping vigilance of the defenders of the fort and their artillery fire caused such disorder among our columns that it was necessary to make use of the reserves. The Alamo was taken, this victory that was so much and so justly celebrated at the time, costing us seventy dead and about three hundred wounded,[3] a loss that was also later judged to be avoidable and charged, after the disaster of San Jacinto, to my incompetence and precipitation. I do not know of a way in which any fortification, defended by artillery, can be carried by assault without the personal losses of the attacking party being greater than those of the enemy, against whose walls and fortifications the brave assailants can present only their bare breasts. It is easy enough, from a desk in a peaceful office, to pile up charges against a general out on the field but this cannot prove anything more than the praiseworthy desire of making war less disastrous. But its nature being such, a general has no power over its immutable laws. Let us weep at the tomb of the brave Mexicans who died at the Alamo defending the honor and the rights of their country. They won a lasting claim to fame and the country can never forget their heroic names.

The enemy, discouraged by this blow that left fateful memories, fled before our forces. Our flanks, however, were, nevertheless, constantly molested by guerrilla bands,[4] which, favored by their intimate acquaintance with the country, the thickets of the woods, and the effectiveness of their rifles, caused daily losses to our troops. It became necessary to remedy this evil. The slow and embarrassing march of the whole army as a unit could have availed but little for such a purpose, for the fact of being together could not stop this evil. Nor was it advisable that our whole army should stop to combat the small guerrilla bands that were almost invisible, allowing the main army of the enemy, now fleeing, to perfect a plan of defence. Brevity was the ruling principle of all my operations, and for this reason I divided the troops available into three divisions, leaving at Béxar a sufficient force under the command of General Don Juan José Andrade to fall back upon.

The first division on our right, under the command of General Don José Urrea, was to operate in the district of Goliad, El Cópano and the whole coast. Its orders were to fight the small groups that were gathering to prevent their acting in concert and becoming a menace, and to clear and free the coast of enemies as far as Brazoria. This division was to rejoin me at San Felipe de Austin, which, situated on the margin of a river, in a central location, and well provided with food, seemed to me very appropriate as a point from which to direct the campaign.

Another division under the command of General Don Antonio Gaona was ordered to our left for the same purpose. With the same objects in view as the first, it was to scour the entire line from Béxar to Bastrop. Although at first he had instructions to continue as far as Nacogdoches, it was always my intention, upon his reaching Bastrop, to have him come to San Felipe, as I did in the end.

Each one of these divisions was in itself sufficient to give battle to the enemy; and, assured now that the army was well protected on its flanks, I had to look for a crossing on the Colorado. The officer whom I sent for this purpose with troops, supplies, and other resources at my command sent me a dispatch that made me believe he was in a serious situation. I issued orders for both the divisions, Urrea's and Gaona's, to march to his assistance, and I myself started out to join him. This I did at the pass of Atascosito on the 5th of April. The enemy who was defending it fled, and the central division of the army crossed the Colorado while the two flank divisions received counter orders instructing them anew to meet me in San Felipe towards which place I was marching.

It is necessary, before proceeding, to pause and review the operations of General Urrea. All of them were brilliant and fortune crowned all his efforts. Dr. Grant was overcome by his division; the coast was cleared of enemies; and those defending Goliad under the command of Fannin abandoned it and fled to Guadalupe Victoria, being forced to surrender at El Encinal in the plain of Perdido.[5] All this contributed in no small manner to the well-earned reputation of that general in the Texas campaign. To me, however, the last incident has brought grave consequences; and it is necessary, therefore, that I be allowed to digress here in order to speak of this matter.

Let it be said now in order to avoid repetition: the war against Texas has been as just on the part of the Mexican government as the lack of the slightest attempt on the part of those who forced it upon Mexico has been to try to justify their action. Few of the colonists, properly speaking, have taken up arms in the struggle. The soldiers of Travis at the Alamo, those of Fannin at Perdido, the riflemen of Dr. Grant, and Houston himself and his troops at San Jacinto, with but few exceptions, were publicly known to have come from New Orleans and other points of the neighboring republic exclusively for the purpose of aiding the Texas rebellion without ever having been members of any of the colonization grants.

Some Mexicans,[6] partisans of a former system of government, thought, perhaps in good faith, that the only effect of fanning the fire of war in Texas would be a political change in accord with their opinion. Their shortsighted ambition must be a terrible lesson to them as well as a source of eternal remorse. Too late, they now deplore having placed in jeopardy the integrity of our national territory.

Our country found itself invaded not by an established nation that came to vindicate its rights, whether true or imaginary; nor by

Mexicans who, in a paroxysm of political passion, came to defend or combat the public administration of the country. The invaders were all men who, moved by the desire of conquest, with rights less apparent and plausible than those of Cortés and Pízarro, wished to take possession of that vast territory extending from Béxar to the Sabine belonging to Mexico. What can we call them? How should they be treated? All the existing laws, whose strict observance the government had just recommended, marked them as pirates and outlaws. The nations of the world would never have forgiven Mexico had it accorded them rights, privileges, and considerations which the common law of peoples accords only to constituted nations.

NOTES

1. Many years later, while in exile, Santa Anna said, referring to the number of men, "I gathered and organized the expeditionary army of Texas, consisting of eight thousand men, in the city of Saltillo." "Diario de mi vida política y militar, "in Genaro García, *Documentos inéditos ó muy raros para la historia de México*, 36 vols. (Mexico: Vda. de C. Bouret, 1905–11), 2:33.

2. "To the proposals to surrender he replied always that every man under his command preferred to die rather than surrender the fort to the Mexicans." Ibid., p. 34.

3. "Not one remained alive but they disabled over a thousand of our men between dead and wounded." Ibid., p. 35.

4. There seems to be no evidence in the English accounts of the campaign that the Texans resorted to the use of guerrilla bands.—Carlos E. Castañeda.

5. "Fannin, who occupied the town of Goliad went out to meet General Urrea with 1500 filibusters and six pieces of artillery." García, *Documentos inéditos*, 2:35.

6. Santa Anna is hinting at Zavala, who left Mexico City and joined the Texans. He was the first vice-president of Texas.—Carlos E. Castañeda.

XENOPHOBIA
AND THE WAR OF 1847

Frederick C. Turner

Frederick C. Turner is a professor of political science at the University of Connecticut. He is a student of demography, Church ideologies, nationalism, and comparative politics in Latin America and the author of several articles on politics in Mexico, Chile, and Brazil. This selection was taken from his book The Dynamic of Mexican Nationalism. *Turner examines the several factors that fostered nationalism and xenophobia, especially those resulting from the loss of Texas and California. The Mexican's awareness of their powerful northern neighbor and their pride in the tenacity of common soldiers like the Niños Héroes are underscored in this essay. In addition, a comparison of this account of the early development of Mexican nationalism with others describing the growth of United States nationalism in the nineteenth century suggests a basic difference in the collective thinking of the two peoples (see note 1).*

EXTRAPOLATING from the national history of the United States, it would be easy for North Americans to discount the potential influence of foreign states in shaping national attitudes.[1] The strength, independence, and long isolation of the United States make it difficult for most Americans to conceive of the sentiments of fear, anxiety, and belligerence that an overpowering and apparently hostile state may provoke in a neighboring populace. Between 1810 and 1910, the power of the United States, as measured by such standards as territorial size, population, and economic potential, increased decisively, and in so doing it provided Mexico with that strong neighboring state that the colony of New Spain had lacked. Successive friction between the

United States and Mexico in the nineteenth century gave all Mexicans an opportunity to work in a common cause, and, whatever the motives of the United States government or its citizens, it also gave advocates of Mexican nationalism a set of historical precedents on which to base claims for the need for national unity.

Friction underlay the initial cordiality between the United States and Mexico. The achievement of independence from European control and the mutual desire to maintain that independence gave Mexico and the United States nominal claim to a common experience and a common interest in 1821. Iturbide declared his admiration for Henry Clay and his appreciation of Clay's championship of Mexico in Congress. What benefit the United States had derived from common experience, friendly declarations, and early American recognition of Mexican independence was undone in large part, however, during the first fifteen years of Mexican-American relations. By the time of Joel R. Poinsett's arrival in Mexico in 1825, a number of conflicts were evident. The United States resented growing British influence in Mexico, and both Mexico and the United States feared that the other was planning to seize Cuba. The differences between North American democracy and Protestantism and the aristocratic dominance and Catholicism of Mexico became sharper as the danger of Spanish reconquest receded. Poinsett failed to dispel this discord but rather increased the hostility by his intervention in Mexican politics. The friction caused by Poinsett's promotion of democracy and American business interests, his countering of British activity, and his siding with the York Rite Freemasons of Mexico against those of the Scottish Rite was increased still further by the second United States minister, Anthony Butler. Butler was, as North American historian Justin H. Smith readily admits, "a national disgrace . . . personally a bully and swashbuckler, ignorant of the Spanish language and even the forms of diplomacy . . . wholly unprincipled as to methods, and, by the testimony of two American consuls, openly scandalous in his conduct."[2] Poinsett's attempt to purchase Texas and Butler's open advocacy of annexation by the United States increased Mexican fears of Yankee expansion.

The historical causes of the Texas secession in 1835, the annexation of Texas to the United States in 1845, and the War of 1846 to 1848 in which Mexico lost the California territory do not have as much bearing on Mexican nationalism as do the causes that the Mexicans themselves have attributed to them. J. Fred Rippy may be essentially correct in saying that the early settlers in Texas "were entirely innocent of conspiracy or of ulterior motives of any sort."[3] Justin H. Smith attempts objectivity in his exhaustive study of *The War with Mexico* when he lays blame for the Texas secession primarily on Mexican politicians and the Mexican military.[4] The overwhelming opinion among most Mexicans, however, has been that the United States encouraged secession, annexation, and war in order to expand its territory. The majority of them would accept the blunt statement by José Vasconcelos, in his popular *Breve historia de México*, that "the Texas colonists were the advance guard of yankee imperialism."[5] Even writers who do not speak of imperialism, such as Carlos Bosch García in his objective and unemotional *Historia de las relaciones entire México y los Estados Unidos, 1819–1848*, can find good reason to fear American acquisitiveness in the pro-Texas and pro-expansion American press.[6]

The loss of Texas, New Mexico, and California has furthered Mexican nationalism in at least four ways. First, it provided an outside focus in the Republic of Texas and the United States against which Mexicans of the time could join in opposition. All classes and groups can set aside their struggles with one another to oppose a foreign foe, and as they continue to oppose forces from outside the national unit over a period of time, their makeshift cooperation proves the feasibility of internal unity. The need to resist foreigners leads to ideological emphasis on the need for unity to make that resistance effective.

At first glance, it seems that Mexicans had little to rally them to a national cause, considering the perfidy and incompetence of Santa Anna and the series of defeats like that at San Jacinto, where Texans, with 3 men killed and 18 wounded, managed to kill nearly 400 Mexicans, wound 200, and take 730 prisoners. What is under consideration is the feeling of common purpose that grows up among the inhabitants of a state, and this feeling is furthered by mutual fear of renewed foreign oppression or a shared sense of wounded pride as well as by a shared joy in common victory that in itself removes the original cause of joint action. It is quite natural that promoters of nationalism should re-examine their history with the idea of pointing out the positive achievements of the national group. It would be a far different matter, however, to say that all feelings of national community that arose among men in the earlier period could be motivated only by victory. The loss of Texas, New Mexico, and California may have increased Mexican nationalism at the time, even though the final proof of Texas' self-assertion and the apparent inefficiency of the central government stimulated *cacique* autonomy and the assertion of *patria chica* loyalties in the aftermath of the War of 1847. It is possible, of course, that the war had no positive immediate effect on Mexican nationalism but rather destroyed loyalties to the national state by demonstrating the state's ineffectiveness. Although the war may or may not have initially stimulated any great degree of national loyalty, the fact that factionalism was not immediately reduced indicates the extent of the divisions within Mexican society and the limited effectiveness of xenophobia in counteracting them.

Second, the loss of Texas, New Mexico, and California provided Mexico with a permanent focus for xenophobia, a focus made particularly effective where low educational levels made most of the population lacking in reasoned analysis and historical objectivity. The "myth of the treasure of Texas and California"[7] remains a potent emotive force in Mexican society. Mexicans can still be rallied by a sense of their lost territory, and when something goes wrong in Mexico, it is possible to say, "Yes, but that would not matter if we had Los Angeles or San Francisco or Houston." The incompetence of Santa Anna can be left unnoted when prominent writers like José Vasconcelos continue to stir Mexican nationalism with references to "Yankee imperialism."

Third, the loss of half of her territory deprived Mexico of the need to incorporate it into an effective national unit. After 1848 the Indians of the north became the gringos' problem. Only massive border fortifications could have prevented the westward movement of individual Anglo-Saxons, particularly after the discovery of California gold, and if Mexico had retained title to her northern territories, she would only have been faced with the problem of incorporating yet another disparate group into her national community.

Finally, it may be argued that the territorial losses proved to be one of the most conclusive of a series of recognized needs for national unity. The Texas secession was the result of an internal conflict that directly alienated a large part of Mexico's territory and, to the extent that the war with the United States was brought on by Mexican intransigence over the Texas issue, indirectly alienated California as well. Furthermore, internal conflicts prevented Mexico from putting up an effective military or diplomatic resistance to United States expansion. Mexicans were increasingly to reflect Justo Sierra's fear that the United States would absorb Mexico and extinguish her nationality if she were found weak. Like a variety of other events in the nineteenth century, and like the violence and destructiveness of the Revolution of 1910, the early losses of territory to the United States indicated the need for an effective unification of the Mexican citizenry.

In retrospect, the war with the United States injected the Mexican people with a deep national consciousness. Although Santa Anna tried to save face after the 1847 defeats by associating his personal honor with the national honor of Mexico,[8] his symbolic importance to the Mexican national community is that of a scapegoat and an "anti-hero" against whom Mexicans join in disgust. Mexicans look back with little pride on their generals and on the outcome of major battles, but they take pride in the tenacity of their common soldiers. Recent Mexican accounts consciously appeal to nationalist sentiments by charging American soldiers with pillage, by accusing General Winfield Scott of stealing Mexican archives, and by denouncing "the lack of patriotism" that some Mexicans displayed in collaborating with the United States "enemy."[9] The American attack on the Military College at Chapultepec Castle on September 13, 1847, gave Mexico a new set of national heroes in the Niños Héroes, the young cadets who died fighting the American invaders. In order to prevent the Yankees from defiling his country's flag, Cadet Juan Escutia wrapped himself in the Mexican colors that flew above the castle and leaped to his death from the battlements. Mexico today celebrates the Niños Héroes in popular textbooks, in colorful pictures with which children decorate their homes, and even in cinema newsreels that show the president of Mexico awarding swords on September 13 to the contemporary cadets of the Colegio Militar.

Anyone wishing to promote a sense of Mexican nationalism by stimulating fear of the United States can find ample precedents following the War of 1846 to 1848. After the acquisition of Texas and California, a vocal minority within the United States supported annexation of all Mexico. The Gadsden Treaty of 1853, although drawn up primarily to settle boundary disputes and to facilitate a southern railroad route for the United States, did add more Mexican territory to the United States. The desire for right of transit and protection on the Isthmus of Tehuantepec aroused some fear of American expansion, for Nicholas P. Trist was authorized to pay extra for the right and certain rights were later incorporated into the Gadsden Treaty. Since these rights were not canceled until 1937, Mexicans had a number of years in which to ponder the potential limitations on their sovereignty.

Mexican conservatives even see Secretary of State William H. Seward's efforts to aid Benito Juárez and remove the French from Mexico as undue American influence. Mexican writers such as Rafael de Castro originally justified French intervention and the monarchy of Maximilian as necessary for the realization of Mexican nationalism by claiming that they would prevent United States invasion and cure Mexico's "social disorganization."[10] Although standard Mexican histories now approve and give importance to Secretary Seward's diplomatic pressure on Napoleon III,[11] a more conservative line of Mexican thinking represented by José Vasconcelos still violently resents the United States "interference." Vasconcelos, as quoted by Erico Verissimo, expresses this viewpoint when he says, "the year 1865 saw the Empire consolidated. But unfortunately the Civil War in the United States ended that same year with the victory of the Unionists, and the first thing they did was to invoke the Monroe Doctrine, threatening us with the invasion of Mexico by Grant's troops."[12]

The final assertion of United States government influence before the conciliatory policies of the Díaz regime eased official Mexican-American relations occurred in 1877, when talk of war arose from President Rutherford B. Hayes's need to divert attention from his doubtful electoral victory. In response to bellicose North American statements, Díaz sent General Treviño to the border to establish order and to counter a possible United States offensive. It is a mark of the increased national unity that Mexico had achieved from its previous friction with the United States and from other sources that this order rallied Mexicans from all factions solidly behind Díaz.

A number of other irritants in Mexican-American relations promoted nationalistic sentiment among particular groups of Mexicans. Raids of American filibusters such as those of William Walker into Sonora in 1853, Callahan and Henry in 1855, or the Crabb expedition of 1857 in which over sixty filibusters were shot after surrendering stirred a national consciousness in the inhabitants of the northern states and rekindled general fears of annexation. The fact that Yucatán remained neutral and maintained its own agent in Washington during the War of 1847 exemplified the divided nature of the Mexican polity. Not only did the inhabitants of Yucatán feel an intense local loyalty that separated them from the inhabitants of Mexico living outside the peninsula, but the Yucatecos themselves were also typically split by the division between the Spanish and Maya populations and the sharp rivalry between the city of Campeche and the rest of the peninsula.[13] When an Indian uprising in 1848 made the inhabitants of Yucatán seek annexation to the United States, Mexicans in touch with the Yucatán situation were made additionally aware of the need to forge a truly national state.

The mounting number of claims by and against American citizens for damage to property, seizure of cargoes, personal injury, or imprisonment forced many Mexicans to turn for settlement to their national government, thus developing a personal stake in the effectiveness of that government. Claims involving officials of the American government sometimes aroused considerable public bitterness, as did those involving Consuls John A. Robinson and Francis W. Rice. It was from a variety of lesser incidents that directly involved only a small number of Mexicans—the filibuster raids and the international claims—and from events of more general relevance—the loss of Texas, New Mexico, and California; Seward's Mexican policy; and Díaz' dispatch of General Treviño—that Mexicans became increasingly aware of their powerful neighbor.

NOTES

1. For the United States, nationalistic feelings were certainly heightened by the wars with Britain which began in 1775 and 1812, although significant groups within the United States preferred to move to Canada after independence, to trade with Britain during Jefferson's Embargo, or to oppose the War of 1812 at the Hartford Convention. Despite incipient conflicts with Britain, settled by the Webster-Ashburton and Clayton-Bulwer treaties, and even the potential intervention of European powers in the Civil War, the geographic isolation of the United States formed a severe barrier to foreign invasion until the radical improvements in world-wide transportation in the twentieth century. The Mexican and Spanish-American Wars hardly threatened United States territory. The effect of our own western frontier was far more significant in shaping American attitudes and values than fear of strong foreign states. The very fact that the growing strength of the United States as compared to that of Canada and Mexico relieved American citizens of potential anxiety in the nineteenth century was in itself a source of anxiety for those neighboring states.

2. Justin H. Smith, *The War with Mexico*, 2 vols. (New York: Macmillan Co., 1919), 1:62.

3. J. Fred Rippy, *The United States and Mexico* (New York: Alfred A. Knopf, 1926), p. 8.

4. While fully cognizant of Smith's painstaking scholarship, Mexicans

find his work to be "a late expression of Manifest Destiny." See Silvio Zavala, "La historigrafía americana sobre la guerra de 47," *Cuadernos Americanos*, 38 (March–April 1948): 202–5.

5. José Vasconcelos, *Breve historia de México*, 3d ed. (Mexico: Editorial Continental, 1959), p. 327. A more specialized tirade which, in bitterly emphasizing the frictions in Mexican-American relations from the early nineteenth century to 1959, concludes that the United States has risen to greatness largely at the expense of Mexico is Mario Gill, *Nuestros buenos vecinos*, 4th ed. (Mexico: Editorial Azteca, 1959). Gill's treatment of the Texas secession and the War of 1847, on pp. 17–89, exemplifies those accounts that consciously try to arouse fierce Mexican pride and xenophobia. The Cuban regime of Fidel Castro has republished a special edition of *Nuestros buenos vecinos*.

6. Carlos Bosch García, *Historia de las relaciones entre México y los Estados Unidos, 1819–1848* (Mexico: Escuela Nacional de Ciencias Políticas y Sociales, Universidad Nacional Autónoma de México, 1961), pp. 173–78.

7. Jorge Carrion, "Efectos psicológicos de la guerra de 47 en el hombre de México," *Cuadernos Americanos* 37 (January–February 1948): 127, 131.

8. *Al pueblo mexicano: Relación de las causas que influyeron en los desgraciados sucesos del día de agosto de 1847* (Mexico: Imprenta de Vicente García Torres, 1847), p. 8.

9. Alberto María Carreño, *México y los Estados Unidos de América: Apuntaciones para la historia del acrecentamiento territorial de los Estados Unidos a costa de México desde la época colonial hasta nuestros días* (Mexico: Editorial Jus, 1962), pp. 154–56.

10. J. Rafael de Castro, *La cuestión mexicana, ó esposición de las causas que hacian indispensables la intervención europea y el restablecimiento de la monarquía en México como unicos medios de salvar la nacionalidad y la independencia del país* (Mexico: Imprenta de J. M. Andrade y F. Escalante, 1864), pp. 70, 87.

11. See Alfonso Toro, *Compendio de historia de México: La revolución de independencia y México independiente*, 11th ed. (Mexico: Editorial Patria, 1959), p. 534.

12. Quoted in Erico Verissimo, *Mexico*, trans. Linton Barrett, (New York: Orion Press, 1960), p. 197.

13. Ricardo Molina H ¨ubbe, "Yucatán en el siglo XIX," *Ciencias Políticas y Sociales* 2 (January–March 1956): 104–5, 121–27. See also Nelson Reed, *The Caste War of Yucatan* (Stanford, Calif.: Stanford University Press, 1964).

TREATY OF
GUADALUPE HIDALGO

Rodolfo Acuña

The Treaty of Guadalupe Hidalgo ended the war between Mexico and the United States. Under the terms of the treaty the Rio Grande was recognized as the border of Texas, and much of the present American Southwest was ceded to the United States for $15 million. In this excerpt, Chicano activist-historian Rodolfo Acuña describes the content of that treaty, especially Articles 8 and 9 and the Statement of Protocol for the omitted Article 10. Acuña argues that these articles guaranteed the political and economic rights of the Mexican American who lived in the occupied and ceded territory, and that had they been enforced, the articles would have protected the cultural integrity of the Chicano people. Instead, the U. S. government violated the treaty terms, and cultural genocide and political and economic discrimination resulted. The reader should note Acuña's final reference to the cultural bias and "racism" of Anglo-American historians. Whatever the truth of Acuña's interpretation, it is apparent that Mexico's past is a living past, not only in Mexico but also in the United States. The author of this selection has published several textbooks on Mexican Americans for the elementary and secondary schools of California. This selection was taken from Acuña's Occupied America: The Chicano's Struggle toward Liberation, *published in revised form as* Occupied America: A History of Chicanos.

By LATE AUGUST 1847, the war was almost at an end, with General Winfield Scott defeating Santa Anna in a hard-fought battle at Churubusco. It placed the Anglo-Americans at the gates of Mexico City. Santa Anna made overtures for an armistice, and for two weeks negotiations were conducted. However, Santa Anna reorganized his defenses during this period, and, in turn, the Anglo-Americans renewed their relentless attacks. On September 13, 1847, Scott drove into the city. Although the Mexicans fought valiantly for their capital, the battle left 4000 of their men dead with another 3000 taken prisoner. On September 13, before the occupation of Mexico began, the *Niños Heroes* (the Boy Heros) fought off the conquerors and leapt to their deaths rather than surrender. These teenage cadets were Francisco Márquez, Agustín Melgar, Juan Escutia, Fernando Montes Oca, Vicente Suárez, and Juan de la Barrera. They became "a symbol and image of this unrighteous war."[1]

Although the Mexicans were beaten, fighting continued. The presidency devolved to the presiding justice of the Supreme Court, Manuel de la Peña y Peña. He knew that Mexico had lost and that it was his duty to salvage as much as possible. Pressure mounted, for the United States was in control of much of present-day Mexico.

Nicholas Trist, sent to Mexico to act as peace commissioner, had been unable to start negotiations until January 1848. Trist arrived in Vera Cruz on May 6, 1847, where he had a "vigorous but temporary tiff with Scott." Negotiations were conducted through the British legation, but were delayed by Trist's illness. This delay compromised a speedy settlement, and after the fall of Mexico City, Secretary of State James Buchanan wanted to revise Trist's instructions. He ordered Trist to break off negotiations and come home.[2] Polk apparently had begun to consider demanding more territory from Mexico and paying less for it. Trist, however, with the support of Winfield Scott, decided to ignore Polk's order, and he proceeded to negotiate on the original terms. Mexico, badly beaten, her government in a state of turmoil, had no choice but to agree to the Anglo-American's proposals.

On February 2, 1848, the Mexicans agreed to the Treaty of Guadalupe Hidalgo, in which Mexico accepted the Rio Grande as the Texas border and ceded the Southwest (which incorporates the present-day states of Arizona, California, New Mexico, Utah, Nevada, and parts of Colorado) to the United States in return for $15 million.

Polk was furious about the treaty; he considered Trist "contemptibly base" for having ignored his orders. Yet he had no choice but to submit the treaty to the Senate. With the exception of article X, the Senate ratified the treaty on March 10, 1848, by a vote of 28 to 14. To insist on more territory would have meant more fighting, and both Polk and the Senate realized that the war was already beginning to be unpopular in many sections. The treaty was sent to the Mexican Congress for its ratification; although the Congress had difficulty forming a quorum, the agreement was ratified on May 19 by a 52 to 35 vote.[3] Hostilities between the two nations were now officially ended. Trist, however, was branded as a "scoundrel," because Polk was disappointed in the settlement. There was considerable support and fervor in the United States for the acquisition of all Mexico.[4]

Contrary to popular belief, Mexico did not abandon its citizens who lived within the bounds of the new U. S. territory. The Mexican negotiators were concerned about the Mexicans left behind, and they expressed great reservations about these people being forced to "merge or blend" into Anglo-American culture. They protested the exclusion of provisions that protected the Mexican citizens' rights, land titles, and religion.[5] They wanted to know the Mexican's status, and they wanted to protect his rights by treaty.

The provisions that specifically refer to the Mexican and his rights are found in articles VIII and IX and the omitted article X. Taken in the context of the reluctance of Mexican officials to abandon their people to a nation that had virtually no respect for Mexicans, it is easier to understand why Chicanos are so angry about violations to their cultural identity.

Under the Treaty of Guadalupe Hidalgo, the Mexican left behind had one year to choose whether to return to the interior of Mexico or to remain in "occupied Mexico." About 2000 elected to leave; however, most remained in what they considered *their* territory. This situation was very similar to that of other conquered people, for the legality of the forced seizure is still an issue.

Article IX of the treaty guaranteed Mexicans "the enjoyment of all the rights of citizens of the United States according to the principles of the Constitution; and in the meantime shall be maintained and protected in the free enjoyment of their liberty and property, and secured in the free exercise of their religion without restriction."[6] This article and the United States' adherence to it have long been debated by scholars. Most sources admit that the Anglo-Americans have respected the Chicano's religion; on the other hand, Chicanos and well-known scholars contend that the rights of cultural integrity and rights of citizenship have been constantly violated. Lynn I. Perrigo in *The American Southwest* summarizes the guarantees of articles VIII and IX, writing: "In other words, besides the right and duties of American citizenship, they [the Mexicans] would have some special privileges derived from their previous customs in language, law, and religion."[7]

In spite of these guarantees, Chicanos have been subjected to cultural genocide, as well as to violations of their rights. *A Documentary History of the Mexican Americans*, published in 1971, states:

> As the only minority, apart from the Indians, ever acquired by conquest, the Mexican Americans have been subjected to economic, social, and political discrimination, as well as a great deal of violence at the hands of their Anglo conquerors. During the period from 1865 to 1920, there were more lynchings of Mexican Americans in the Southwest. But the worst violence has been the unrelenting discrimination against the cultural heritage—the language and customs—of the Mexican Americans, coupled with the economic exploitation of the entire group. Property rights were guaranteed, but not protected, by either the federal or state governments. Equal protection under law has consistently been a mockery in the Mexican-American communities.[8]

Just as controversial is the explicit protection of property. Although most analyses do not consider the omitted article X, this article had comprehensive guarantees protecting "all prior and pending titles to property of every description."[9] When this provision was deleted by the U. S. Senate, Mexican officials protested. Anglo-American emissaries reassured them by drafting a Statement of Protocol on May 26, 1848, which read:

> The American government by suppressing the Xth article of the Treaty of Guadalupe Hidalgo did not in any way intend to annul the grants of lands made by Mexico in the ceded territories. These grants . . . preserve the legal value which they may possess, and the grantees may cause their legitimate (titles) to be acknowledged before the American tribunals.
>
> Conformable to the law of the United States, legitimate titles to every description of property, personal and real, existing in the ceded territories, are those which were legitimate titles under the Mexican law of California and New Mexico up to the 13th of May, 1846, and in Texas up to the 2nd of March, 1836.[10]

It is doubtful, considering the Mexican opposition to the treaty, whether the Mexican Congress would have ratified the treaty without this clarification. The vote was close. The Statement of Protocol was reinforced by articles VIII and XI, which guaranteed Mexicans rights of property and protection under the law. In addition, court decisions have generally interpreted the treaty as protecting land titles and water rights. Nevertheless, the fact remains that property was seized

and individual rights were violated—largely through political ma-
nipulation.

It is one thing to make a treaty and another to live up to it. The
United States has had a singularly poor record in complying with its
treaty obligations, and as subsequent chapters will show, nearly every
one of the obligations discussed above was violated, confirming the
prophecy of Mexican diplomat Manuel Cresencio Rejón who, at the
time the treaty was signed, commented:

> Our race, our unfortunate people will have to wander in search of hospi-
> tality in a strange land, only to be ejected later. Descendants of the
> Indians that we are, the North Americans hate us, their spokesmen
> depreciate us, even if they recognize the justice of our cause, and they
> consider us unworthy to form with them one nation and one society, they
> clearly manifest that their future expansion begins with the territory that
> they take from us and pushing [sic] aside our citizens who inhabit the
> land.[11]

CONCLUSION

Manuel Cresencio Rejón affirms the legacy left behind by Anglo
conquest and violence. Mexicans were the victims of unjust aggressions and transgressions against them and their nation.
Mingled with feelings of Anglo-American racial and cultural
superiority, the violence created a legacy of hate on both sides
that has continued to the present. The image of the *Tejano* had
become that of the obnoxious, rude oppressor throughout Latin
America, whereas most Anglo-Americans considered Chicanos
as foreigners with inferior rights. As a result of the Texas War and
the Anglo-American aggressions of 1845–1848, the occupation of
Chicano territory began, and colonization started to take form.
The attitude of the Anglo, during the period of subjugation following the wars, is reflected in the conclusions of the noted Texan
historian and past-president of the American Historical Association, Walter Prescott Webb:

> A homogenous European society adaptable to new conditions was
> necessary. This Spain did not have to offer in Arizona, New Mexico, and
> Texas. Its frontier, as it advanced, depended more and more on an Indian
> population. . . . This mixture of races meant in time that common sol-
> diers in the Spanish service came largely from pueblo or sedentary Indian

stock, whose blood, when compared to that of the plain Indians, was as ditch water. It took more than a little mixture of Spanish blood and mantle of Spanish service to make valiant soldiers of the timid pueblo Indians.[12]

A new era had begun, and according to the Anglo-American, it had a homogenous and racially superior people to lead it. The conquest laid the framework of the colony and justified the economic and political privilege established by the conquerors. Most Anglo-Americans, historians and laymen alike, are inflicted with a historical amnesia as to how they acquired it and how they maintained control over the conquered land and people.

NOTES

1. Alfonso Zabre, *Guide to the History of Mexico: A Modern Interpretation* (Austin, Texas: Pemberton Press, 1969), p. 300.

2. Dexter Perkins and Glyndon G. Van Deusen, *The American Democracy: Its Rise to Power* (New York: Macmillan Co., 1964), p. 237.

3. Robert Selph Henry, *The Story of the Mexican War* (New York: Frederick Ungar Publishing Co., 1950), p. 390.

4. See John D. P. Fuller, *The Movement for the Acquisition of All Mexico* (New York: Da Capo Press, 1969).

5. Letter from Commissioner Trist to Secretary Buchanan, Mexico, 25 January 1848, Senate Executive Document no. 52, p. 283.

6. Wayne Moquin et al., eds., *A Documentary History of the Mexican American* (New York: Frederick A. Praeger, 1971), p. 185.

7. Lynn I. Perrigo, *The American Southwest* (New York: Holt, Rinehart, and Winston, 1971), p. 176.

8. Moquin, *Documentary History*, p. 181.

9. Perrigo, *American Southwest*, p. 176.

10. *Compilation of Treaties on Force* (Washington, D.C.: Government Printing Office, 1899), p. 402; quoted in Perrigo, *American Southwest*; p. 176.

11. Antonio de la Pena y Reyes, *Algunos Documentos Sobre el Tratado de Guadalupe Hidalgo* (Mexico: Secretaría de Relaciones Exteriores, 1930), p. 159, quoted in Richard Gonzáles, "Commentary on the Treaty of Guadalupe Hidalgo," in Feliciano Rivera, *A Mexican American Source Book* (Menlo Park, Calif.: Educational Consulting Associates, 1970), p. 185.

12. Walter Prescott Webb, *The Great Plains* (New York: Grosset & Dunlap, 1931), pp. 125–26.

MEXICO'S TRAGEDY

Justo Sierra

Justo Sierra (1848–1912) was one of the foremost intellectuals of the Porfiriato. He was known as a novelist, essayist, poet, historian, and educator. Sierra contributed articles on philosophy, jurisprudence, law, and history to several journals and newspapers, including La Tribuna *and* La Libertad. *As a historian he edited the monumental work of the Porfirio Díaz period,* México, su evolución social. *He also wrote two books on Mexican history,* Evolución política del pueblo mexicano *and* Juárez, su obra y su tiempo. *The following selection was taken from Sierra's classic liberal history entitled* The Political Evolution of the Mexican People. *In it Sierra details, from a Mexican point of view, the important events between 1835 and 1848. It illuminates how internal political events in Mexico were related to the Texas secession (e.g., how the dissolution of the federalist Constitution of 1824 gave an air of legality to the Texas separation). Note also the continuous theme of Mexicans as a people defeating themselves, rather than being defeated by outsiders. An interesting comparison can be made between Sierra's description of Santa Anna and North American accounts. In his conclusion Sierra suggests a kind of moral compensation and fatality in history. Perhaps the mood of the final paragraph is more revealing than its content.*

THE FIRST THREE DECADES of our history as a nation were overcast by the menace and fear of a conflict with Spain. But, after the death of Ferdinand VII, the rise to power of the reform party in Spain and a terrible civil war changed entirely the situation which had produced the abortive attempts at reconquest. Assaults on the supremacy of the Church and clergy became progressively more drastic and were followed by frightful bloody riots. By comparison, the efforts of our York party to found a lay government in Mexico were mild and innocuous. Any further attempt at reconquest was out of the question. The next step, then, was recognition of the former colonies' independence, and this step was taken by the minister José María Calatrava toward the end of 1836 when solemn diplomatic sanction was accorded to relations between Spain and Mexico. Had this been done ten years earlier, a great deal of grief and woe would have been avoided.

The truth is that federalism and sympathy with the United States to the point of seeking an alliance with them—notions cherished by the founders of our early liberalism—were natural consequences of Spain's attitude. When this began to change, our anxieties turned northward, where the Texas problem loomed on the horizon, scarcely eclipsing, however, the colossus of might and ambition that towered beyond. A war with Texas did not preoccupy the Mexicans; what did overcast the entire period of centralism was the fear of a war with the United States. The fear was well founded: the United States could easily cut off our meager revenues and our communication with the outside world by seizing our unfortified ports, so that we would have to devour ourselves in desperate civil strife. Fortunately for Mexico, the war came as a direct invasion which, while shamefully laying bare some of our intimate weaknesses, stirred our blood, arousing the valor of the most self-abnegating people in the world—for the masses had no positive blessings to defend, nothing but what was abstract or emotional—and the disorganized nation achieved a measure of cohesion at last.

The most redoubtable legacy left to us by Spain was the vast stretch of desert along our northern frontier, beyond the Rio Grande and the Gila, uninhabited and in the main uninhabitable, with extensive belts of fertile land and others hopelessly sterile. The distances separating these regions from our political center and the fact that most of our population was rooted to the soil and the rest sparsely scattered made it impracticable for us to exploit resources which, in any case, were still largely a matter for conjecture. What was certain was that the Anglo-Americans' formidable expansion would sooner or later engulf those regions. The easternmost, Texas, fell so naturally within the scope of that irresistible thrust that our statesmen should have considered only the best way to give away, literally, the land we could never occupy by inviting the whole world to colonize it—the Russians, the French, the English, the Spaniards, the Chinese— thereby erecting a Babel of peoples as a dike to stem the tide of

American expansion. But it is easy to prescribe with hindsight; our fathers, prejudiced and necessarily ignorant as they were, could have taken no such step; our knowledge is the consequence of their mistakes.

A thousand little attempts at encroachment made it abundantly clear that the United States coveted Texas, fertile, well-watered, and teeming with cattle, from the day that the expanding nation reached the state's borders. The Spanish government stood staunchly on its rights and was very cautious and parsimonious in granting concessions. The concession that gave rise to the American colonization of Texas was granted to the father of Stephen F. Austin and permitted him to settle three hundred Catholic families in the province. The Mexican government, feeling the need of amity with the United States and lacking the power to assert its rights, confirmed the grant but failed to enforce the restrictions. Texas was soon dotted with small but growing American colonies. Grants made to Mexican citizens, such as those to Zavala and others, were sold to Americans, who promptly settled in the fecund region. The danger was patent and considered so imminent, a law passed in Bustamante's first administration prohibited the acquisition by foreigners of lands within the limits of the frontier states. This law was aimed at the Americans, who nevertheless continued to seep into Texas and to form colonies there, despite the military posts established by General Mier y Terán. The state, then conjoined with Coahuila, first took part in political affairs by siding enthusiastically with the revolution instigated by the smugglers of Vera Cruz against Bustamante's strict administration in 1832 and headed by the inevitable Santa Anna. The following year Texas declared itself, *moto proprio*, separate from Coahuila. Zavala, who owned land in Texas, moved by self-interest, by his Jacobin's venomous hatred for Catholicism (which in that day, to be sure, took on in Mexico the aspect of a vast superstition), and by his congenital affinity, as a Yucatecan, for loose federation, states' rights, and even for local autonomy and secession, carried the grim tidings of centralism's triumph to the Anglo-American colonists. Excited by his eloquence, and by Austin's, and counting on strong support from the United States, the Texans decided to secede from Mexico and declare themselves independent. This was a sad but unavoidable turn of events. Multiple ties bound the Texans to their blood brothers, but no ties at all to the Mexicans. What made our case worse was that the rupture of the federal pact gave a perfectly legal character to the separation—

which was sure to occur sooner or later, anyhow. Even if the Constitution of 1824 had been legally reformed, the states of the Federation were clearly under no obligation to remain in the union unless they ratified a new agreement; as parties to a contract, they were at liberty to renew it or not, as they saw fit. Texas seceded without going through the formality of refusing to renew the contract because the Constitution was not reformed—it was abolished. Centralism was proclaimed, and an assembly convoked to stamp a seal of sanction on a *fait accompli.*

If our statesmen had been wise enough to see the matter in this light, if, accepting the secession as legal, they had set about extracting the best possible advantage from a settlement with Texas, the ensuing war, with its aftermath of shame and ruin, could have been averted, and also the conflict with the United States, which was the ineluctable consequence of that war.

The separatists seized San Antonio; receiving constant shipments of arms from the United States, they awaited the Mexican armies. The preparation of an army that was to fight a national war (for most Mexicans so considered the war with Texas) afforded Santa Anna and his cronies an opportunity for rich pickings. The country's fate was still in the hands of the moneylenders. The exchequer could not even take care of current expenses. Waste, disorder, and the tremendous deficit added by each triumphant revolution to the deficits incurred by previous revolutions made it necessary to resort to the implacable usurers of Venice, who built their fortunes out of our misfortunes. New taxes were levied, one on top of another, but the masses were unproductive. They produced solely for the landowner, who, by means of the rural system—the proprietor's store, his vouchers, his special currency for each type of transaction, and at times the practice of fostering alcoholism—kept the country laborer (and this means more than half the population) in bondage for debt and degraded. Thus, the peon paid indirectly the taxes assigned to his master. And the man who was free, who had his own little independent business, paid excises and tolls that devoured two-thirds of his profits and caused him to look on contraband as a deliverance. The head-tax in some states and the requisitions of the Church added the final cogs to the monstrous machine calculated to crush all liberty, just as it crushed every effort at economic independence, every attempt at saving. The Mexican has never known what it means to save, has never saved anything. The middle class, both rural and urban—the farmowner, the prosperous artisan, the storekeeper—was the perpetual victim of the tax system, the eternal plotter of new revolutions, always hoping that the triumph of a new order would bring him relief. This class, moreover, was the one that suffered perpetual exploitation at the hands of the guerilla chief, the general, the prefect, the governor. The merchant and the landowner were engaged in a desperate struggle with the government. They robbed their extortioners any way they could and cheated the law religiously. Abandoning their businesses, little by little, to the foreigner—the hacienda, the farm, the food store to the Spaniard (who had already returned), the clothing and jewelry shops to the Frenchman, the mines to the Englishman—they at last took refuge en masse in the bureaucracy, that superb normal school for idleness and graft which has educated our country's middle class. All this serves to explain why the Congresses would authorize the contracting of loans amounting to only a few hundred thousands of pesos, of which no more than forty-five percent was received in credit, with an interest not exceeding four percent per month and a term of six months until the entire sum must be repaid! Under this system, we were defeated before we ever started. Santa Anna, in San Luis Potosí, before taking the field managed to collect funds which were always exhausted, frittered away, in less than a month's time. He procured these funds from the clergy, from the concessionaires of the mints, and from private persons, who received, in return for a mess of pottage, national properties of the highest value (the salinas of Peñon Blanco, for example). Even so, the army was able to move from one place to another only with the most agonizing hardships. And nobody got paid.

The campaign in Texas made two things manifest: (I) the incapacity of the seceded state to defend itself alone, for the victorious Mexican army traversed a good part of the territory between the Rio Grande and the Sabine, and (2) the political and military ineptitude of that general who, though experienced only in civil war and barracks mutiny, was exalted by the Mexican masses as a military genius. His policy of shooting prisoners, laying waste the countryside and burning the towns roused the Texans to fury and added flaming indignation to the self-interest that had moved the Americans to sympathize with the Texans, who rightly appealed to the humanitarian sentiments of the civilized world for judgment against the savage invader. And the culmination of his strategy was a mad risk that turned a triumphal march into a shambles at San Jacinto, where the contingent that he led was annihilated and himself taken prisoner. Fear of losing his life impelled him to convert partial defeat into general catastrophe, and, in obedience to his order as President of the Republic and Commander in Chief, the army under General Vicente Filísola came back across the Rio Grande. Thus, the whole state of Texas was abandoned. In reality, the military problem was ended so far as this rebel state was concerned. Any further attempt to recover it would mean an encounter, face to face, with the United States. . . .

It is true that history, which in our day strives for scientific precision, should shun emotion and concentrate on establishing facts, analyzing them, and fitting their salient characteristics into a synthesis. But there are too many periods in our history when the repetition of the same errors, the same evils, over and over in dismal monotony, afflicts and oppresses our hearts with sorrow and shame. What a waste of energy, what a loss of vitality in the endless spilling of blood, the endless strife! How many humble homes darkened forever, how many, how incalculably many individual tragedies! And all to prepare the way for the ultimate humiliation of our country! The bandit who infested every road became indistinguishable from the guerrilla chief, who became a colonel, who between one tumult and another became a general, and between one revolution and the next, an aspirant to the Presidency. And each of them carried on the point of his bayonet a declaration, and in the wallet of his counselor—whether priest, lawyer, or merchant—a plan, and on his banner a constitution, all guaranteed to bring felicity to the Mexican people, who, trampled and macerated underfoot everywhere and by everyone, dragged themselves from the bloody mire to earn their daily morsel by drudging like beasts of burden or to earn oblivion by fighting like heroes. The period between the French and American wars was one of the darkest in our tragic history. There would be another one like it later, but then a ray of light would glimmer on the horizon. Now there was nothing but the black night. . . .

The United States had tried since the birth of the Mexican Republic to acquire the territory between Louisiana and the Rio Grande, from the river's source to its mouth. Poinsett had offered to buy Texas from the Mexican government; the leaders of the Democratic Party, which was strongest in the states of the South, never gave up the idea of acquiring it, either by agreement or by force. Soon they added to this ambition that of acquiring all the Mexican territory on the Pacific north of the tropic of Cancer, to forestall, they said, its acquisition by

England or some other nation. In short, their doctrine was that all territory adjoining the United States which Mexico could not effectively govern should belong to the Americans.

Aggression was retarded by treaties and the practices of international equity, by the anxiety of England and France over the Union's expansion, and by the opposition of the Whig Party, led by Henry Clay, great conscience and great orator, to the pro-slavery, secessionist Democratic Party; but the trend of events made war inevitable.

If the opposing parties in Mexico had not used the Texas question as a political club, each accusing the other of traitorous intentions, catastrophe might have been avoided. The incontrovertible right of Texas to secede once the federal pact was broken should have been recognized to begin with, and the differences between the American political parties should have been exploited.

But no, the constant specter of war with Texas, which seemed certain, and with the United States, which seemed probable, served Santa Anna's purposes. It gave him an excuse to station the ghost of an army, starving and almost unarmed, on the Rio Grande, so that he could incessantly demand funds, which he incessantly frittered away.

In the field of international equity our diplomacy won consistent victories over the Americans. A series of impeccably reasonable notes remonstrated against the unceasing attacks on the dignity of the Mexican Republic which had been countenanced by the government in Washington. Open meetings in some cities of the Union urged war with Mexico and the annexation of Texas, and a sort of armed emigration toward the latter region was organized, a threat which not even Daniel Webster's talents could find excuses for.

But the course of events was inexorable. Over and beyond the issue of illicit aid to Texas (for whether Texas was regarded as a rebel state of Mexico or as an independent nation at war with a friendly nation, the aid was illicit) there arose the issue of annexation. And even if the Texans were within their rights in seeking to join the United States, the Americans had no right to proceed with annexation before arriving at an understanding with regard to mutual responsibilities. President Tyler's Secretary of War, John Calhoun, who would be the Moses of the secession movement, negotiated a treaty of annexation with Texas, which the Senate in Washington refused to approve and which shocked France and England—both had recognized the independence of Texas—into offering us their services as mediators in order to avert further insults. Meanwhile, Santa Anna made preparations to resume the war with Texas as soon as the armistice should expire, and thereby brought down the fulminations of the American plenipotentiary, who candidly bared his government's intentions by warning that any invasion of Texas would mean war with the United States. This was understood by the Mexican government, which had previously warned that the admission of Texas to the Union would be answered with a declaration of war. The whole question hung on the presidential election in the United States. If Polk, candidate of the Democrats and of the South and with a platform calling for annexation, should be elected, conflict was inevitable. If Clay should win, peace was assured. Polk won by fewer than 40,000 votes out of a total of 2,060,000. This spelled disaster for Mexico. One thing was clear, however: the cause of annexation and war in the United States was not a national but a Southern cause. . . .

Meanwhile, the war had become a fact, although hostilities had not yet commenced. Paredes, anxious to repair his irreparable guilt, was accumulating supplies and slowly sending reinforcements to the frontier. But the Mexican generals were never able to muster a numerical superiority in troops that was sufficient to overbalance the American superiority in armament. At the beginning of May, the Mexican Commander in Chief, General Mariano Arista, resolved to chase the invader from the soil of Tamaulipas, pushing him back across the Nueces River into Texas. He crossed the Rio Grande with an army the same size as the enemy's and was defeated in hot battles on two consecutive days. Forced to retire to Matamoros, he fell back on Linares. This disaster was owing to the incompetence of Arista and his staff and the superiority of the American artillery.

The outcome of these battles inspired President Polk to declare, with a cynicism unexampled in history, that a state of war existed because the Mexicans had invaded Texas and that it must be prosecuted until peace was secured. The Mexican government declared war formally in June, adducing such moderate and sensible reasons, founded on justice, that not a single honest conscience in the United States or Europe could fail to admit that we were in the right.

The country, horrified by our defeats, now burst into flame. Revolution, breaking out at Guadalajara, clamored for Santa Anna, of all men. The minute he got out of sight, the country became obsessed by a vague belief that he could work miracles. He was our man for emergencies, our *deus ex machina,* our savior who never saved anything. What to do? Paredes needed near him a force strong enough to cope with the rebellion, and yet he needed all available forces in the north. He sent some, badly armed, badly supplied, in the direction of San Luis Potosí. One of these brigades, when it was about to march, declared for the Federation and for Santa Anna. The government of Paredes, his Congress, his monarchists, disappeared as if by magic; they never should have appeared in the first place.

The new military revolution took the form of a reaction against monarchism, and while Santa Anna, who had been advised be-forehand, was on his way home in the company of General Almonte, for the time being an ardent republican, his allies in the capital convoked a Congress and declared the Constitution of 1824 to be in effect. The departmental committees were accordingly suppressed, and, as a manifestation of the return to pure federalism, Valentín Gómez Farías, leader of the reformist party, was brought in to head the Cabinet.

Santa Anna arrived; the Americans, with the most cunning Machiavellianism, had let him through, as if they were tossing an incendiary bomb into the enemy's camp. The month of August 1846 was coming to an end. What did this man bring to us, he who had so often been vilified by the common people, he whose statues they had dragged in the dust and who was, for all that, persistently regarded by them as a Messiah? What did he bring us, this betrayer of hopes, this champion of any cause that might serve his greed or his ambition, what did he bring to the desperate situation, to that army vanquished before any battle by nakedness and hunger, without confidence in its officers and without faith in victory? He brought but a single purpose: to be, redeeming his sins, a soldier for his country. Alas, this soldier who was not good enough to be a general was going to be Commander in Chief.

Paredes had left more than half a million pesos in the exchequer, and by the time Santa Anna arrived it had all been spent. But he set about concentrating troops in San Luis Potosí for a march on Monterrey. With three thousand men and provisions for eight days he finally started out, he who had been up to now nothing more than a revolutionary chieftain. Meanwhile, Mexico was in the throes of an electoral campaign. The radical element, it appears, with the protec-tion of the authorities, prevented the moderates from voting and *ad terrorem* triumphed at the polls. Even the liberal journals protested. But the hour for men of action had come, and the reform party got set to give the clergy the deathblow.

When Santa Anna had barely started his march he learned that Monterrey had capitulated and that Ampudia's division, with the honors of war, was falling back on Saltillo. In this new and bloody episode of the war our eternal improvidence undid us. The soldiers fought bravely, some of the officers on both sides performed deeds of heroism, but the enemy's superior staff and his superior artillery were effective again and again. And the story would be the same, over and over, to the end.

Santa Anna was a whirlwind of energy at San Luis Potosí. He begged incessantly for money or took it where he found it. His army grew to fifteen or twenty thousand men, what with merciless levies in the surrounding regions and the addition of some state troops and the remnant of the Division of the North. And as the army grew, his demands took on colossal proportions. The situation of the country was this: our ports were blockaded, most of the states paralyzed, the northern ones lost; Yucatán, seceding again, declared itself neutral so as not to fall into the Americans' power; the deficit soared to seven to eight millions; the press clamored against the government; the people of the capital formed battalions of militia, some to support the dominant reformists, others, of the middle class, to prevent any sacrilege against the clergy, who, less from patriotism, perhaps, than from fear, parted, sobbing bitterly, with tiny fractions of their fortune.

The Congress met [December 6, 1846]. The reformists were in majority, and even the opponents of reform were liberals. In the closing days of the year Santa Anna was named President and Gómez Farías Vice-President. Things looked ominous to the clergy and to the great mass of the people who, whether liberal or conservative, regarded the economic power of the Church as an inviolable institution.

Gómez Farías and his advanced thinkers arrived at an agreement with Santa Anna: the property held in mortmain by the clergy was to be taken over and either sold directly until fifteen million pesos had been obtained or sequestered until a loan was elicited. This was a drastic measure, but nobody denied the government's right to decree it. Let us recapitulate briefly. The clergy's possessions were not private, but corporative property; they were, therefore, subject to special restrictions which the State had the right to impose. The clergy's possessions could not, under mortmain, be sold, and so added nothing directly to the circulation of wealth. The government, then, for the common good could change or modify this condition. The clergy's possessions had been acquired through donations, either from the king or with his consent. And these were all definitely revocable. The Spanish kings stood firmly on their prerogatives in this matter. When His Most Catholic Majesty Charles III confiscated the entire property of the Jesuits in his dominions, nobody denied his right to do so. What was criticized was the way he used this right.

The reform party's aims were threefold: political, social, and patriotic. The party considered the clergy's influence to be pernicious, since it was to the Church's advantage to keep the classes in the *status quo*, which meant keeping the lower classes immersed in religious superstition and the upper classes innoculated with the fear of new ideas. The party considered the Church's privileges to be the principal barrier against the advent of a democracy, in which all would be equal, and felt that so long as the clergy remained the dominant financial power in the country they could never be stripped of these special privileges. And the political aim was to do just that. As for the social aim, the same economic problem was involved. Until the vast mass of landed wealth under mortmain could be brought into circulation there could be no general prosperity; governments and private persons alike acted as parasites on the Church. Nor could there be any betterment of class conditions or any social progress. The patriotic aim was to save the very life of the country by securing the financial resources needed to organize an army for defense and to maintain it and move it about. The usurers would lend no money, preferring to wait till the famished Treasury got desperate enough to borrow one peso and pay back one hundred. The clergy would lend scarcely enough to suffice for a day. The recently enacted tax on incomes and rents brought in nothing. It was impossible to collect taxes systematically in the country's disrupted condition. There was but one thing to do: secure enough money to defray expenses for a year. And the only rich treasure belonged to the Church.

The opposition in the Congress consisted of moderate liberals. The majority consisted of radicals known as "reds"—"pure ones," they were called by the people. Both factions agreed on the necessity of stripping the Church of its privileges and landed wealth. But some of the moderates insisted that an indemnity must be paid, and this would mean a compromise with the Church. The pure ones countered that the Church would never consent to anything but an accomplished fact; this had been its invariable policy. The moderates, even those who held no brief for indemnity, were unanimously in favor of postponing the measure. Such a step, they predicted, would be futile or even disastrous at this juncture; there would be no buyers; the reform party was not strong enough to enforce its will, and the consequence would be civil war. But the reform party was confident of its strength because Santa Anna was on its side, confident that buyers would appear because the sequestered properties would be offered at prices so low that the clergy themselves would buy them back. So the law was passed (January 1847). The ministers of the government girded themselves for the struggle with the clergy; protests in the form of pronunciamentos began to erupt here and there; some legislatures approved, and some refused to promulgate the law; the rabble, egged on by monks of the lowest type, swarmed through the streets of the principal cities, crying, "Long live religion, and death to the pure ones!" The whole country was in tumult.

What the government offered was too precarious to provoke any demand; nobody wanted to buy. And Santa Anna never ceased to ask for money. Finally, exasperated by the attacks of the press, which furiously criticized the new law and berated the Commander in Chief for his inactivity, he decided to go out and meet the American army, to cross a fearful desert without tents or adequate supplies, without having given his troops the rudiments of military training. With eighteen thousand men he marched across that interminable stretch of desolation, dust, and thirst, toward Saltillo (February 1847), and by the time he made contact with the enemy he was already beaten. He had lost four thousand men in his battle with the desert. The enemy had chosen an admirable position for defense (La Angostura), and there sustained two tremendous assaults. If the Mexican army had been led by a real general instead of by an officer who, though extremely brave, was vain, unstable, and ignorant, the assault would have been concerted instead of planless and chaotic, and Taylor would have retreated to Saltillo. The Mexican soldier proved his good qualities in this frightful carnage. He is a soldier who, when hungry and weary, still fights on with courage and ardor. But, subject to sudden fits of despondency, like all the undernourished, and to panic, like all the high-strung, when he loses confidence in his officer or his leader he deserts; remembering that he was carried off by the levy and educated by the rod, he runs away.

Santa Anna was like him; Santa Anna embodied all the defects of the Mexican and one good quality: intrepid disdain for death. A fit of despondency when the battle was at its height moved him to beat a retreat. And he turned back across the desert, where sickness, nakedness, hunger, and desertion made a last assault on that bloodstained, gaunt column straggling under a pitiless sun, in a perpetual cloud of dust that tormented and very nearly devoured it. Santa Anna was fleeing from probable victory, on his way to certain defeat. He was fleeing toward the City of Mexico, where his power was threatened and where he had addressed a bulletin announcing his victory— cream of the jest! True, he had not been vanquished by the enemy: he had been vanquished by himself.

Mexico, at the same time, was likewise vanquishing itself. In the last days of February, while the national army was meeting disaster at La Angostura, a new American army occupied Tampico, previously abandoned, and disembarked on the coast near Vera Cruz. Thus the invasion took a new direction, from the east instead of the north. Vera Cruz was defended by a mere handful of men. It was imperative to contain the enemy till a new army could come to the rescue. The government, still trying to put the law disposing of Church property into effect, lived in a state of constant alarm. Battalions in which men of the upper class predominated were hostile to reform; these, petted by the clergy and promised backing, refused to obey orders to move on Vera Cruz. The mutiny declared itself to be a protest against the continuance in power of Gómez Farías, against the January law, against the Congress. There were incessant skirmishes in the capital, very little bloodshed. The youths from wealthy families who made up these battalions were popularly known as *polkos*, and with this name they pitted themselves against the pure ones. Santa Anna, chosen by the two factions as arbiter, arrived in the City of Mexico, took over the Presidency, and, furious at learning that Vera Cruz had surrendered, left the Presidency *ad interim* in the hands of General Pedro María Anaya, and went forth to cut short the American advance on the capital, beyond Jalapa (his home ground), after abrogating the law which had caused so much unrest.

With his usual access of energy, he soon managed to assemble an army on the rim of the Hot Country. He, and he alone, was in a position to choose the field of battle, among any number of strategic sites along the rugged staircase that climbs to the plateau. He chose the worst and was utterly routed. The same vain pretense, the same petulance, so characteristic of the Veracruzan, that had often defeated him before defeated him again. And still his ardor and activity succeeded in producing a new army out of the very fragments of the old, a feat that amazed General Scott, who advanced on the capital, scattering conciliatory and soothing proclamations to the four winds. He said that he came as a republican, to make war on the monarchist faction, and that no one could have more respect than he for religion and for the Catholic Church. And yet, the monarchist faction, headed by Paredes, had done nothing but sabotage the defense of the frontier. It was the liberal party, aided by some of the military, that was conducting and organizing the defense of the country; many leading reactionaries cooperated, but not as a party. Scott pretended to be unaware of these facts; in truth, the invaders were disappointed to find themselves face to face with the federalist reformers who shared so many ideas with the people of the United States and who took them for a model.

When the invaders occupied Puebla, the decision was made to defend the capital, and the Federal District was marshaled for the struggle. Among the intellectuals there was little or no faith: "The result is foregone," so their minds ran.

> [It is] impossible to vanquish an army that can be reinforced endlessly from the north and from the east. And what if we do lose lands that never belonged to us except in name: Texas, California? Perhaps that would be an advantage; a reduction in size might make for cohesion, concentration, strength.

But the people felt they must beat the Yankees. The people were not afraid; the vague terror that a series of defeats inspires in the masses was not present here.

"The Americans are not really winning; rather the Mexicans are defeating themselves with disunity, disobedience, and mistakes; all that is needed is a unified effort and that handful of intruders will disappear." So thought the people in their hate and contempt for a race incompatible in customs, language, and religion. They failed to recognize what was admirable in that valiant and level-headed handful of intruders who, taking advantage of the superiority of their armament and their cohesion and of the inefficiency of Mexican generals and the damaging dissensions of civil war, had penetrated to the heart of the country, sweeping all before them.

When Scott reached the Valley of Mexico popular excitement rose high. Why should we not be victorious? Here was a veteran's division containing the survivors of La Angostura, commanded by General Valencia, who now tried to outrival Santa Anna, and the President made moving speeches to them. Here were the civic militia, the *polkos*, in a picturesque camp, which the flower of high society turned into a continuous gaudy picnic, with the boys receiving, in the presence of their sweethearts and mothers, the eucharistic communion as the supreme viaticum for country and for glory.

The stolid invaders took a position on the lowest spurs of the mountains rimming the Valley on the south, where they could safely pick a time and a route to their liking. The core of the defense was Valencia's division, which took a bad position (Padierna) vulnerable to the invaders. The Commander in Chief ordered him to abandon it; the ambitious subaltern balked. Santa Anna, who probably did not care much what happened to Valencia, failed to enforce his order and watched the first day's battle, but not the second day's disaster. The defeat at Padierna entirely disrupted the defense, and the invaders would have entered the city in pursuit of the fugitives if they had not been exhausted by the heroic stand made against them at the convent and bridge of Churubusco. They were turned back at the southern fortifications. The invading army consisted of fewer than ten thousand combatants, and the same number, more or less, were pitted against them during those two terrible August days, when the Mexican army lost five to six thousand men—the best, no doubt. The American officers' superior tactics were demonstrated throughout the Valley campaign, in which they defeated our army piecemeal, always with stronger forces. Curious facts: Scott said in his reports he had captured two ex-Presidents of Mexico (Anaya and Salas); how surprised he would have been if he could have known he had two future Presidents among his officers—Franklin Pierce and Ulysses S. Grant.

Scott asked for an armistice, which was easily arranged. The object was a meeting of an envoy of the United States with Mexican commissioners in order to bring to an end what the American general justly termed "an unnatural war." The envoy, Mr. Trist, demanded a strip of our northern frontier which included New Mexico and the Californias. Our commissioners refused to concede anything except Texas, bounded by the Nueces, and a part of Upper California. The negotiations ended; the armistice expired, and Mexico's fate was decided in the first half of September. Santa Anna's eternal incapacity to concentrate his defense caused him to leave Casa Mata and Molino del Rey weakly guarded; a triumphant defensive fight could not be sustained on the offensive and was turned into rout. The same thing happened a few days later when Chapultepec was taken. The salient episode of these bloody battles was the defense of Chapultepec's summit by the cadets of the Military College; some of them died there. This simple and sublime act was the most glorious of all the brave acts in the entire war, on either side.

On September 15 of this same year of 1847, the victorious army occupied the capital. Scattered attempts at popular resistance were quickly quelled. Santa Anna, in disgrace, resigned as President of the Republic and headed east. A few days later, Manuel Peña y Peña, the Chief Justice, got himself recognized as President by most of the country, assembled some troops, called the governors together, arranged for the Congress to meet, and organized a government that could enter into negotiations with the commander of the invading army. There was a group in the Congress that passionately opposed the idea of peace, the idea that was incarnate in Peña y Peña and in his minister Luis de la Rosa and later in the Provisional President, General Herrera. They and nearly the whole moderate party had desired this peace from the first, foreseeing what was bound to happen. Now they were determined to secure peace in spite of the fulminations of the military and the theatrical eloquence of some deputies. Even before the annexation of Texas, peace was urgent; after that, imperative; after the war, our only salvation. The war had left us without soldiers (9,000 men dispersed about the country), without artillery, without rifles (less than 150 in the armories).

The principle that a country must never cede territory is absurd, and no country, once invaded and conquered, has been able to sustain it. The true principle is quite different: a country in the grip of dire necessity can and should cede a part of its territory in order to conserve the rest.

With these convictions the eminent jurists representing us entered into negotiations with the American envoy Trist, a highly deferent man, and were surprised to learn that the victors had not increased their demands to any extent since their decisive triumphs in the Valley. The discussions produced, one month later, the Treaty of Guadalupe Hidalgo. The Mexicans disputed each demand, yielding only to compulsion. Meanwhile, the national government was in Querētaro, struggling to stay on its feet amidst anarchy and the hostility of the principal states and latent insurrection in others, amidst penury and prostration. If it should fall, the Republic would fall with it. On February 2 the Treaty was signed. We lost what we had already lost in fact: California, New Mexico, Texas, the portion of Tamaulipas beyond the Rio Grande. The rest of the occupied territory was to be delivered to us shortly, together with an indemnification amounting to fifteen million pesos. This was not a price paid for one ceded territory which was already in the Americans' possession (and they delivered to us much that we had thought lost forever)—this was payment for damages caused by the war, and so vital that the government could not have survived without it and the consequences would have been chaos, dismemberment, and annexation. This was a painful treaty but not an ignominious one. A comparison with the treaty between France and Germany at Frankfurt, and with that between the United States and Spain at Paris, will enable us to judge our forefathers with more fairness. They did what they should have done, and did it well.

Mexico, a weak country because of its scant and sparse population, still partly ignorant of cultured life and of patriotism in its fullest meaning, has been vanquished in all its international wars, though never really conquered. But there is a fatality about the country, a sort of malign influence on its invaders which would seem to have some mysterious relation to justice. French intervention in Mexico led to the Franco-Prussian war; American invasion led to the War Between the States. From the disruption of political parties in the United States there arose the resolutely antislavery Republican Party, which opposed the spread of the black social plague to the newly acquired territories, and against this group the South, feeling itself strong (for to make itself strong it had insisted on the War with Mexico) resorted to arms. The Mexican War was the school for the future generals of the American Civil War.

MEXICAN LIBERALISM

Harold E. Davis

Harold E. Davis is Emeritus University Professor of Latin American Studies at the American University in Washington, D.C. He is a specialist in Latin American government and politics, inter-American relations, and political and social thought in Latin America. His many books include Latin American Social Thought, The Americas in History, Latin American Leaders, *and* Government and Politics in Latin America. *In the following essay Professor Davis surveys the main ideas of Mexico's more important liberal thinkers.*

MEXICO PRODUCED a number of outstanding Liberal spokesmen during these years, as well as one of the best American representatives of traditionalist thought, the historian of independence and organizer of the Mexican Conservative party, Lucas Alamán. But first let us note the thought of three Liberal advocates of quite different types: José María Luis Mora, Ignacio Ramírez and Manuel Crescencio Rejón.

José María Mora (1794[?]–1850), in his life and in his writing, gives us an expression of Mexican economic and political Liberalism during the troubled quarter century that followed independence. Mora spoke for that part of the Mexican elite who were willing to break with the authority of Church and crown in trying to apply the Liberal principle of freedom in politics, religion, and economics.

His moderate Liberalism was characterized by an aristocratic or class-conscious temper. But it also breathed something of the spirit of the historicism of Friedrich Karl von Savigny and the Compte de

Volney, as well as that of the liberal political economy of Adam Smith and Jeremy Bentham. He believed in progress and in the perfectibility of man and society; but when forced to choose between liberty and order, he chose order. His writing also reveals the race-consciousness characteristic of the social thought of his day. Recognizing the Indians as Mexico's greatest social problem, like Domingo Sarmiento in Argentina and Antonio Saco in Cuba, he believed that to develop, Mexico should emphasize her European character. "The name of Mexico is so intimately linked with the memory of Cortes," he wrote, "that while the latter exists the former will not perish."[1]

Mora was the theoretician of Mexican political Liberalism in the years immediately following independence, playing an active part in developing the federalist constitution of 1825 and in later restoring federalism after its abrogation by Santa Anna. As a minister in the Cabinet of Valentín Gómez Farías (1832–1834), he was identified with the short-lived anticlerical reforms of that administration. The anonymous *Catecismo político de la federación mexicana* (1831) is generally attributed to him.[2] This pamphlet presented federalism as a logical application of Liberal political principles which asserted that decentralization lessened the danger of generating arbitrary political power. In a spirit somewhat similar to that of the authors of the United States federal constitution, Mora wrote that federalism was a means of preventing the demagogic forces (the local caudillos) from capturing control of the state. Federalism also appealed to him as a hierarchical structure of the state through which the criollo leaders might govern with law and order, holding in restraint the threat of social revolution ever present in the subjugated Indian masses. In accordance with this view of limited democracy, he advocated a suffrage limited to property owners. His principal reform objectives were to destroy the privileges of the two most powerful institutions in Mexican society, the Army and the Church.

Consequently, Mora displays much of the Liberal, but little of the romantic, even in his historicism. Supremely confident in the power of reason, he rejected Bolívar's dream of a united Spanish America as "the greatest of deliriums." Mexico, he was sure, would have its own future as a separate nation. The memory that his family had been ruined financially by the destruction attending the Hidalgo uprising may have caused him to fear popular movements that might bring the repetition of such a violent mass movement. This fear was not unusual among his social class, whether or not they had suffered personally.

The distinctive thing in Mora's case was that his keen social perception led him to see that in order to avoid such revolutions the governing class must rule democratically, extending the realm of freedom by progressive measures.[3]

Manuel Crescencio Rejón (1799–1849), another of the Mexican Liberals, was the principal originator of the broad judicial process called the *amparo*, a Mexican juridical innovation subsequently copied elsewhere in Latin America. Under this process an individual may defend his constitutional rights against governmental action of almost any kind. It has sometimes been compared in its scope and importance to the writ of Habeas Corpus, and the comparison is not inappropriate, much as the two procedures differ.[4] Rejón was also one of the early Mexican proponents of freedom of the press. Known as one of the *Puros* among the Liberals, he was a federalist, an advocate of direct elections, and like Mora a collaborator with Valentín Gómez Farías in restoring the federal constitution of 1824. In 1840 he was a minister in the Gómez Farías government. Yet in 1844, as minister of foreign affairs, Rejón supported Santa Anna in his opposition to the United States in the Texas question, later (1846) defending this action in what is one of his more important written works.[5]

His full name was Manuel Crescencio García Rejón y Alcalá, though he was usually known as Manuel C. Rejón or Crescencio Rejón. Born in the year 1799 in the village of Bolonchenticul, near Mérida, in Yucatán, he was the son of Manuel García Rejón, descendant of an old Yucatán family, and Bernarda de Alcalá, of the Canary Islands. In Mérida he studied in the Seminario Conciliar de San Ildefonso and pursued studies under two Yucatán philosophers who had embraced ideas of the Enlightenment: Vicente María Velásquez and Pablo Moreno. He was encouraged in his studies and aided financially by a wealthy young priest, José María Guerra, who later came to be bishop of Yucatán. Both Velásquez and Moreno were ardent defenders of the Indians of Yucatán and espoused the ideas of Bartolomé de las Casas. A group of young men who gathered around them included, in addition to Rejón, Andrés Quintana Roo and Lorenzo de Zavala. The group, most of them destined to national fame, came to be known as the San Juanistas, a name derived from Velásquez's parish of San Juan Bautista.

Rejón completed his studies in philosophy in 1819 at the age of

twenty. Two years later he participated in the independence movement of 1821, working through the Masonic Lodge in support of the
Iturbide movement. He then went to Mexico as a member of the
national Congress. But he soon became a critic of Iturbide and was one
of those members who absented themselves from the Congress that
approved Iturbide as emperor. He was a member of the commission
which drew up the Constitution of 1824, becoming one of a trio of
early federalists with Ramos Arizpe and Prisciliano Sánchez. In this
connection he defended the principle that the judicial authority ema-
nates not from the executive or legislative, but "directly from the
people" (*immediatamente del pueblo*).[6] Rejón also urged the adoption of
Liberal economic and fiscal policies, especially in foreign commerce
and in respect to a merchant marine. His greatest influence, however,
was in the fields of law and politics.

His thought shows a number of intellectual influences in addition
to those of his teachers, Moreno and Velásquez. To the eclectic Victor
Cousin, he owed some of his moderate characteristics. John Locke and
the eighteenth century British jurist Sir William Blackstone, both of
whom he cites in defending his action in issuing certain controversial
decrees of 1844, influenced his political and legal thinking. He was
also familiar with the Constitution of the United States, to which he
frequently refers.

In the final analysis, the essentials of Rejón's thought may be
summed up in five basic principles, all characteristic of the evolving
liberal ideology: (1) the popular basis of the judicial authority, (2) the
constitutional right of the individual citizen for protection against
arbitrary action of government, (3) the fundamental importance of
freedom of the press, (4) the essential need for decentralizing political
authority to prevent authoritarianism, and (5) the fundamental importance of national loyalty (and of the nation) as the basis of all
rights.[7]

Ignacio Ramírez (1818–1879) was Mexico's Voltaire. A generation later
than Mora, Rejón, and Ramos Arizpe, he speaks for a mid-century
Mexican Liberalism in full vigor. As Minister of Justice and Public
Instruction under President Benito Juárez, he was responsible for
carrying out the Laws of Reform, including the suppression of
monasteries. In this connection, as well as in other ways, his anticlericalism, verging on atheism, earned him the popular sobriquet, *El*

Nigromante (The Necromancer). Diego Rivera may have overdramatized this religious nonconformity of Ramírez by putting his phrase "*Dios no existe*" (God does not exist) in a controversial mural in the Hotel del Prado in Mexico City, a painting depicting leaders of Mexican reform. Yet, although the text of the address has been lost, this appears to have been what he said in a speech in the Academy of Letrán.

There is no question that he pursued the rationalism of his age to a position of pantheism, if not atheism. It is unfair to his thought as a whole, however, to confine its significance to this one, somewhat exceptional position. Atheism, as a not unnatural accompaniment of Liberal romantic thought, deserves special attention. But what Ramírez and his like really meant was that reason (the science or reason of the universe) was the supreme good. His speech is best understood as a violent protest against the Church's opposition to the Liberal reforms, especially in the field of education, *El Nigromante's* special concern.

Ramírez was much more than an anticlerical. A mestizo by birth, but Spanish (criollo) in culture, he sympathized with the Indians and admired those Spaniards, such as Bartolomé de las Casas, who had defended them. His Liberalism included vigorous advocacy of universal suffrage, freedom of speech, and religious freedom.[8]

Miguel Ramos Arizpe (1775-1843) was another of the early Mexican intellectual Liberals coming out of the generation of independence. His career exhibits several aspects interesting for the thought of his time. A revolutionary priest, he was excommunicated for his heretical ideas, yet served for years as Dean of the Cathedral of Puebla, and in his later years was for a time Minister of Justice and Ecclesiastical Affairs.

Born in San Nicolás de la Capellanía, now Ramos Arizpe, Coahuila, he was the youngest son of a family of modest means. He was educated for the priesthood, receiving the degrees of Licenciado (1807) and Doctor of Canon Law (1808) at the University of Guadalajara. Competing for a vacancy in Canon Law at the Cathedral of Monterrey, he won first place in the competition; but the bishop (as before) refused to appoint him, sending him back to his obscure parish, Real de Bourbón. In 1810, however, the Municipal Council of Saltillo named him deputy to the Cortes called by the rebels against

Napoleon in Spain. There he quickly emerged as a leader of the American deputies. He stayed in Spain for eleven years, including twenty months in prison after the restoration of Ferdinand VII. Known as a defender of the Constitution of 1812, he was repeatedly asked while in prison whether sovereignty resided in the king or in the nation. His answer: "*Aqui cerrado no lo puedo saber; dejenme Vstedes salir y ver la sociedad, y volveré al punto a la prisión a contestar.*"[9]

NOTES

1. Quoted by Arturo Arnáiz y Freg, in *José Maria Luis Mora* (Mexico: Universidad Nacional, 1941), pp. xvi–xvii.

2. Samuel Ramos, *Historia de la filosofía en México* (Mexico: Imprenta Universitaria, 1943), p. 109.

3. The author has not been able to determine whether the complete works of Mora have been published. Some of his writings are found conveniently in *Ensayos, ideas y retratos*, edited with a prologue by Arturo Arnáiz y Freg (Mexico: Universidad Nacional, 1941); *El Doctor Mora Redivivo. Selección de sus obras. Estudio critico de Genaro Fernández MacGregor* (Mexico: Botas, 1938); and *José María Luis Mora, Ensayos, ideas y retratos* (Mexico: Universidad Nacional de México, 1964). *México y sus revoluciones*, 3 vols., appeared in Paris in 1836, and two volumes of *Obras sueltas* were published there in 1937 by Rosa. Biographies and critical studies include *El Doctor José María Luis Mora, Homenaje de la Universidad Nacional de México* (Mexico: Universidad Nacional de México, 1934); Salvador Joscano, *Vida del Dr. Mora* (Mexico: Biografías Populares, no. 1, 1936); and Charles A. Hale, *Mexican Liberalism in the Age of Mora, 1821–1853* (New Haven: Yale University Press, 1968).

4. Ignacio Burgoa, *El juicio de amparo*, quoted in *Manuel Crescencio Rejón: pensamiento político*; prólogo, selección y notas de Daniel Moreno (Mexico: Universidad Nacional Autónoma de México, 1968), p. xxviii.

5. Manuel Crescencio Rejón, *Justificación de la conducta de Manuel Crescencio Rejón, desde 1841 hasta la fecha* (New Orleans, 1846); reproduced in Daniel Moreno, ed., *Manuel Crescencio Rejón: pensamiento político*.

6. Ibid., p. xiv.

7. In addition to Daniel Moreno's collection, *Manuel Crescencio Rejón: pensamiento político*, see Rejón's speeches in Carlos A. Echánove Trujillo, ed., *Manuel Crescencio Rejón. Discursos parlamentarios (1822–1847)* (Mexico: Secretaría de Educación Pública, 1943).

8. Ignacio Ramírez, *Ensayos, Prólogo y selección de Manuel González Ramírez* (Mexico: Ediciones de la Universidad Nacional Autónoma, 1944).

9. Quoted in Vito Alessio Robles, *Miguel Ramos Arizpe, Discursos, memorias e informes* (Mexico: Universidad Nacional Autónoma de México, 1942), p. xxxv.

LUCAS ALAMÁN,
MEXICAN CONSERVATIVE
Charles A. Hale

Charles A. Hale is professor of history at the University of Iowa. He is a specialist in Mexican intellectual history and is the author of several articles on Mexican liberalism and the methodology of intellectual history. The following description of Alamán's conservative historiography was taken from Hale's Mexican Liberalism in the Age of Mora, 1821–1853. *The reader should note Alamán's view of history, especially his Hispanophile bias and his theory of Mexico's dual revolution. This study of Alamán's historical views clearly illustrates how interpretations of the past are often conditioned by present concerns.*

THE CHIEF CONSERVATIVE SPOKESMAN was Lucas Alamán, undoubtedly the major political and intellectual figure of independent Mexico until his death in 1853. A man of indefatigable energy and diverse talents, Alamán was not only a prolific writer, whose works fill twelve stout volumes, but also the guiding force in several administrations and an active promoter of economic development.

One can follow a rough pattern in Lucas Alamán's life that runs from activist to writer, from statesman and entrepreneur to *pensador*. It is important to note that his conservatism hardened only in the 1840s, particularly after 1846. The great bulk of Alamán's writing was done in his later years. Besides his histories, he was generally acknowledged to be the editor of *El Tiempo* and of *El Universal*. History was Alamán's principal weapon and the cornerstone of what could be called conservative political philosophy in Mexico. *El Tiempo* announced its ap-

Reprinted from Charles A. Hale, *Mexican Liberalism in the Age of Mora, 1821–1853* (New Haven: Yale University Press, 1968), pp. 16–22, by permission of the publishers.

pearance in Burkean terms by explaining that its title signified a search in the past (*tiempo pasado*) for lessons to guide in the present (*tiempo presente*), which in turn contains the seeds of the future (*tiempo por venir*). Destructive natural phenomena, such as earthquakes and volcanic eruptions, it added, cannot be a model for human development. "We thus reject from our ideas of progress all violent and revolutionary means."[1]

On September 16, 1849, *El Universal* opened its attack on Mexico's accepted revolutionary tradition by asserting that Miguel Hidalgo's Grito de Dolores should no longer be considered Independence Day. Instead, there appeared on September 27 an article entitled "The Great Day of the Nation," commemorating Agustín de Iturbide's entry into Mexico City in 1821. The liberal newspapers *El Siglo* and *El Monitor* rose immediately to the defense of Hidalgo and of September 16, and a fierce debate ensued. It was symbolic of the broader conflict of ideas over the social and political bases of independent Mexico and the country's relation to its colonial and Hispanic past.

Alamán announced on several occasions that the purpose of his historical writing was to combat popular disrespect for Mexico's Spanish heritage and the idea that independence constituted a necessary break from it. He set out to demonstrate through history that Hernán Cortés was the founder of the Mexican nation, that three centuries of colonial rule had been on the whole beneficial and progressive, and that Mexico's only road to salvation in the present crisis was to reject liberal and disruptive doctrines and return to time-honored practices. By 1851 Alamán was claiming success for his efforts and pointed to recent patriotic orations as evidence.[2] Alamán's conservative appeal through history had begun on February 18, 1844, when he proposed to the Ateneo Mexicano, a group of scholars and men of letters, that he prepare ten "dissertations" covering "our national history from the epoch of the Conquest to our day." He completed this effort nine years and eight volumes later, a few months before his death in June 1853.[3]

Alamán's treatment of New Spain in his *Disertaciones* focused on Cortés and the Conquest. His approach was largely biographical, not unlike that of his contemporary, William H. Prescott. Alamán emphasized the constructive as well as the military and destructive achievements of Cortés and described in detail his organization of the government of Mexico City, his agricultural and mining enterprises, and his founding of charitable institutions.[4] It should be added that

Alamán's historiographical mission to solidify Cortés' stature served a practical purpose as well. Alamán had served during two decades as agent for the Sicilian Duke of Terranova y Monteleone, the present heir to Cortés' huge sixteenth-century feudal patrimony. As early as 1828, Alamán defended Monteleone's holdings against liberal attacks on the grounds "that we are not the nation despoiled by the Spaniards, but one in which everything originated with the Conquest."[5]

Characteristic of Alamán's historical argument was the third volume of *Disertaciones* (1849), devoted entirely to a history of peninsular Spain between 1500 and 1810. It was as if he were deliberately baiting the liberal Hispanophobes of his day. Spain and Mexico were one historically, and Mexicans should recognize their tie to the great tradition of the Catholic Kings and the eighteenth-century Bourbons. Still, Alamán's treatment of the Colony in *Historia*, Vol. 1, was balanced, and it is cited and even translated today as a perceptive and useful synthesis. He accorded high praise to the civilizing efforts of the early missionaries, the Jesuits, and a handful of statesmanlike viceroys; yet he was not blind to the principal colonial grievances.

Being a Creole aristocrat himself, Alamán recognized the political and social inferiority imposed on the Creoles. He often spoke, too, of the industriousness of that group. He had no sympathy for Spanish restrictions on colonial industry and agriculture. Moreover, he condemned the Inquisition, though he regarded the church, spiritual and temporal, as the soul of Mexico's Hispanic heritage. For him, independence was both inevitable and beneficial, prepared for by three centuries of generally enlightened and progressive policies. It was not independence itself that Alamán questioned, but rather the use it had been put to by republican Mexico.[6]

Alamán made most effective use of history as a weapon in his interpretation of the Revolution for Independence. The force of his argument was not based on mere polemic but rather on the documentation and detail of his five large volumes. His *Historia de Méjico* remains the standard treatment of the 1810–21 period, and it has never been equaled by a "liberal" version. This fact may reflect the durability of Creole conservatism in the Mexican tradition. The interpretation embedded in Alamán's narrative is clear and unequivocal: there was not one revolution; there were two. The first was led by Miguel Hidalgo in 1810 and lasted ten years till it disintegrated in 1820; the second took place briefly in 1821 under Agustín de Iturbide. In no way, asserted Alamán, could the first revolution be considered a war of "nation against nation," nor was it "a heroic effort of a people struggling for their liberty," trying to "shake off the yoke of an oppressor power." Hidalgo's insurrection was rather a "rising of the proletarian class against property and civilization," led by many "lost souls or ex-criminals noted for their vices." This first revolution caused a "reaction of the respectable segment of society in defense of its property and its families," which "stifled [1820] the general desire for independence." Moreover, "the triumph of the insurrection would have been the greatest calamity that could have befallen the country."[7]

Lucas Alamán grew up in a wealthy and distinguished family in the prosperous mining city of Guanajuato, which was the first target of the Revolution of 1810. As a youth of seventeen he experienced siege by Hidalgo's Indian hordes and saw the death of the enlightened Spanish intendant Riaño, a family friend. Alamán escaped with his family to Mexico City, but, he wrote in 1849, the "shout of death and destruction . . . still resounds in my ears with a terrible echo." His memories of 1810 were revived by the entry of the American army into Mexico City in September 1847. Though his house escaped sacking, he noted that some of his neighbors were not so fortunate.[8] Alamán concluded that Father Hidalgo was merely a demagogue, appealing to mob anarchy and the exaggerated democratic doctrines of the French Revolution. His use of the Virgin of Guadalupe as an emblem was a blasphemous linking of religion and violence. After disorder had been unleashed by Hidalgo, it was impossible for more disciplined leaders like José María Morelos and Ramón López Rayón to control its fury. Alamán found admirable qualities in several of the later insurgent leaders, but the movement as a whole could be termed a disaster.

The second revolution was the climax of Alamán's *Historia*. It was a frankly conservative movement directed against the anticlerical and democratic principles of the Spanish cortes (assembly) and the Constitution of 1812, both of which had been reactivated in 1820. Independence was achieved as a mere breaking of political ties with Spain. Iturbide was correct, maintained Alamán, in refusing to recognize a connection between the 1810 insurrection (against which he had fought as a royalist commander) and his harmonious movement. Independence was thus "brought about by the same people who until then had been opposing it."[9] Alamán was explicit in denying the "vulgar error" current in 1821 that independence was a resurgence of the pre-Conquest nation of Anahuac after three centuries of Spanish oppression. The nation that emerged in 1821 was for Alamán the product of sixteenth-century conquest, guided by Hispanic principles of authority, religion, and property. Alamán summed up his position in words his friend Manuel Terán had used in 1824: "I have never considered myself other than a rebellious Spaniard."[10]

This interpretation of the Revolution for Independence was tied closely to an Iturbide cult which flourished in the conservative writings of 1846 to 1853. Not only did he emerge as the hero of Alamán's *Historia* and as the subject of much praise in the conservative press, but he was the focus of Luis G. Cuevas' *Porvenir de México*, which was subtitled a "judgment on [Mexico's] political state in 1821 and 1851." The work was a long nostalgic essay, evoking the halcyon days of 1821 when Mexico was a great and extensive nation, strong from the unifying and conservative principles of Iturbide's Plan of Iguala. Though both Cuevas and Alamán were harsh in their judgment of Iturbide's self-styled empire, clearly it was not his actions in detail that mattered, but rather the principles he espoused and the social groups he represented. Mexico's present anarchy did not begin in 1821, but rather with the overthrow of Iturbide by men "who had embraced unthinkingly the system of changing everything" and had thus negated "union which is the strength of nations."[11]

The political use of history by the postwar conservatives posed a challenge to liberal and republican Mexico. The liberals were asked to acknowledge the inner contradictions of the independence movement, to choose, as it were, between Hidalgo and Iturbide. Should the nation find the principles of reconstruction in the Indian upheaval of 1810 and the revolutionary idea of popular sovereignty? Or, should the 1821 movement be the model, acknowledging the social supremacy of Creole aristocrats, established church, and traditional views of authority? The dilemma this conservative challenge posed for the liberals can be seen by a brief consideration of their interpretations of the Revolution for Independence before 1847. In general, the revolution had been accepted as an integral movement, begun by Hidalgo and completed by Iturbide. Beginning with the multivolume chronicle of Carlos María de Bustamante in the 1820s and continuing with the Independence Day orations of subsequent years, the emphasis was clearly on the heroic achievements of Hidalgo and Morelos. Yet, the revolutionary years could be referred to as one movement, embodying the forces of liberalism, progress, and popular sovereignty against three hundred years of Spanish tyranny.[12]

NOTES

1. *El Tiempo*, 24 January 1846.
2. See Alamán's letter to Monteleone, 3 December 1851, in *Alamán, Documentos diversos*, 4 vols. (Mexico: Editorial Jus, 1945–47), 4:604.
3. Alamán, *Disertaciones sobre la historia de la república megicana, desde la época de la conquista que los españoles hicieron . . . hasta la independencia*, 3 vols. (Mexico, 1844–49). See notice in *El Siglo*, 9 June 1844.
4. Alamán, *Disertaciones*, 2:1–126. Alamán acknowledged his debt to Prescott and annotated the Spanish translation of the latter's *Historia de la conquista de Méjico*, 2 vols. (Mexico, 1844).
5. Alamán, "Esposición que hace a la cámara de diputados del congreso general el apoderado del Duque de Terranova y Monteleone," *Documentos*, 3:47. In a letter of 3 December 1851, Alamán claimed that his historical writings had helped gain public acceptance of the duke's holdings (ibid., 4:604).
6. See Alamán, *Historia de Méjico*, 5 vols. (Mexico: 1849–52), 1:83, 346; 5:109–10; also *El Tiempo*, 25 January 1846. His disillusionment with Mexico's misuse of the gift of independence was baldly stated as early as 1835 in "Borrador de un artículo que salió como editorial de un periódico en 1835 con motivo del aniversario de la independencia," *Documentos*, 3:349–50.
7. See Alamán, *Historia*, 4:722–24; also 5:352. Alamán was reiterating the arguments of royalist propagandists in 1810. In fact, there is a striking parallel between the "psychological warfare" conducted by the post-1847 conservatives and by the 1810 royalists. Both appealed with great effectiveness to Creole social conservatism. See the interesting discussion by Hugh M. Hamill, Jr., "Early Psychological Warfare in the Hidalgo Revolt," *Hispanic American Historical Review* 41 (1961):206–35.
8. Alamán, *Historia*, 1:379; "Autobiografía," *Documentos*, 4:14; letter to Monteleone, 28 September 1847, in ibid., p. 450–51. Alamán remarked ironically that the American occupation of Mexico City on September 16 was perhaps a form of divine retribution, commemorating Hidalgo's insurrection (*Historia*, 2:225).
9. Alamán, *Historia*, 4:725; 5:108, 351–52; also "Noticias biográficas del Lic. D. Carlos Ma. Bustamente," *Documentos*, 3:308.
10. See Alamán, *Historia*, 1:190 n. Alamán found Bustamente, the chronicler of the wars of independence, particularly guilty of the Aztec myth. See "Noticias," *Documentos*, 3:327.
11. See Luis G. Cuevas, *Provenir de México*, ed. Francisco Cuevas Cancino (Mexico: Editorial Jus, 1954), pp. 148, 198. Further examples of the effort to glorify Iturbide can be seen in *El Tiempo*, 6 and 26 February 1846 and 30 March 1846; *El Orden*, 27 September 1853. Alamán found ridiculous the makeshift "coronation" and the tawdry imperial trappings. See Alamán, *Historia*, 5:624–41.
12. Carlos María de Bustamente, *Cuadro histórico de la revolución de las América mexicana*, 6 vols. (Mexico, 1823–32); Mariano Otero, "Discurso que en la solemnidad del 16 de septiembre de 1841 pronunció en la ciudad de Guadalajara," *El Siglo*, 22–23 October 1841, and "Oración cívica," ibid., 23

September 1843; Andrés Quintana Roo, *Discurso pronunciado . . . en el glorioso aniversario del 16 de septiembre de 1845* (Mexico, 1845); Manuel Díaz Mirón, *Discurso que pronunció el 16 de septiembre de 1845, aniversario del grito de Dolores* (Veracruz, 1845), p. 6.

PART III
LA REFORMA AND THE FRENCH INTERVENTION, 1855–76

IN 1846, WHILE WAR WAS CONTINUING between Mexico and the United States, the monarchist party of Mariano Paredes was overthrown. Gómez Farías returned to power and immediately restored the liberal and federalist Constitution of 1824. With the restoration of federalism in the national capital, liberal party movements and administrations gained strength in many of the provinces; Michoacán and Oaxaca, for example, acquired liberal governors. The governor of Michoacán was the anticlerical scholar Melchor Ocampo. In Oaxaca a forty-one-year-old Zapotec Indian, Benito Juárez, was appointed governor (see Reading 14). By 1854 these men had joined with others in launching the Liberal Revolution of Ayutla. Their movement and this era of Mexico's history is collectively known as the Reform (see Reading 13).

Like the French Revolution, the Reform had as its primary objective the destruction of feudalism. In Mexico, however, the religious princes were more the object of liberal attacks than were the aristocrats of the First Estate of France. The anticlericalists hoped to reduce the power of the Church in politics and education and redistribute its corporate wealth among an emerging group of middle-class property owners. The Reform was to be Mexico's bourgeois revolution. Constitutional government would guarantee individual liberties and freedoms, curtail the authoritarian rule of the Church and its allies in the army, replace local anarchy and arbitrary presidential rule with parliamentary democracy (see Reading 15), and promote economic progress and equality.

But the Reform proved to be costly and only partially successful. Reforms led to civil war and bloodletting, which in turn led to the French Intervention and more bloodletting (see Reading 16.) Government under the Constitution of 1857 continued to be dictatorial. Property was not redistributed—in fact, a whole new generation of hacendados emerged. There was no social justice for the Indian, and when the Reform was over, peonage was more widespread and entrenched than ever. And the Church, although it lost much of its material wealth in the fighting, was still a political and educational force in the life of the nation.

Yet the Reform and the ensuing French Intervention were significant in at least two ways: the Reform actually delivered political and economic power to an emerging middle-class group of mestizos and new creoles; and the Mexican people, united in a common campaign against the French Empire, became aware, for the first time, of their national identity. With the departure of the French in 1867 the rule of Benito Juárez was restored. The army was reduced, railroad building was begun, the national finances were restructured, and in education the National Preparatory School was established as a model for the nation. When Porfirio Díaz issued his Plan de Tuxtepec in 1876, the foundations for a modern mestizo nation had already been established.

REFORMS

Víctor Alba

In this selection from The Mexicans, *Víctor Alba (see also Reading 1) surveys Mexico's history from the Plan of Ayutla in 1854 to the coming of the Porfiriato in 1876. Alba details the laws of the Reform, especially noting the anticorporate features of the* Ley Juárez *and the* Ley Lerdo. *He also describes the three-year civil war of La Reforma, in which the clerics, led by Félix Zuloaga in Mexico City, fought against the liberal government of Juárez. As Alba indicates, the national treasury was exhausted by the civil war; a default on foreign loans set up the conditions which made the French intervention almost inevitable. When the French and Maximilian were defeated in 1867, the liberal rule of Benito Juárez was restored.*

The reader should be prepared to ask several questions when reading the Alba selection. What, for example, was the role of the government of the United States toward Mexico throughout this period? How did that role affect Mexico's destinies during the war of La Reforma, the French Intervention, and the coming of Díaz in 1876? How does Alba explain the failure of Napoleon III and Maximilian? Why did the French Intervention serve to particularly discredit the conservatives and clerics? Why does Alba call the Ley Lerdo *an example of dogmatism? How did the Reform stimulate the development of latifundism and create a new middle class of profiteers?*

THE LOSS OF THE NORTH disturbed Mexican political society for some time. Presidents came and went: Manuel de la Peña y Peña, José Joaquín de Herrera, and General Mariano Arista. Conservative rebellions and Indian uprisings followed one upon another. Industry was paralyzed; a shortage of funds hindered attempts to attend to the needs of education. After Arista, the inevitable Santa Anna returned to power in 1853; this time in a kind of delirium of splendor. He

---

Reprinted from Víctor Alba, *The Mexicans* (New York: Frederick A. Praeger, 1967), pp. 63–77, by permission of Phaidon Press Limited and Holt, Rinehart and Winston.

established a "perpetual" hereditary dictatorship, persecuted the press, sold new blocs of national territory to the United States, and insisted upon being addressed as "Your Serene Highness." The liberals coalesced and prepared a coup in 1854, which they announced, as usual, in a plan—the Ayutla Plan—and bitter civil war ensued. Until that time, coups had been short-lived: either they never reached the battle stage or the battles were few. Now, however, a series of skirmishes went on for years all across the countryside of Mexico, especially on the northern plateau, once the geographical center of the country but then a frontier region.

By 1857, the liberals had momentarily triumphed, but in many regions the conservatives refused to lay down their arms and they never ceased to plot. The liberals realized that this chaotic situation could not be corrected without basic reform of the political structure. Some of them, strongly influenced by Proudhon, went so far as to advocate reform of the social structure. In 1857 they tried to bring about such reforms legally through a new constitution—the panacea of the Latin American—a true declaration of principles. They were young intellectuals, self-educated or trained in the more modern provincial institutes set up by Gómez Farías, instead of in the old universities, from which came the conservative intellectuals. Melchor Ocampo (1814–61) was the social theorist of this group; Benito Juárez (1806–72) was its statesman; Ignacio Ramírez (1818–79), who wrote under the pseudonym of the "Necromancer," fired some punishing salvos at the Church and religion; and Ignacio M. Altamirano (1834–93) and Guillermo Prieto (1818–97) were its poets. This generation of romantics, many of whom often risked their lives and one of whom, Melchor Ocampo, was murdered by soldiers, refused to be defeated by rebellions or to be dazzled by university scholars. General Ignacio Comonfort (1812–63) had headed these liberal followers of the Ayutla Plan. When he became president, however, he came to an agreement with his enemies, the embattled conservatives, in order to restore peace after three years of fighting. But one man never lost his faith in the liberal cause: Benito Juárez (1806–72), then president of the Supreme Court, who was the constitutional successor in the event of the absence or death of the president. When, in 1858, Comonfort went into exile, the republic found itself with two presidents: Felix Zuloaga, backed by the conservatives and the army in the capital, and Juárez, the legal successor. Juárez and his partisans, the most exalted liberals, the most romantic provincial intellectuals, refused to yield. They

rounded up small armies, packed the whole government into carriages, the administration into several wagons, and wandered over
the countryside behind their troops. They were beaten at Salamanca,
were almost captured and executed at Guadalajara, sought sanctuary
in Veracruz, which Juárez reached after taking ship in Manzanillo on
the Pacific Coast and crossing the Isthmus of Panama against the rip
tide of immigrants heading for California.

In Veracruz, Juárez put some political content into his government by issuing the laws that became known as the Reform. Thus he
completed in 1859 the work begun by Gómez Farías in 1833 and
continued by a few laws passed in 1856 and by the constitution of
1857. Primarily, Juárez was trying to affirm the supremacy of the state
over the Church. The new laws secularized the life of the country,
nationalized the property of the clergy, and separated Church and
state.

By the summer of 1861, although earlier their generals had been
defeated, the liberals had reorganized and returned to the fight; in the
end, they conquered almost without having won a battle.

The essence of the Reform is embodied in two laws: the first was
the so-called Ley Juárez, which abolished the jurisdiction of the
ecclesiastical courts over members of the Church in civil cases. (Juárez
was particularly concerned with establishing the equality of all Mexicans before the law.) The second was the Ley Lerdo, drawn up by
Miguel Lerdo de Tejada (1812–61) and passed in June, 1856. This
outlawed corporations, religious or otherwise, from owning property
other than that indispensable to their immediate needs, such as
church buildings. At that time, the Church owned lands valued at
some $300 million. The law ruled that this property must be sold at
public auction unless previously bought by renters. Lerdo believed
that a class of small and medium landholders would be created by this
legislation, in cities and rural regions alike, and that their taxes would
augment the national income. Clearly, the law was inspired by the
auctions held during the French Revolution and by the dissolution of
the property of the Church decreed in Spain by Prime Minister Mendizábal some thirty years earlier. Lerdo hoped, too, that the lands so
acquired would serve as security for loans which he felt confident he
could float in the United States. The law made no explicit mention of
the importance of diminishing the economic and political power of the
Church, for the liberals preferred to present their measure as being
exclusively an economic one. But on those grounds, during debate on

the bill, only Ignacio Ramírez, the aforementioned "Necromancer," foresaw that, instead of creating new landowners the legislation would increase the holdings of the *latifundistas* and, far from impoverishing the Church, would make it the "banker for the nation," with funds from the sale of its properties. And that is what happened.

The Church, however, was not yet aware that it would, and besides, it did not wish to appear defeated. When the measure became law, the Archbishop of Mexico refused confession and burial in consecrated ground to anyone who bought ecclesiastical properties, and he excommunicated those who refused to resign their positions in the government (which required an oath of support of the law). More moderate lay Catholics argued that some of the Church's wealth was being used to succor the poor and that the Ley Lerdo would cut off this charity.

All in all, urban estates worth 10 million pesos and rural estates worth 2 million were expropriated from the Church. The wealth of the clergy was so great that it worried even a conservative like Alamán, who had pointed out years earlier that the clergy had grown rich not only from the ecclesiastical lands, but more especially from mortgages on the property of the faithful that the Church held. (These were not touched by the Reform laws.)

A war between the liberals and the conservatives, instigated by the Church, went on for three years. The Ley Lerdo, vigorously applied and reinforced by other legislation, gave the liberals the means to carry on the conflict. But the ultimate effects of the law were not those envisaged by its author. The Reform laws contained a threefold negation, as Octavio Paz has said: they denied the Spanish heritage, the indigenous past, and Catholicism, which had served to reconcile both heritages. In addition, the Reform tried to create in Mexico what the French Revolution had created in France—a class of small landowners, especially in the rural regions. In France, however, not only was the property of the Church released from mortmain but that of the nobility too, but in Mexico, non-Church property was left untouched. The juridical base of the Reform was the liberal conviction that the soil and subsoil are property of the nation, granted for use by the state as a concession, with the state retaining the option of expropriating it in the national interest. The Reform laws did not propose to change the social structure by any measure as radical as those advanced in revolutionary France; rather, they simply aimed to alter the political structure by taking away the economic power wielded by the Church and hoped to encourage industry and small landownership.

Yet the dogmatic liberals did not confine themselves to expropriating Church property. They also declared the *ejidos*, the public lands, the property of the whole nation. These communes of the Indians, in existence since the colonial era, were now to be distributed among the Indians who had been cultivating them. The result was that the Indian, who had never known private ownership, soon found himself faced with ruin, handicapped by debts, isolated from the old *ejido* institutions that had once protected him, and forced to sell the land he had acquired—after which he had to work it for the benefit of a new master. For the same people, many of them Spaniards, who had bought Church lands now bought the lands that the Indians had been granted but did not know how to cultivate on their own. In this fashion, as Ramírez had predicted, the dogmatism of the liberals— their blind faith in the concept that the Indians were the equals of all other citizens, needing no special protection or teaching—reinforced latifundism. For naturally the *latifundistas* were easily able to expand their holdings at the expense of the Indians, and as late as the Díaz regime the Ley Lerdo was used to destroy existing *ejidos* and accumulate land. Before the passage of the law, there had been three large groups of landowners: the Church, the ranchers and *hacendados*, and the Indians and mestizos on the *ejidos*. After the law, only the hacienda owners and ranchers remained. By the time of the Revolution of 1910, the number of haciendas had doubled from 6,000 to 12,000 and the big ranches from 15,000 to 30,000, until 97 per cent of the cultivated land in the country was in the hands of 1 per cent of the people.

The Ley Lerdo thus became a tragic example of how dogmatism—in this case, the application of liberal dogma that envisaged equality between the Indians and hacienda owners—can be so twisted from its original purpose of helping the poor as to benefit the rich at the poor's expense. And thus was independent Mexico's fundamental problem—Church-state relations—transformed into an agrarian problem after the Reform. Thousands of property owners were able to enlarge their holdings and turn them into haciendas. These huge estates became enormous, self-contained, autarkic production units. On the other hand, the people on the *ejidos*, which had previously been juridical entities with some influence, lost that status; the Indian found that he was abandoned, and he became a *de facto* serf of these new *latifundistas*. Later, the lesson of this development was taken to heart, and it helped to free the Mexican Revolution from the dogmatism that made the liberals of 1857 unwitting accomplices of the most regressive of great landowners.

In spite of their blunders, however, the liberals had not forgotten the Indians completely. The constitution of 1857 provided that no Indian would be obliged to lend his personal services without just recompense or without his full consent. In no case could the law authorize contracts resulting in loss of freedom—whether in fulfillment of a religious vow, in serving an apprenticeship, or in labor. "Free labor and free industry" was the liberal slogan.

The liberals had a left wing of their own, who saw the need "not to destroy, but to generalize property." Ponciano Arriaga (1811–65) was the exponent of this view. Others, influenced by utopian socialists, favored dividing property and establishing a rural middle class. Esteban Avila, governor of Aguascalientes, promulgated a law in 1861 that levied a tax on large landholdings in order to force the *latifundistas* to sell land to small farmers. But the law never worked effectively.

In the course of the three-year civil war that followed the Reform of 1857, the Mexican mentality underwent a change that would prove to be lasting. For one thing, both camps were led by young generals and politicians; the graybeards did not predominate. For another, because the liberals needed money to pay their troops and support their government, Juárez, impelled as much by this need as by loyalty to liberal principles, responded to pressure from his generals by speeding up and generalizing the expropriation of Church property. Even before the expropriation law was made public, the liberals had seized the wealth of the churches in many cities and villages. In the heat of the battle, they had also executed the armed priests encountered in conservative ranks. And as a consequence, the Mexican lost his superstitious reverence for the clergy and learned that he could fight against the Church and survive.

None of the liberal leaders amassed fortunes for themselves, but they could not prevent many of their followers from doing so. This created a new middle class of war profiteers, ready to support the liberals out of self-interest. Indeed, this wealthy middle class managed to remain in power until the Revolution. For their part, the conservatives found that the clergy were turning their moveable wealth over to the faithful for safekeeping. But when the war ended, the faithful joined the liberal side in great numbers to avoid having to return the wealth entrusted to them, and they made common cause with those liberals who had grown wealthy from the property of the clergy.

In the final analysis, the interests of both parties overrode the national interest. To raise money, Miguel Miramón (1832–67), the clever and audacious general who led the conservatives, sold national bonds at an infinitesimal price to a Swiss broker named Jenker, who began at once to make Mexico's business his business. On the liberal side, Ocampo signed a treaty (the McLane-Ocampo agreement) that permitted passage of people from the United States across the Isthmus of Tehuantepec in perpetuity, hoping by this means to stave off American intervention, which was being hinted at; in return, the government in Washington promised to pay $2 million and agreed to indemnify citizens who had suffered damage in the Mexican War. The U.S. Senate refused to ratify the treaty because the Northerners believed it would favor the South.

At long last the war ended. The liberal generals entered Mexico City amid loud cheering and the proffers of laurel crowns. Juárez arrived a few days later, minus the brass bands, dressed in black, and riding in his black berlin, which had traveled over half of the country. For the first time, Mexico had a president dressed in mufti. But of all her presidents, he was the one who had been most involved in war.

Indeed, the conflict had no sooner ended than the conservatives began to prepare for a new thrust. They hoped that this time it would be definitive.

In time, the Reform laws might have profoundly affected Mexico's structure, as Ocampo had hoped. In his view, the laws were not drawn up to diminish the authority of the Church so much as to create new landholders and prevent the rise of economic forces stronger than the state. But time was not on Ocampo's side. As soon as the Reform laws were applied, they provoked a strong reaction from the unseated but not vanquished Church and from the conservatives. This reaction was to reach its apex with the establishment of a Mexican Empire ruled by an emperor imported from Europe. That, in turn, ignited a new civil war, and the Reform laws could be applied in a normal way only at the end of that long conflict. Even then, a dictatorship was needed to apply them, using the laws to keep the Church neutral rather than as an instrument for transforming the country.

Mexico's treasury was empty. Proceeds from the sale of Church property, instead of being used to build schools and roads, had been diverted to finance a civil war. Many liberals were demanding a dictatorship, but Juárez, who had fought to defend the constitution, intended to be a democratic executive. He called an election and was returned to office, only to be beset by criticism from a congress made up of impatient young men.

Juárez granted amnesty to the conservatives under sentence of death. But, in the north, bands of guerrilla priests still scoured the land. In 1861, they captured and executed three of the strongest leaders in the liberal camp: Ocampo, General Santos Degollado, and General Leandro Valle. Meanwhile, Spain, France, and Great Britain were demanding indemnities and apologies for the damage done to the property of their nationals during the civil war. With the coffers empty, Juárez was forced to decree a two-year suspension of payments on foreign debts. At that very moment, civil war broke out in the United States. Juárez realized then that he was standing alone against the possibility of foreign intervention.

The possibility was strong indeed, and it was provoked by the conservatives. Juárez proposed an accord with England and, to prove that the nation was without funds, offered the British an opportunity to supervise customs, but the Mexican congress rejected the agreement. Meanwhile, Spain, France, and England had agreed to "teach Mexico a lesson" and by the Treaty of London undertook to intervene to protect their interests. In January, 1862, the first detachments landed at Veracruz—Spaniards under the command of General Juan Prim (who, years later, was to depose Isabel II and die at the hands of an assassin). To justify their presence in Mexico, the three powers issued a manifesto declaring that their expeditionary forces had been sent "to preside over . . . the country's regeneration." To the Spaniards and English, regeneration meant paying the debts owed them. But to the French under Napoleon III, it meant effecting a plan concocted by a group of Mexican exiles and implanted in the Emperor's and the Empress Eugenie's heads to establish a vast Catholic empire, stretching from Texas to Panama, facing the Protestant Anglo-Saxon republics to the north. This idea had been fathered by Archbishop Labastida of Puebla and General Juan N. Almonte (1803–69), who had turned to Paris for help. Their patron was the Duc de Morny, an associate of the Swiss banker Jenker, who by now held $15 million in Mexican bonds.

The plan, reported to Juárez, offered him a stratagem. He sent his foreign secretary to General Prim to inform the general of France's secret designs, and soon afterward, in April, the English and Spanish troops withdrew, while a new French army landed at Veracruz. General Almonte, arriving with it, had hardly set foot ashore before he acted out an old dream by proclaiming himself president. The Mexican exiles in Paris had felt confident that the people would welcome the French invaders and support them with arms. Trustingly, therefore, the French advanced toward Puebla, halfway between Veracruz and the capital. There, an army of seasoned guerrilla fighters met and defeated them with fieldpieces bought in Europe forty years before, after Waterloo. Napoleon III was shorn of his illusions, but he did not care to lose his prestige. He dispatched 30,000 more troops.

Juárez levied new taxes and ordered a general mobilization. The results were not encouraging. The country was exhausted. A new attack on Puebla settled into a two-month siege, which ended with the surrender of the Mexican defenders of the city—almost the whole of the regular army. Troops were taken prisoner and sent to France. One of their officers, Porfirio Díaz (1830–1915), eluded capture and remained in the country. Only 14,000 men were left to Juárez, and not a single, trustworthy general. Knowing that he could not defend his capital, Juárez moved the government northward to San Luis Potosí. The French entered Mexico City on June 7, 1863, where they were welcomed cordially by the clergy and the old conservatives.

The Mexicans had made a fool of Napoleon in the beginning; now he intended to make fools of the Mexican conservatives, just as he had deceived the Spaniards and the English. General Forey, commander of the invading army, decreed that ecclesiastical properties were not to be handed back to the Church, since he had discovered that many Frenchmen were the buyers of those properties.

All in all, the French turned out to be far too radical for the conservatives' taste. In order to checkmate them, a group of conservative notables hastened to offer the crown of Mexico to a European prince, the Archduke Maximilian of Austria (1832–67). Maximilian was a vacillating man, but he was also a man of good will, better than those who invited him. He insisted on a plebiscite to demonstrate whether or not the Mexican people wanted him as their monarch. Bazaine, the new French general, received instructions from Paris to organize the plebiscite:

Meanwhile, Juárez was traveling from city to city, trying to recruit soldiers, rally support, and raise money. In the north he stood almost alone; in the south, Porfirio Díaz held Oaxaca, and the old general Juan Alvarez (1790–1867) was in command of Guerrero. The rest of the country was in the hands of the conservatives, who were busy jailing and executing liberals. Maximilian, persuaded that the favorable plebiscite was genuine, sailed for Mexico with his wife, Carlotta. In preparation for their arrival, peons from the haciendas built a stone bridge called the Emperor's Bridge (still in use) along the road from Puebla, so that the imperial cortege would not need to ford a river.

In a sense, this moment—when Juárez and the liberals seemed to be conquered, abandoned, and without prospects—marked the beginning of the Mexican's grasp of his nationality. No longer was it a question of battles between parties, of ideological rivalries, or of factions—though to be sure all those things were still operative. Above and beyond everything else was the fact that the country was occupied by foreign forces, that an alien monarch was to govern it, and that the people, worn out by three years of civil war, seemed resigned to this. Yet out of that discouraging and defeating situation, the people emerged on their own, with no outside help, to no great fanfare, with a stubborn will to resist, choosing their own officers and leaders from their ranks, in the midst of intrigue, heroism, cowardice, maneuvering, ambition, bungling, firmness—all the acts and attitudes that cluster around moments of great historical tension. The revolt against the Empire was the first episode in Mexico's history of which Mexicans felt proud. Possibly it was the first moment when many, very many, Mexicans really felt that they were Mexicans.

All illusions were shattered. The conservatives lost theirs in the discovery that Maximilian was not a firm monarch but a dreamer and a liberal; Maximilian's vanished when he realized that he had not been called by the people and that it would be difficult to reign as an enlightened and progressive sovereign. He managed to persuade Napoleon to station troops in Mexico until 1867, even though the cost of their upkeep tripled the country's foreign debt. He tried to establish a reform government composed of moderates; he refused to return clerical property; and he even attempted to impose religious freedom. The Church began to favor attacks against Maximilian, and it was declared from the pulpit that the emperor was syphilitic, which was why Carlotta had borne him no children. Meanwhile, Maximilian concentrated on drafting laws—seven volumes in all—in the belief that he could solve his problems by legislation.

By about 1865, Maximilian had overcome almost all opposition.

Even the liberals were applying for posts in the bureaucracy, the only source of income for the middle class. Just then the Civil War in the United States ended, and the government in Washington (which had never recognized Maximilian) began to aid Juárez. The Juarists were able to collect large supplies of munitions at the frontier; General Bazaine showed his brutality by executing them; and the people blamed his acts on Maximilian, although the true source was Napoleon, who wanted to finish Juárez off as quickly as possible so that he could withdraw his own forces. The number of guerrilla fighters multiplied, and the Juárez armies were reborn. Victor Hugo wrote to Juárez from his home on the Isle of Guernsey that he was fighting *à coups de montagne*. Carlotta sailed for Europe to ask for help and went mad there when her pleas were denied.

Maximilian was prepared to abdicate, but the conservatives organized so many demonstrations of loyalty that they persuaded him to remain. He was alone, for at last the French had sailed for home. Finally, the conservative army met defeat at Querétaro; the emperor was taken prisoner and executed with his generals. For the second time, Juárez entered the capital, as always riding in his black, dust-covered berlin. The wandering government had come to rest.

From top to toe, the Empire had been an artificial creation, put together to destroy liberalism. The religious newspaper *La Sociedad* had written: "The European political world must prevent America from becoming democratic in every sense and from submitting to the single and dangerous influence of Washington." Yet Maximilian had wanted to rule as a liberal, and even his general, Miguel Miramón, recognized when he took command of the imperial government in its last days that "no government has ever consolidated its hold on the country, because none has taken care to adapt the individual well-being to that of the public." In 1865, Maximilian had manumitted the serfs on the haciendas by decree, but the landowners refused to comply with his law. His plan to protect the Indians, the only people who welcomed him with some enthusiasm (perhaps because he was blond or a new incarnation of the old pre-Cortesian myth of Quetzalcoatl), proved abortive, too. Maximilian had fixed the working day at ten hours, shorter than was common then; he had forbidden strikes, but he had also abolished the hated company stores. These regulations were fixed by fiat, like the order that every hacienda with twenty or more families of peons and every factory with 100 operators must establish a school. They were never obeyed.

Maximilian started with many ingredients for success: a good army, the support of the Church and of France, and the war-weariness of the people. But aligned in opposition were a stubborn and dedicated group and the disadvantages of his own weak character, burdened with good intentions. He alienated the Church by failing to return its property. His Mexican generals found they had to play second fiddle to incompetent French officers, and, to add insult to injury, they had to support them because France controlled the revenues. Maximilian also made a number of mistakes: he granted high government posts, such as director of colonization and head of the land office, to Confederate generals and politicians who sought sanctuary in Mexico after the American Civil War and sold them land cheaply so that they could establish themselves in Cordova and Coahuila. They went down with the Empire. (Of course, the Mexicans hated the Confederate immigrants, because they feared that if their influence grew strong, they would try to establish slavery.) Another of Maximilian's mistakes was to negotiate with Juárez—to no avail—instead of taking the logical course of capturing him at any cost. In the end, the conservatives respected Maximilian's memory less than the liberals, whom he had impressed by his refusal to escape after defeat and by his yielding of the position of honor before the firing squad to a Mexican, his own general Miramón.

None of these events had succeeded in dividing the people. The Empire had made liberalism identical with national independence in their eyes. When Juárez returned to power, he found his country devastated, but united. For the first time, it would be possible really to govern the country. In fact, Juárez made every effort to create not only a government but an administration as well. He understood that he could not leave the Indians without safeguards, and, accordingly, he tried to keep the *ejidos* operating, even at the cost of not applying that part of the Reform laws which decreed the distribution of communal lands. In 1867, Juárez was re-elected president and immediately encountered opposition from his own partisans, who before long branded him a dictator.

During the regime of the conservatives, most of the *caciques* were liberals. But now that the liberals were in power, bossism was slated for extinction, for, as someone said, a central *cacique* was about to take the place of the local *caciques*. Matías Romero (1837–99), secretary of the treasury, succeeded in imposing on the country a degree of austerity and in combating administrative corruption. Industry and commerce began to recover, thanks in great part to the disappearance of the guild system, which had survived in various forms after independence. British engineers resumed their work of building a railroad from Veracruz to Mexico City, which was started in 1837 and opened, finally, in 1873.

Juárez had said that he would welcome Protestant ministers to his country because they would teach the Indians to read instead of demanding money from them for the saints. Now he made a vigorous effort to organize a school system. He appointed Gabino Barreda (1818–81) to do the job. Barreda had recently returned from Paris where he had been a disciple of Auguste Comte. Seven years later Mexico had 8,000 schools with some 350,000 pupils out of a school-age population of 2 million.

The army that won the victory for Juárez had numbered 90,000 men. He discharged 60,000 without pensions, provoking many mutinies and executions of insubordinates. Juárez wanted to have done with militarism, but he never achieved his wish. Porfirio Díaz, a very popular general whom Juárez distrusted, saw his chance in the discontent of the army and the *caciques*. He ran against Juárez in the next election and was defeated. In 1871, Juárez decided to run again. Sebastián Lerdo de Tejada (1820–89), a trusted friend, also ran against him, thus, with Díaz, splitting the liberal party into three factions. As none of the three candidates received a clear majority, congress chose Juárez as president. Lerdo became president of the Supreme Court (which meant he was vice-president). Díaz rebelled, was defeated, and went into hiding. Then, just as the country seemed about to enter upon a period of order, Juárez died of a heart attack. Lerdo succeeded him and was later elected president.

The new president's first act was to grant an amnesty to the Díaz rebels. But though he was highly intelligent and a fine orator, Lerdo was a complete failure as chief executive. Arrogant and vacillating, he alienated all his supporters. When Lerdo ran for re-election in 1876, Díaz proclaimed the so-called Tuxtepec Plan and the slogan "Effective Suffrage and No Re-election" (a motto that his adversaries were to use against him thirty years later). Support for Díaz came from the United States, where businessmen looked mistrustfully upon Lerdo because he refused American railroads permission to continue into the Mexican interior, declaring "Between the powerful and the strong, the desert." In November, Lerdo resigned and left the country. Díaz entered the capital, put down the small force that supported the president of the Supreme Court, and proclaimed himself president.

His inauguration marked the beginning of a period of contradictions—dictatorship with material progress and civil retrogression. Historians have named this period the Porfiriate.

NOTES FOR MY CHILDREN
Benito Juárez

Benito Juárez (1806–72), the first civilian president of Mexico, was born in the small village of San Pablo Guelato in the southern province of Oaxaca. His parents were full-blood Zapotec Indians. Orphaned at three, young Benito spent his early years living in relative isolation, poverty, and ignorance. After moving to Oaxaca at the age of twelve, he studied at the primary school and the seminary. In 1828 he entered the Institute of Arts and Sciences and graduated with a law degree in 1834; in his subsequent practice he defended the rights of the Indian communities. His political career began with his appointment as regidor (councilor) to the Town Council of Oaxaca in 1831. By 1833 he was serving as deputy to the state legislature. In 1847, he was elected governor of the state. As a liberal governor with an honest and efficient record in government he quickly developed a national reputation. He supported the Plan of Ayutla in 1854, and soon thereafter became president of the Supreme Court in the liberal government of Ignacio Comonfort. With the latter's resignation in 1858, Juárez assumed the mantle of the presidency under the Constitution of 1857. For three years he led the liberal defense of the government against the clerics in the civil war of La Reforma, and he continued to oppose the French during the Intervention. Restored to power in 1867, he remained as president of Mexico until his death on July 18, 1872.

The selection from the Notes *which follows describes Juárez's life from his childhood to his appointment as governor of Oaxaca in 1847. Most of this essay describes his early life and education. This selection affords the reader the opportunity to play psychohistorian and, as such, attempt to determine those psychological and historical conditions which shaped the adult personality of one of Mexico's most important public figures. Of special interest in this context are Juárez's early orphan status, his attitude toward authority figures like the primary school teacher, his mention of his uncle's whipping him (and his own positive attitudes about the "whip"), and his repugnance yet dependence upon religious men, clerics, and the Church. On another level the account is quite informative about the nature of rural education in nineteenth-century Mexico and the dependence of the populace upon religious schools and religious vocations.*

From pp. 29–30, 32–33, 38–40, 49–50, 63, 82–84 in *Viva Juárez!* by Charles Allan Smart (J. B. Lippincott). Copyright © 1963 by Charles Allan Smart. Reprinted by permission of Harper & Row, Publishers, Inc.

AFTER 1857, nearly forty years after he ran away from home, Juárez wrote some autobiographical *Notes for My Children*, which begin as follows:

On March 21, 1806, I was born in the village of San Pablo Guelato, the jurisdiction of Santa Tomás Ixtlán in the state of Oaxaca. I had the misfortune of not knowing my parents, Marcelino Juárez and Brígida García, Indians of the primitive race of the country, because I had hardly reached three years of age when they died, leaving [me] with my sisters María Josefa and Rosa in the care of our paternal grand-parents, Pedro Juárez and Justa López, also Indians of the Zapotec nation. My sister María Longinos, a child recently born, for my mother died in giving her birth, remained in the care of my maternal aunt, Cecilia García. Within a few years my grandparents died, my sister María Josefa married Tiburcio López of the village of Santa María Tahuiche; my sister Rosa married José Jiménez of the village of Ixtlán, and I was left under the guardianship of my uncle Bernardino Juárez, because of my other uncles, Bonifacio Juárez had already died. Mariano Juárez lived apart from his family, and Pablo Juárez was still a minor. . . .

The *Notes* continue:

. . . as soon as I could think at all, I dedicated myself, insofar as my tender age permitted, to work in the fields. In the few intervals in which we were not working, my uncle taught me to read; he showed me how useful and advantageous it would be for me to know the Spanish language, and since at that time it was extremely difficult for poor people, and especially for Indians, to follow any learned career except the ecclesiastic, he revealed that he wanted me to study for ordination. His desire, and the examples that I had before me of fellow countrymen who knew how to read, write, and speak the Spanish language, and of others in the priesthood, awakened in me a vehe-ment desire to learn, with the result that when my uncle called me, to give me my lesson, I myself took him the whip, so that he could beat me if I did not know it; however, my uncle's work, and my own, in the fields, frustrated my ambition, and I advanced very little in my les-sons. Furthermore, in a village as small as mine, which had hardly twenty families, at a time when hardly anyone was concerned with the education of youth, there was no school; and there one hardly ever heard Spanish, because the parents who could pay for the education of their children sent them to the city of Oaxaca for that purpose, and those for whom there was no possibility of paying for board and tuition sent them to work in private homes, on condition that they would be taught to read and write. This was in general the only method of getting an education that there was, not only in my village but also in the whole district of Ixtlán, with the interesting result that at that time most of the servants in the houses of the city were young people, of both sexes, from our district. Thus, from feeling out these facts, rather than from any mature reflection, of which I was incapable, I acquired the conviction that I could learn only by going to the city, and to this end I often urged my uncle to take me to the capital, but either because of his affection for me, or from some other motive, he did not do so, but only gave me hopes that some day he would take me there.

Furthermore, I too was hesitant to separate myself from him, to leave the house that had sheltered me in my orphaned childhood, and to abandon my little friends, with whom I had always had the deepest sympathies, and from whom any separation always wounded me. The conflict that arose within me, between these feelings and my desire to go to another society, new and unknown to me, where I might acquire an education, was cruel indeed. However, my hunger overcame my emotions, and on December 17, 1818, when I was twelve years old, I fled from my house and walked on foot to the city of Oaxaca, where I arrived on the night of the same day.

The *Notes* continue:

I lodged in the house of don Antonio Maza, in which my sister María Josefa was serving as cook. During those first days I worked by taking care of the cochineal, earning two *reales* a day for my keep, while I looked for a house in which to work. At that time there lived in the city a pious and very honorable man who worked as a bookbinder. He wore the habit of the Third Order of St. Francis, and although dedicated to devotions and religious practices, was very broad-minded and was a friend of the education of youth. The works of Feijóo and the Epistles of St. Paul were his favorite reading. This man, who received me into his house, offering to send me to school, so that I could learn to read and write, was named don Antonio Salanueva. In this way I found myself settled in Oaxaca on January 7, 1819.

In the primary schools at that time, Spanish grammar was not taught. Reading, writing, and learning by rote the catechism of Father

Ripaldo was at that time the whole of primary instruction. Inevitably, my education was slow and in every respect imperfect. I spoke Spanish without rules and with all the errors committed by the uneducated. After some time in the fourth class in writing in the school that I attended—as much because of my work as because of the bad method of instruction—I could still hardly write at all.

Anxious to finish my writing lessons quickly, I asked permission to go to another school, believing that thus I could learn more perfectly and rapidly. I presented myself to don José Domingo Gonzáles, as my new teacher was named, and he promptly asked me in what grade I was writing; I answered him, in the fourth. "Well, then," he said, "write me a page and hand it in to me at the hour when the others hand in theirs." When the usual time arrived, I handed in the page that I had prepared in accordance with the pattern he had given me; but it was not perfect, because I was a student and not a teacher. The teacher was annoyed, and instead of showing me the defects that my page had and showing me how to correct them, he only told me that it would not do, and ordered that I be punished.

This injustice offended me deeply, as did the inequality with which the teaching was done in that school, which was called the Royal School: for while the teacher in a separate department taught with care a certain number of children who were called "decent," the poorer youngsters, such as myself, were relegated to another department, under the direction of another man, called the Assistant, who was as little fit to teach, and of as harsh a character, as the master.

Since I was dissatisfied with this deplorable method of teaching, and since there was in the city no other school to which I could go, I decided to leave the school for good, and to practise by myself the little that I had learned in order to express myself in writing, however bad in form that writing might be—as indeed it is to this day. [It was not calligraphically bad, if less formal than many of that time.]

Meanwhile, every day, I saw going to and coming from the Seminary College in the city [*Seminario Conciliar de la Santa Cruz*] many youths who were studying to embrace careers in the Church, and that reminded me of the advice of my uncle, who wanted me to become a priest. Furthermore, it was at that time the general opinion, not only of the common people, but also of those in the upper classes of society, that the religious, and even those who were only studying to become priests, knew a great deal; and I noticed that they were in fact treated with respect and consideration for the knowledge that was attributed to them. This circumstance, more than the idea of my becoming a clergyman, an idea for which I felt an instinctive repugnance, induced me to ask my godfather—for so I shall call don Antonio Salanueva, because he took me to be confirmed only a few days after receiving me into his house—to allow me to go and study in the seminary, assuring him that I should do all I could to make the fulfillment of my obligations to him, in his service, compatible with my dedication to the studies I wanted to undertake.

Since that good man, as I have already said, was a friend of the education of youth, he not only received this idea gladly, but even urged me to put it into effect, saying that since I had the advantage of knowing Zapotec, my native language, I could be ordained, in accordance with the ecclesiastical laws of America, without having to have the patrimony that others needed to live while obtaining a benefice. With my road smoothed in this manner, I began the study of Latin grammar at the seminary, with the rank of *capense*, on October 18, 1821—of course without knowing Spanish grammar or any other of the elements of a primary education. Unfortunately I was not alone in this deficiency, which marked the other students generally, because of the backwardness of public education at that time.

Thus I began my studies under the direction of teachers who, all being clerical, gave me a literary education that was strictly ecclesiastical. In August of 1823 I completed my study of Latin grammar, having passed the two required examinations with the grades of excellent. In that year the course in arts did not begin, and I had to wait until the following year to begin the study of philosophy in the work of Father Jacquier; but before that I had to overcome another serious difficulty that presented itself, as follows: as soon as I finished my study of Latin grammar, my godfather showed great eagerness that I should go on to the study of moral theology, so that in the following year I could begin to receive holy orders. This suggestion was very painful to me, both because of my repugnance to a religious career and because of the low reputation of the priests who had only studied Latin grammar or moral theology, and who therefore were ridiculed by being called "priests of mass and stew," or "Larragos." They were called the first because, on account of their ignorance, they could only say mass to earn a living, and were not permitted to preach or to exercise any other functions requiring instruction and ability; and they were called "Larragos" because they had studied moral theology only in the works of Father Larraga.

As well as I could, I explained this objection frankly to my god-father, adding that not yet being old enough to be received into the priesthood, I should lose nothing by taking the course in the arts. Luckily, my arguments convinced him, and he allowed me to go my own way.

In the year 1827 I finished the course in arts, having maintained in public two theses that had been assigned to me, and having passed two required examinations with the grades of excellent unanimously given, and with other honors given me by my synodical examiners.

In the same year there began the course in theology, and I went on to study that subject, as an essential part of the career or profession to which my godfather wished to destine me, and perhaps that was the reason why he had not insisted that I be ordained previously. . . .

The constitution of 1824 was a compromise between progress and reaction, and far from being the basis of a stable peace and of true liberty for the nation, it was the fertile and enduring seedbed of the incessant convulsions that the Republic has suffered, and that it will still suffer while society does not recover its balance by making effective the equality of rights and duties of all citizens and of all persons who inhabit the national territory, without privileges, without exemptions, without monopolies, and without odious distinctions; or while there remain in force the treaties between Mexico and foreign powers, treaties that will be useless as soon as the supreme law of the Republic is an inviolable and sacred respect for the rights of all men and of all peoples, whoever they may be, provided they respect the rights of Mexico, her authorities, and her laws; or while, finally, there is not in the Republic one single and unique authority, the civil authority as it is established by the national will, without a religion of the state, and wiping out the military and ecclesiastical powers as political entities that force, ambition, and abuse have opposed to the supreme power of society, usurping its rights and prerogatives, and subjecting it to their caprices.

The republican party adopted the name Yorkist party, and from that time onwards there continued a bloody and unremitting struggle between the Scotch party, which defended the past with all its abuses, and the Yorkist party, which sought liberty and progress; but unfortunately, the latter almost always fought at a disadvantage because, enlightenment not having become general in those days, its adherents, with a very few and very honorable exceptions, lacked faith in the triumph of the principles they proclaimed, since they ill understood liberty and progress, and they lightly deserted its ranks, going over to the opposing party, which action confused the efforts of their former fellow partisans, defeating them and delaying the triumph of liberty and progress. This was in general the state of the Republic in the year 1827.

At the beginning of 1833, [he continues] I was elected deputy to the state legislature. Because of the Law of Expulsion of Spaniards passed by the federal congress [1829], the Bishop of Oaxaca, don Manuel Isidoro Pérez, although exempted from this hardship, refused to remain in his dioceses, and departed for Spain. Since there was not now one bishop in the Republic, because the few that there had been had also gone abroad, it was not easy to receive holy orders, and they could only be had by going to Havana or New Orleans; for this purpose it was indispensable to have sufficient resources, which I lacked. For me, this circumstance was highly favorable, because my godfather, recognizing the impossibility of my being ordained, permitted me to continue in my career at the bar. By that time I was supporting myself entirely by my own resources.

In the same year I was named Aide to the Commandant, General don Isidro Reyes, who defended the city against the forces of General Canalizo, who had pronounced for the plan of religion and exemptions put forward by Colonel don Ignacio Escalada in Morelia. From that time, the clerical-military party impudently undertook to maintain by force of arms, and by means of rebellions, their exemptions, their abuses, and all their antisocial pretensions. What gave this rebellion of the privileged classes a pretext was the first step that the liberal party took at that time on the road of reform: repealing the unjust laws that imposed civil coercion for the collection of monastic votive offerings and the payment of tithes.

"In the year 1845," Juárez continues,

there were held elections of the deputies to the departmental assembly, and I appeared as one of the many candidates who offered themselves to the public. The electors resolved on me and I was unanimously elected. Early in 1846 the departmental assembly was dissolved as a result of the military sedition led by General Paredes, who, under orders from the President, don José Joaquín de Herrera, to march to the frontier threatened by the American army, pronounced in the hacienda of the Peñasco in the state of San Luis Potosí, and countermarched towards the capital of the Republic, in order to seize the government, which he did, submitting himself completely to the direction of the monarchist-conservative party. The liberal party did not concede defeat. Aided by the Santa Anna party, it worked actively until it succeeded in overturning the reactionary administration of Paredes and in installing General don Mariano Salas provisionally in the Presidency of the Republic.

In Oaxaca the movement against Paredes was supported by General don Juan Bautista Díaz; there was named [August 11] a Legislative Committee and an Executive Power of three persons who were named by a Committee of Notables. The election fell on don Luis Fernández del Campo, don José Simeón Arteaga, and myself, and we began at once to fulfill the duties with which we had been honored. Informed of this arrangement, the general government decided to dissolve [September 10] the Legislative Committee, and to entrust the executive power of the state to don José Simeón Arteaga alone. I had to return to my legal post in the prosecutor's office, but Governor Arteaga dissolved it in order to reorganize it with other personnel, and in consequence he proceeded to its reorganization, naming me President or Regent—as at that time was named the presiding officer—of the Tribunal of Justice of the state.

The general government called on the nation to elect its representatives with full powers to revise the constitution of 1824 [which meanwhile had been illegally set aside], and I was one [of nine] of those named for Oaxaca, and so proceeded to the capital of the Republic, to fulfill my new duties, early in December [the 6th] of the same year of 1846. At this time the Republic was already invaded by forces of the United States of the North; the government lacked funds sufficient to set up a defense, and it was necessary for the congress to afford the means of acquiring them. The deputy for Oaxaca, don Tiburcio Cañas, took the initiative in authorizing the government to mortgage part of the properties administered by the clergy, in order to provide resources for the war. The proposal was admitted and then turned over to a special commission, to which I belonged, with the recommendation that it be given prompt attention. On January 10, 1847, a report was made on this matter, advising the adoption of this method, and it was brought up immediately for discussion. The debate was extremely long and heated, because the moderate party, which had a large majority in the chamber, put up a strong opposition to the project. At two in the morning of the 11th, however, the report was approved in general, but in the discussion of the particulars, the opposition presented a multitude of amendments to each of the articles, with the unpatriotic purpose that even when it was finally approved the act would have so many hobbles that it would not produce the result that the congress proposed. At ten in the morning the discussion came to a close with the passage of the law, but for the reasons stated it did not issue with the desired amplitude . . .

"From that moment," Juárez continues,

the clergy, the moderates, and the conservatives redoubled their efforts to destroy the law and to eject from the Presidency of the Republic don Valentín Gómez Farías, whom they considered the leader of the liberal party. In a few days they succeeded in realizing their desires by inciting to rebellion a part of the city at the moment when our troops were fighting for the nation's independence on the northern frontier and in the city of Veracruz. This mutiny, which was called that of the Polkos, was viewed with indignation by most of the people; and the rebels, thinking that their plan could not succeed by force of their arms, resorted to subversion, and succeeded in winning over General Santa Anna, who commanded the army that had defeated the enemy at La Angostura, and whom the liberal party had just named President of the Republic over the opposition of the moderate and conservative party; but Santa Anna, inconsistent as always, abandoned his men and rushed to Mexico to give the victory to the rebels. These went to the Villa of Guadalupe to receive their protector, with their chests covered with badges of membership in religious orders and relics of saints, as "defenders of religion and the exemptions." Don Valentín Gómez Farías was removed from the Vice-Presidency of the Republic, and the liberal deputies were attacked and denied the reimbursement that the law allowed them for their subsistence in the capital. We deputies from Oaxaca could not receive any help from our state because there the legislature had been destroyed and replaced by those who supported the rebellion of the Polkos; and as a matter of fact the congress was not holding sessions because it lacked a quorum. I decided to go home and dedicate myself to the practice of my profession.

In August of the same year [1847] I arrived in Oaxaca. Although they were persecuted, the liberals were working actively to reestablish the legal order, and in this effort they were authorized by law, for there existed a decree that, on my motion and that of my associates in the deputation from Oaxaca, was passed and sent by the general congress, condemning the mutiny that had occurred in this state and refusing to recognize the authorities established by the rebels; nor did I hesitate to help in any way that I found possible those who worked for the fulfillment of the law, which has always been my sword and my shield . . .

On November [actually October] 23d we succeeded very well in a movement against the intruding authorities. The President of the Court of Justice, Lic. don Marcos Pérez, took charge of the government; the legislature met and named me Governor *pro tempore* of the state.

The Mexican Constitutional Congress, 1856–1857: A Statistical Analysis

Richard N. Sinkin

Richard N. Sinkin teaches and researches Mexican history at the University of Texas at Austin. This study was originally read at the annual meeting of the American Historical Association in 1971. Professor Sinkin used a quantitative technique known as factor analysis to identify associations or correlations between pairs of variables. The result enabled him to identify group behavior patterns among the delegates to the Mexican Constitutional Convention of 1856–57. This kind of statistical analysis yielded several significant conclusions, including the observation that the liberals of this generation were moving away from earlier liberal federalism toward centralization of power in a national parliament. As Sinkin notes, "The roots of the concentrated authority of the Porfiriato can be found in the centralization of power during the Reform." For further study the reader is urged to consult the document that resulted from this Convention, the Constitution of 1857.

THE SINGLE MOST IMPORTANT DOCUMENT and symbol of the Reform in Mexico in the middle of the nineteenth century is the Constitution of 1857. Because of its importance, it has attracted much scholarly and popular attention, most of which focuses on certain important articles included in the document. The Constitution is noted for the inclusion of the *Ley Lerdo*, which forced corporations like the Church and the Indian communities to sell their property. The Constitution also contained the *Ley Juárez*, which severely limited and circumscribed the privileges of the Church and military. For the first time in Mexican

From Richard N. Sinkin, "The Mexican Constitutional Congress, 1856–1857: A Statistical Analysis" (*Hispanic American Historical Review* 53: 1–26). Reprinted by permission of the publisher. Copyright 1973, Duke University Press (Durham, N.C.).

history, individuals were to be protected by a bill of rights. Complete equality under the law, abolition of slavery, freedom of speech, freedom of assembly, freedom of the press, freedom to teach whatever one wanted, and restrictions on the application of the death penalty—these were some of the individual rights guaranteed by the Constitution. And these rights remained when the Constitution was revised and rewritten in 1916–1917.[1]

Yet, in spite of the significance of the Constitution of 1857, the social composition and voting behavior of the delegates who wrote it have been completely neglected. In general, we have been led to believe that Mexico's constitutions "have been the result of free discussions among men of all political views and all philosophical doctrines."[2] To test this view, the present article analyzes three distinct aspects of the Mexican Constitutional Convention: (1) the social composition of the delegates, (2) their voting behavior, and (3) to what extent social background determined conflict within the Congress. Each element has its own value as an analytical tool; together they indicate much about the nature of Mexican politics in the middle of the nineteenth century.

TABLE I: OCCUPATIONAL STRUCTURE OF CONGRESS

Principal Occupation	Number	Percentage*
Law	35	46
Journalism	9	12
Military	16	21
Medicine	4	5
Education	1	1
Bureaucracy	7	9
Other Professional	3	4
Other Non-Professional	2	3

*Cumulative percentage may vary from 100 because of rounding.

In describing the social composition of the Mexico City Congress, Jesús Romero Flores asserted that the members of the body were "the most distinguished men of the epoch" with "the majority dedicated to diverse occupations: farmers, shop keepers, journalists, and a few military men."[3] Francisco Bulnes, on the other hand, suggested that of the 154 delegates to the congress, 108 were lawyers and the rest were soldiers and bureaucrats.[4] Walter Scholes has also concluded that the delegates were lawyers, journalists, teachers, and government employees.[5] Table I summarizes the occupational structure of those delegates for whom information was available.[6] Although data could be obtained for only half (N = 77) of the delegates, it seems possible to conclude that Romero Flores' description of the social composition of the convention is inaccurate. There were no farmers, few shop keepers, and a large number of military men. Scholes' estimate appears closer to reality, and many of those in journalism, teaching, and the bureaucracy had received legal education prior to entering these occupations, thereby confirming Bulnes' estimate of the number of lawyers. Thus, rather than being a popular convention representing all groups in society, the Constitutional Congress that met in 1856 represented a professional class, and in a county where few could read or write, a social elite.

These data also suggest that although the delegates may have been an elite, they were a young elite, and not the most socially prestigious or politically powerful men of the epoch. The average age of the delegates for whom birth dates are available (N = 64) was 40, and 60 percent of the sample had entered politics within the decade prior to the Congress. Of this young group almost half (47%) resided either in the Federal District and the State of Mexico or the surrounding states (Guanajuato, Michoacán, Puebla, Querétaro, and Tlaxcala).[7] These data may indicate migration patterns in which young provincial professionals moved toward the center in search of employment and advancement. They seem to be men who joined the liberal movement against the dictatorship of Antonio López de Santa Anna because they had found the paths to personal advancement closed to them.

Although the delegates to the Congress were similar in background, there was much conflict during the writing of the constitution. Those who have commented on the subject have identified two groups within the Congress: the moderates (moderados) and the radicals (puros).[8] The problem for the analyst is to identify the issues which created these groups and then to clarify the social composition of the two blocs.

To analyze both the issues and the groupings, I used the roll-call votes taken during the year-long Congress. The official records of the Congress, the Actas oficiales del Congreso Constituyente (1856–1857), contain over 200 roll-call votes. Of these, 161 had statistical significance in terms of opposition voting. From this list of 161 votes,

70 were selected on the basis of a stratified random sampling technique; four votes were chosen for their importance in the literature, and the rest with the aid of a table of random numbers. The use of the Riker coefficient of significance was of limited value. (See Appendix I for a list of the roll calls, their substance, and the Riker indices, which measure "significance" in terms of both participation and cleavage.) These votes were used as the basis for the statistical analysis.[9]

The principal method of analysis used to identify the major issues at the Congress was factor analysis, a technique which measures the underlying relationships among all variables and produces mathematical statements of the common relationships. In this study, factor analysis begins by measuring the degree of association (or correlation) between pairs of variables (here the variables are votes). Then the program analyzes the degrees of association between sets of variables and discovers those sets that vary in similar ways in the body of data. The result is the identification of groups or clusters of variables that are most meaningful in explaining variability in the voting patterns. These groups are called factors. Although it may serve other purposes, the most common use of factor analysis is to reduce an unwieldy mass of data to a few "underlying dimensions" or factors. Individual votes which account for most of the variance within each factor are said to have "high loadings" on that factor. The votes with high loadings are used to define the nature of the factor.[10] Table II gives a summary of the votes with high loadings ($\geq \pm 0.5$) on the five factors that emerge from the factor analysis of the roll-call voting at the Constitutional Congress (for the absolute mathematical relationships on the five factors, see Apendix II).[11]

Factor I reveals some fascinating relationships. Votes with high loadings are: the defeat of Article 15 of the projected constitution, which would have permitted the unrestricted establishment of non-Catholic religions in Mexico; the establishment of freedom of education; the defeat of trial by jury in criminal cases; a defeat of an attempt to bring to the floor the discussion on whether to abolish mutilation as a punishment for crimes; a secret vote giving the Constituent Assembly the right to expel cabinet ministers from the hall when the Congress discussed their office; the establishment of jury trials in cases involving federal courts; a defeat of an article establishing trial procedures for high government officials; a defeat of an article which would have abolished shackles, chains, and irons as legitimate punishments for crimes; a defeat of an attempt to remove the cities of Cuernavaca and Cuautla from the State of Mexico and give them to the State of

Table II: Summary of High Loadings in Rotated Factor Matrix*

Roll Call	I	II	III	IV	V
4. Executive Council (Defeated)				x	
5. Repeal Executive Budget (Defeated)				x	
6. Approval of Viduarri (Defeated)				−x	
9. Congressional Autonomy				−x	
13. Mail Seizure (Defeated)					−x
17. Freedom of Religion (Defeated)	−x				
18. Freedom of Education	−x				
21. Trial by Jury (Defeated)	−x				
22. Discuss Abolition Mutilation (Defeated)	−x				
23. Expulsion of Ministers	x				
24. Unicameral Legislature	−x				
25. Procedure: To Debate Death Penalty Abolition				−x	
26. Abolition of Death Penalty				−x	
27. Size of Congressional District			x		
29. Residency Requirements for Congress		−x			
31. Congress has Authority to Allow States to Divide			x		
29. Jury Trial in Federal Cases	−x				
41. Prohibit State Alliances		−x			
46. Limit Tax Powers of Congress (Defeated)		−x			
47. Trial of Government Officials (Defeated)	−x				
50. Prohibit Shackles, Chains, and Irons (Defeated)	−x				
56. D. F. in Querétaro (Defeated)		x			
57. Cuautla and Cuernavaca to Guerrero (Defeated)	−x				
58. Maintain Boundaries of State of Mexico	x				
62. Licenses by Congress	x				
64. Death Penalty Time Limit (Defeated)					x
67. Remove all Congressional Residency Requirements (Defeated)		x			
69. State Support for Clergy (Defeated)		x			

*Loadings with negative signs have an inverse relationship to those with opposite signs on the same factor.

Guerrero; a vote to uphold the present boundaries of the State of Mexico (including Cuautla and Cuernavaca); and, finally, an authorization of Congress to issue licenses to high government officials to leave the capital.

A superficial perusal of these votes suggests no immediate relationship. There seems to be a mixture of votes relating to religion, criminal punishments, congressional power, and local boundary disputes. The issue of church and state can be dismissed immediately as the principal dimension of conflict because only two votes pertained (the defeat of religious toleration and the establishment of non-Catholic education). Similarly, geographical boundaries applied only to the two votes on the size of the State of Mexico. On the other hand, the large number of votes on crimes and criminal procedure suggests that law and order may have been the principal issue.

A careful reading of the debates on all the votes further clarified the significance of Factor I. One delegate, José María Castillo Velasco, said of the importance of Article 15 (Religious Toleration): "The question before us is not a truly religious one, but rather essentially social and political."[12] The debate focused principally on the effects religious toleration would have in Mexico. Toleration will "bring on rebellion," predicted Marcelino Castañeda. And he concluded: "Ultimately, fellow delegates, the domestic home will disintegrate into chaos. . . ."[13] José María Lafragua, Minister of *Gobernación* and delegate to the Congress, articulated the central fear underlying the debate on Article 15, arguing that religion per se was not at issue; instead, it was a question of law and order. Admitting alien religions into Mexico would bring on national disintegration. "The Indians," he warned, "are agitated, and for this reason it is very dangerous to introduce a new element which will be exaggerated by the enemies of progress in order to immerse us in a truly frightening anarchy."[14]

Fear of anarchy pervaded the debates on the other votes with high loadings on Factor I. Freedom to teach without restrictions other than public morality received support because an educated public would be a public less prone to civil disturbance. And Mexico had experienced its share of political turmoil; in the thirty-five years from the Plan of Iguala to the Constitutional Convention, Mexico had forty-four changes of government. As Manuel Soto put it: "civilization is impossible without the development of intelligence." In the case of trial by jury, the defeat was motivated by an intense distrust of the popular instincts. Ignacio Vallarta, in attacking the article, argued that Mexico was still in an infancy "corrupted by an uninterrupted series of rebellions" and that to allow trial by jury would only perpetuate the anarchy. Similarly, Prisciliano Díaz González attacked the attempt to remove the cities of Cuautla and Cuernavaca from the State of Mexico and incorporate them in the State of Guerrero on the grounds that such a move would produce rebellion, chaos, and anarchy. The vote to maintain the present boundaries of the State of Mexico was thus a vote to preserve law and order. These votes, seen in relationship to the votes on chains and irons, cruel and unusual punishments, and trials of government officials, strongly suggest that the major dimension of conflict at the Constitutional Convention of 1856–1857 was a fear of anarchy, or "Law and Order."[15]

Other votes in Factor I—on the expulsion of ministers from the Chamber during debates, the establishment of the unicameral legislative body, and the power of Congress to issue licenses to high government officials should these officials want to leave the Federal District—all suggest that the solution to the problem of Law and Order was to be found in congressional power.

Hence, the votes with high loadings on Factor II become increasingly important. Factor II clearly concerns the composition and power of the unicameral Congress. Two of the five votes deal directly with residency requirements for election to Congress; another is a defeat of an attempt to limit the tax powers of the legislative branch of government; and the defeat of the attempt to move the Federal District to Querétaro was motivated directly by the fear that to do so would weaken the prestige and power of the legislature.[16] Thus the second principal dimension of conflict was the "Power of Congress."

Factor III identifies a centralist-federalist split in the Constitutional Convention. Each of the three votes with high loadings on Factor III involves the relationships between the national power (Congress) and state government. In every case the Congress decided that power would rest ultimately with the national government, thus calling into question the shopworn assumption that the Reform liberals were also federalists.

Indeed, the loadings on Factor IV suggest that the major conflict was not whether power would reside at the national level or the state level, but rather whether it would be exercised by the President or the Congress. The defeat of Comonfort's executive council and the vote on repeal of the executive budget indicate that Congress saw itself not only as a constituent assembly but also as a legislative body. Congress even went so far as to issue a declaration (Vote 9) prohibiting the executive from making objections or observations about the decrees and resolutions of the Constitutional Congress. The vote to annul Santiago Vidaurri's unilateral and illegal unification of the states of

Nuevo León and Coahuila was not only an attack on the northern caudillo's federalism, but also a direct confrontation with President Comonfort's policy of conciliation with the local chief. Thus Factor IV can be labeled "Congress vs. the President."

Taking Factors II, III, and IV together suggests a strong centralist tendency in the Constitutional Congress. In reaction to the excessive executive power exercised by Santa Anna, the liberals of the 1850s wanted power vested in the Congress. They feared excessive local power and arbitrary presidential absolutism equally; they wanted above all regularized, effective, and legitimate central government. An all-powerful unicameral Congress was their solution.

Factor V has four high loadings, three of which concern the application and limitation of the death penalty. The fourth vote is a defeat of an article which would have permitted the national government to seize personal mail "in times of grave crisis." Although mathematically independent of Factor I, Factor V bears a close relationship in meaning. The partial abolition of the death penalty engendered the same kind of debate on law and order as did the votes that loaded highly on Factor I.[17] Yet the factor analysis identified the death penalty as an independent dimension, and it deserves separate treatment. Factor V is therefore labeled "Death Penalty." Ultimately the Constitutional Congress abolished the death penalty, but only upon the completion of a national penitentiary system.

Thus the factor analytic process was able to identify five principal dimensions of conflict within the Constitutional Congress. Statistically the most important was "Law and Order." The other four were: Power of Congress, Centralism versus Federalism, Congress versus the President, and the Death Penalty. (See Table III for the distribution of variance in the rotated factor matrix.)

One issue that did not appear as an independent dimension of conflict was the Church-State conflict. Walter V. Scholes has argued that "in the minds of the leaders *the* question was the clerical one."[18] And Justo Sierra has characterized the politics of the period as a "war between the lay and the ecclesiastical state."[19] While it is true that the Constitutional Congress met in the midst of a vicious Church-State struggle, the statistical analysis suggests that it was not a major source of conflict within the Congress. In fact, the delegates were of a similar mind on the need to break the political and economic powers of the Church, and the votes on these issues, such as the limitation of ecclesiastical privileges and the disamortization of Church property,

TABLE III: DISTRIBUTION OF VARIANCE IN ROTATED FACTOR MATRIX*

Factor	% of Total Factor Variance	% of Total Variance
I. Law and Order	35.8%	14.9%
II. Power of Congress	19.4	7.1
III. Centralism vs. Federalism	15.2	5.2
IV. Congress vs. President	14.5	4.0
V. Death Penalty	15.1	3.8
	100.0%	35.0%

*Rotating the factor matrix reduces the percent of variance explained by Factor I while increasing the percent of variance explained by the other factors.

were nearly unanimous.[20] The Church-State issue can most profitably be considered as an integral part of the larger issue of the ordering and stabilizing of Mexican society and politics. The struggle to secularize society was thus a function of the rationalization and restructuring of power in the state.

Factor analysis not only provides a means of identifying the underlying dimensions of conflict within the Congress, but also it supplies a technique for grouping delegates by how they vote on any one factor. It gives each delegate a score on the factor, and delegates with similar scores can be considered to form a voting bloc.

Almost all the literature on the Congress mentions a split between two competing blocs: the moderates and the radicals. Although no one provides a formal list of the groups, invariably men such as Ponciano Arriaga, Francisco Zarco, Ignacio Ramírez, and José María Mata are linked with the radicals. Others—such as Marcelino Castañeda, Antonio Aguado, Juan Barragán, and Mariano Arizorreta—are usually classified as moderates.[21] An analysis of the factor scores on Factor I of the 70 delegates who voted more than 50 times does not confirm this judgment.[22] Grouped together at the positive (i.e., "Radical") end of the scale are Ignacio Ramírez (as expected) and Marcelino Castañeda (unexpectedly). Zarco and Mata both score at the opposite end of the scale. Ponciano Arriaga falls in the middle. The factor scores thus indicate that on the issue of Law and Order the moderate-radical split does not exist. The factor score distribution graph (see Figure 1) further suggests that no groupings are easily identifiable.

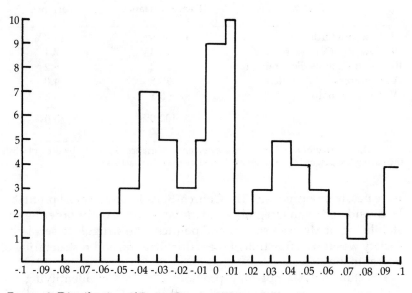

FIGURE 1. Distribution of Factor Scores on Factor I.

TABLE IV: COMPARISON OF Q-ANALYSIS AND FACTOR SCORES

+High Loadings	Factor Score	−High Loadings	Factor Score
Arriaga	.0150	Guerrero	−.0132
S. Degollado	−.0306	Quintana	.1034
Mata	−.0076	Rosas	.0100
Payró	−.0391	Villagrán	.0017

Nor does a factor analysis using the delegates instead of the votes as variables indicate a clearly defined "moderate-liberal" split.[23] In this Q-analysis, those with high positive loadings were Ponciano Arriaga, Santos Degollado, José María Mata, and Gregorio Payró. Those with negative high loadings were Benito Quintana, José de la Luz Rosas, Rafael María Villagrán, and Francisco Guerrero. Table IV compares the factor scores of each bloc. In both cases the relationships are too slight to identify a defined cleavage within the Congress. Instead, we may conclude that the conflict in the Congress was among constantly shifting coalitions.

The statistical analysis of the Mexican Constitutional Convention of 1856–1857 yields a number of significant conclusions.

1. The delegates were young professionals. Most had law degrees even though they may have practiced another profession. They seem to have formed an upwardly mobile social elite that had found the path to further advancement closed to them by what they viewed as the tyranny of unchecked authority. Thus one of their central concerns was the protection of individual liberties.

2. At the same time, they divided on how far the process was to proceed. Although almost all the delegates agreed that the powerful corporate interests had to be subordinated to the state, they disagreed sharply on how much individual liberty could be permitted. The Law and Order issue indicated that they disagreed, not on the need for stability, but rather on what would produce instability.

3. The liberals of the middle 1850s were moving away from the earlier liberal federalism. The loadings on Factors II, III, and IV indicate that one goal of the delegates was the establishment of a rational and regularized political system in contrast to the prevailing alternation of anarchy and presidential absolutism. A powerful national congress, regularly elected and supreme in authority, was seen as the optimum solution.

4. Even though Law and Order proved to be the principal dimension of conflict within the Congress, it did not produce a clearly defined moderate-radical voting bloc split. Neither regional identification, nor occupation, nor age, nor social status played a major role in determining voting positions. Instead, voting seems to have been issue-oriented. The idiosyncratic nature of the voting patterns may be attributed to the obvious social uniformity of the Congress.

The Constitution of 1857 was written at a critical moment in Mexican history. Less than a decade before, the country had lost half its territory to the "Manifest Destiny" of the United States. As a result, many Mexicans had begun to doubt if Mexico would continue to exist as a sovereign nation. Both liberals and conservatives reacted to this psychological crisis by calling for strong government. But for the conservatives strong government meant a return to the authoritarianism of the colonial period, with Santa Anna ruling as "His Most Serene Highness." For the new generation of liberals strong government meant rule of law, not rule of men; it meant power concentrated in a permanent revolutionary assembly controlled by a new political elite, not in the hands of a dictator; and it meant equality under the law, not arbitrary exile and imprisonment. Although law and order were equally the goals of the liberals in 1857, the subsequent decade of civil war begun by the Reform War (1858–1860) and finished by the French Intervention (1862–1867) made order more important than law. When the wars were over and the liberal triumph assured, the Constitution of 1857 stood as a national symbol. Power, however, was completely in the hands of the executive, where it has remained ever since. The liberal attempt at parliamentary democracy had failed, only to be replaced by another solution to the problem of law and order: the constitutional dictatorship. The roots of the concentrated authority of the *Porfiriato* can be found in the centralization of power during the Reform.

NOTES

1. The best studies of the Constitutional Congress are Emilio Rabasa, *La constitución y la dictadura* (1912; reprint ed., Mexico: Editorial Porrúa, 1957); Daniel Cosío Villegas, *La Constitución de 1857 y sus críticos* (Mexico: Editorial Hermes, 1957). For the debates see Francisco Zarco, *Historia del Congreso Constituyente (1856–1857)* (Mexico: El Colegio de México, 1956). Also see Colegio de Abogados de México, *El Constituyente de 1856 y el pensamiento liberal mexicano* (Mexico: M. Porrúa, 1960); Manuel Loza Macías, *El pensamiento económico y la Constitución de 1857* (Mexico: Editorial Jus, 1959). For a comparison with the Constitution of 1917, see H. N. Branch, trans., *The Mexican Constitution of 1917 Compared with the Constitution of 1857* (Washington, D.C.: Government Printing Office, 1926).

2. Jesús Romero Flores, *Comentarios a la historia de México* (Mexico: Libro Mex, 1958), p. 152.

3. Ibid., pp. 154–55.

4. Francisco Bulnes, *Juárez y las revoluciones de Ayutla y de la Reforma* (2d

ed., Mexico: Editorial H. T. Milenario, 1967), p. 168. Bulnes goes on to suggest that most of those who practiced law did so in the pay of the government because (1) ecclesiastical lawyers handled the big cases and (2) there were too many lawyers for the small job market.

    5. Walter V. Scholes, "Church and State at the Mexican Constitutional Convention, 1856–1858," *Americas* 4 (October 1949): 151–74. Also see Wilfrid H. Callcott, *Church and State in Mexico, 1822–1857* (Durham, N.C.: Duke University Press, 1929), pp. 268–69.

    6. Socio-economic data for this study were taken from biographical dictionaries. Among the most useful were *Diccionario Porrúa de historia, biografía, y geografía de México* (Mexico: Editorial Porrúa, 1965, and supp., 1966); Alberto Leduc, et al., *Diccionario de geografía, historia, y biografías mexicanas* (Mexico: Vd. de C. Bouret, 1910). A total of seventy-one state biographical dictionaries were consulted. The absence of a formal archive made the task of gathering socio-economic data extremely sketchy and must be used with great caution, they are more valuable than appears. Rarely did more than ninety delegates vote on an issue and, in general, it is for these men that data exist. These data must, therefore, be taken as a general order of magnitude rather than as a precise tabulation.

    7. The youngest delegate discovered was twenty-one; the oldest, seventy-five. State representation of the delegate was, in most cases, the same as residency. Six delegates represented more than one state or territory, and in all these cases the state of birth was chosen as the state of representation. For purpose of analysis the delegates were assigned to the following regional categories: Pacific North (Baja California, Sinaloa, Sonora, Jalisco, Colima); North (Chihuahua, Coahuila, Aguascalientes, Durango, Nuevo León, San Luis Potosí, Tamaulipas, Zacatecas); Center (Guanajuato, Michoacán, Puebla, Querétaro); Pacific South (Chiapas, Guerrero, Oaxaca, Tehuantepec, Yucatán); Core (México, Distrito Federal). Cross-tabulations using a NUCROS computer program of several socio-economic variables (age, occupation, region, number of years in political activity) and "participant" categories (number of votes and number of participations in debates) failed to identify significant relationships.

    8. See, for example, Bulnes, *Juárez*, pp. 162–85; Scholes, "Church and State," p. 152 n. 3; Cosío Villegas, *Constitución*, pp. 82–83; Rabasa, *Constitución*, pp. 30–45.

    9. The techniques for selecting votes to be used in roll-call analysis are in Lee F. Anderson et al., *Legislative Roll-Call Analysis* (Evanston, Illinois: Northwestern University Press, 1966), pp. 77–87. The following procedure was used to select roll calls in the Mexican Congress: (1) Since the principal concern of the study was conflict, only votes with 10 percent opposition voting were included. The procedure produced a universe of 161 roll calls. (2) This number was then reduced to 70 for two reasons: (a) the large number of duplicate votes and (b) the large amount of time required to code all the roll calls. (3) Four roll calls were then selected for their importance in the literature (votes no. 1, 2, 8, 17). The 66 others were selected with the aid of a table of random numbers. The result was a stratified random sample. The Riker Coefficient of Significance proved inadequate for selecting the final 70 roll

calls because the number of voting delegates fell during the year-long Congress, thereby skewing "significance" chronologically. For the computer program to compute the Riker Index, see ibid., p. 186.

10. There are several other techniques available for analyzing voting behavior, especially Guttman scaling and cluster-bloc analysis. After experimenting with these techniques, I found factor analysis gave a clearer picture of the dimensions of conflict within the Congress. The best work on factor analysis is R. J. Rummel, *Applied Factor Analysis* (Evanston, Ill.: Northwestern University Press, 1970), but also see Benjamin Fruchter, *Introduction to Factor Analysis* (New York: Van Nostrand, 1954). Two important concepts basic to factor analysis are (1) variance—a standard statistical measure of the degree of dispersion of the values of a variable—and (2) correlation—the amount of variance shared by two variables. Although factor analysis has the useful property of reducing large numbers of variables to a smaller number of factors, it has one major weakness in roll-call analysis: it treats all votes as occurring simultaneously, thus neglecting the influence an early vote might have had on succeeding votes. Nevertheless, since most of the votes used in this study occurred within four months of one another, time was judged to be an insignificant element. Also, were time significant, it would appear as a factor in the factor matrix.

11. The votes were coded in the following manner: yes $= +1$, not voting $= 0$, no $= -1$. The table is drawn from the results obtained using the packaged computer program MESA1 of the University of Texas Computation Center. This technique produced a matrix of Pearson product-moment correlations and used the highest squared multiples in the diagonals of the correlation matrix. This matrix was factored by the principal components procedure. The matrix included only the votes of the 70 delegates who voted more than 50 times. As a check on the validity of this technique, I ran four EDSTAT programs (devised by the Department of Educational Psychology, University of Texas) with 1's in the diagonals and (a) using all 134 voting delegates, (b) using only the 70 "participant" delegates, (c) excluding missing data, and (d) including missing data. In all runs 15 factors with positive eigenvalues of ≥ 1.5 were extracted, which accounted for 67.9 percent of the total variance in MESA1. Significantly, in all five runs the same votes loaded highly on Factor I. The reason the MESA1 results are being used in this study is that they more clearly delineated Factors II through V than did the EDSTAT program. For the purposes of this paper, the orthogonally rotated (VARIMAX) factor matrix was more useful than the unrotated matrix. In the unrotated matrix Factor I remained essentially the same; in the rotated matrix Factors II through V became more clearly delineated. (See Rummel, *Applied*, chap. 16, for discussion of orthogonal rotation.) Oblique rotation was not used since I was looking for "independent" dimensions of conflict. It should be noted that in the final MESA1 run, vote no. 70 had to be dropped from the matrix for mathematical reasons. The procedure seemed acceptable, since the vote had low loadings in all the EDSTAT results.

12. Zarco, *Historia*, p. 568.

13. Ibid., pp. 549–51.

14. Ibid., p. 630.

15. Ibid., pp. 718, 748, 1073–77. It is important to note that the naming of Factor I would have been impossible without the debates. Only through a careful study of the debates did the underlying relationships of the votes that loaded highly on Factor I become clear. On the techniques, difficulties, and the artistry needed to name factors, see Rummel, *Applied*, pp. 472–89.

16. For the debates on the location of the Federal District see Zarco, *Historia*, pp. 1110–15.

17. See ibid., pp. 782–89, 1208–9.

18. Scholes, "Church and State," p. 152 n. 5. Italics are his.

19. Justo Sierra, *The Political Evolution of the Mexican People*, trans. Charles Ramsdell (Austin: University of Texas Press, 1969), p. 270.

20. For a discussion of the unanimous and near-unanimous votes, see Bulnes, *Juárez*, pp. 182–85.

21. The only informal list I was able to locate of the moderates and radicals is found in Cosío Villegas, *Constitución*, p. 79. The difficulty with using his list in a factor analysis is that with the exception of Marcelino Castañeda, the men listed as moderates had fewer than fifty votes.

22. The factor scores are taken from the EDSTAT program using the seventy participant delegates. They were not transformed and are derived from the rotated factor matrix.

23. A Q-factor analysis consists of factor analyzing a matrix in which "variables" refers to entities, in this case the seventy participant delegates. The loadings thus measure association among delegates on a given factor. See Rummel, *Applied*, pp. 195–96, 241–43; Anderson et al., *Roll-Call Analysis*, pp. 142–43, 165.

FRENCH IMPERIAL POLICY
IN MEXICO

Jack A. Dabbs

Jack A. Dabbs is a professor of Spanish at Texas A&M University. He is a student of history, anthropology, literature, and linguistics, and is also a specialist in namelore. Professor Dabbs collaborated with Carlos Castañeda on several bibliographies of manuscript collections, including The Guide to the Latin American Manuscripts in the University of Texas Library; The Manuel E. Gondra Manuscript Collection; *and* Independent Mexico in Documents.

In the following essay Dabbs explains why French colonial rule did not succeed in Mexico and suggests that the choice of Mexico was a bad one for the French. Dabbs also notes how the presence of French soldiers, politicians, and engineers left an impact on Mexican culture, especially in language, literature, philosophy, architecture, and engineering. Mexican intellectuals and philosophers are still influenced more by Continental ideas coming from France and Spain than those originating in Anglo-America.

WITH RESPECT TO HIS ADMINISTRATION in Mexico, as well as that of Maximilian, it is very attractive to take advantage of hindsight to criticize and to point out errors. As far as the French in Mexico were concerned, the existence or lack of individual errors is almost inconsequential. No matter what brilliant actions on the part of Bazaine or of Forey, the French intervention was doomed to failure. For France to send troops four thousand miles from home to occupy and hold so huge a country was out of the question. Only one such experiment has succeeded: England held most of India for a century and a half, but in most of the sub-continent the English only held control over allied native princes with whom they maintained treaties. They did not try

Reprinted from Jack A. Dabbs, *The French Army in Mexico, 1861–1867* (The Hague: Mouton & Co., 1963), pp. 279–86, by permission of the publishers.

to make over India into a new England. A common complaint against French colonial policy, however, has been that it has called for a revision of native governments on the French model, the installation of French officers in even minor offices, and the imposition of French law over the new areas.

In Mexico that policy was not followed. The French plan hoped to avoid conflict over the Monroe Doctrine by setting up a new government by "elections" rather than by incorporating the land into the French Empire. In such a case the new government, popularly chosen, could not be challenged. The French would withdraw, and Mexico would be only *de facto*, not *de jure*, under French influence. Statements on a broad level early in the intervention have been reviewed in earlier chapters. Even as late as 1866 official policy stated by the Chief Minister in Paris maintained no suggestion of a permanent French military force:

> We went there not to bring about a monarchical proselytism, but to obtain reparation and guarantees which we ought to claim, and we sustain the government which is founded on the consent of the people because we expect from it the satisfactions of our wrongs, as well as the securities indispensable to the future.[1]

No responsible official ever maintained a suggestion of a permanent French occupation or further direct French control than a transitional military government. The incorporation of some individuals to the armed forces of the Mexican Empire was not the same thing because it involved an oath of allegiance and a transfer of loyalty.

The French went to great pains to obtain a ballot by which they could show that the Maximilian Empire was elected by a popular vote and represented the will of the public. This vote was criticized more in Europe than in the United States, but for the same reasons. French representatives corresponding with agents of the United States often spoke of the popular choice of Maximilian; but the United States agents, when they did mention it, disclaimed its significance: The inconsistency between this policy of the United States and the acceptance of balloting done in the ex-Confederate States during the military occupation of the South by Federal troops is obvious, but no longer of moment.

> The United States . . . are of opinion that such an acceptance could not have been freely produced or lawfully taken at any time in the presence of the French Army of invasion.[2]

The French program might have succeeded if the Civil War had resulted in a separate nation along the Gulf of Mexico. But the effort of the Confederate States failed, and the Mexican Empire thereafter had to face uniformly strong opposition from the North.

Apart from the opposition of the United States there is some reason to believe that the experiment might have succeeded. In 1864, with little aid from the North, Juárez was almost driven out of Mexico, and the army was almost destroyed; only with the material aid that began in 1865 on a large scale did his fortunes improve. Without that aid Juárez could not have continued the struggle, and organized resistance would have dissolved. With the United States next door, aid to the patriots was inevitable in United States interests. Only an extremely weak or a treacherous American administration would have failed to secure a native government on its southern border.

Napoleon, or his advisors, in his effort to extend French influence, counted too heavily on the weakness of the two divided armies of the northern neighbors. A more careful study of world geography would have shown several parts of the earth more favorable for an extension of French economic materialism, and the positivists in the Paris government should have understood them better. The intervention in Indo-China was more successful because there was no strong nation to protect the peninsula. France had an equal chance with England to extend her possessions in Africa, but the English, with a better understanding of world forces, seized the healthiest part of Africa, leaving the less desirable to the other nations. The French were well advised in their seizure of Madagascar; there were no protecting forces; and only rivalry with Russia and England kept Iran from falling to France, and the Pacific Islands were for the taker to choose. But in America the choice of Mexico was a particularly bad one—the area lay immediately adjoining the strongest nation in the New World. If Napoleon had made an attack on a South American country, he might have had better chance of success. If he had attempted to seize one of the latter, for example, he would have come nearer his military goals. Whatever the intentions of the United States, it would have been physically impossible for them to give aid to one of the South American countries on the scale that Mexico received it. Except for Brazil, all were much smaller, and the same number of troops could have maintained order better.

But the idealistic purposes of Napoleon, and perhaps the more mundane ones of the Duc de Morny and unofficial advisors, overrode the pragmatic positivism of the time. Napoleon hoped to raise Latin prestige in the New World by inserting a block or dam to retard the United States' expansion into Latin America. The logical place to begin was in Mexico, not in South America. Once he stopped the expansion, then French culture as well as industry and economic influence could increase their rôle.

The story would have been different if the French had provoked an outright invasion by American Federal troops. Mexico could not have come out of such an occupation without territorial loss. The United States Government was in the hands of expansionists, but, fortunately for Mexico, the energy was finding an adequate outlet in the development of the West at that time. Nonetheless, considering the weak position of the northern states, the exploratory filibustering expeditions, and the projected railroads to the Gulf of California, it would have been almost impossible for Mexico to have rid herself of American allies without divorcing herself at the same time of Sonora, Lower California, Chihuahua, or all three. The decision of Napoleon to withdraw without a fight saved Mexico territorial loss, and Napoleon evidently knew it.

The French definitely were overextended in Mexico. It would have taken twice as many troops to police the country. There were two alternatives: They could have made use of local armies to a greater extent; Márquez, Mejía, and even Vidaurri, Lozada, Uraga, Ugarte, and López could probably have maintained armies in their own way that could have controlled whole states, leaving the French fewer key positions. But the French policy and philosophy were too idealistic and anti-clerical to allow such a condition. They could not bring themselves to allow the Mexican generals to operate in their own way; they had to impose French rules of conduct, and it cost them heavily. Again the liberal philosophy of the Revolution succumbed before the realistic requirements of the situation.

Another alternative was open. The French might very well have given up the whole of Northern Mexico and concentrated their efforts on a smaller scale in the South. The Yucatán Peninsula and the States of Chiapas and Tabasco could have been occupied effectively from the beginning, but it was not in the plan. The Mexican conservatives wanted the French in Mexico proper, and the legendary mines of Sonora kept all eyes peeled on the north. Yucatán could have become a last refuge, and the Imperial court and the French very likely could have held out there for a very long time if the threat of the northern neighbor did not materialize. But again the drawback was that a withdrawal to Yucatán could have left a vacuum in Mexico that would have furnished an open invitation for American troops to march south.

The only answer was a withdrawal.

SUGGESTED ALTERNATIVES

The work of the Intervention was a permeation of French influence into every phase of life. Many public officials received training in governmental administration that continued into later presidencies. French literature was more widespread than ever; the language was more common; and, after the initial period of patriotic hatred subsided, more people began to recognize the improved way of life that the French had brought. They left the metric system of measurements firmly seated as the official one. They modified the architecture from the Spanish drabness. They stimulated literature and the arts and brought new philosophical systems, particularly the positivist, as the last word and the magic key to man's conquest of nature.

More interesting, however, is the failure of the intervention to remedy the social ills. In particular the allies seriously disappointed the Indians.[3] They had for the first time a deliverer who made a show of bringing them freedom. But the deliverers soon fell into the slough of Mexican custom and failed to carry out their promise.

Once Maximilian entered upon his duties and abjured the support of the arch-conservatives, but while he still had the support of the French army, he had the one great moment since 1521 to raise the Indians out of the mires into which society had forced them. For a period of over a year Maximilian owed nothing to the conservatives, and he could have founded his empire on Indian support that would have immeasurably strengthened his position and drained the Juarist armies of their manpower. By an Indianization of the Empire, it could have come much nearer success.

The position of the Indian in Mexico differed greatly from that in the United States. When English colonists with their legal authorities reached the New World, they met Indian leaders and recognized them as sovereign groups with whom they made treaties, recognizing the chiefs as sovereign heads of state—hence the common expressions the Cherokee Nation, the Iroquois Nation, and the Tuskarora Nation.

That the settlers violated the treaties is another matter. After 1776 the United States continued this legal status, recognizing Indians as non-citizens, later to be segregated in restricted areas or reservations, where they did not have voting privileges.

In the Spanish realms, however, colonization began earlier and continued more of the feudal line of thought. There was at first a lively debate, but it settled with recognition of the Indians as subjects of conquest. When the conquistadores took new land, they asked or forced the Indians to accept the King of Spain as their liege lord and accept a feudal allegiance to him. Thereafter as long as they did not revolt, Indians were subjects of the King, and elaborate laws tried to protect them from exploitation. That they *were* exploited by Spaniards is another matter. With the independence of Mexico and the rest of Spanish America, this relationship continued. Indians of Mexico were considered citizens. They could enjoy most of the privileges of citizenship provided they fitted themselves into the social and cultural patterns of creole society and gave up their Indian identity. Exploitation of the Indians was extra-legal. The Indians maintained many separate enclaves with their own language and customs, but they had practically no political organization. When they took part in politics, it was because a leader from the creole society called them to follow him on a campaign. They did not follow through political conviction.

The French military leaders, with a rare insight far ahead of the rest of Western Europe or America, had a certain vision of the basic problem; and they tried to organize separate battalions of Indians without Mexican (creole) officers, rather using French officers at first and trying to develop non-commissioned officers, later officers, from the ranks. These battalions made a good start, but later on recruiting dropped off. In these battalions Spanish was still the means of communication. The battalions made a good showing, but the whole enterprise was contrary to creole social patterns and was not supported by the Conservatives. When the French began to prepare for a withdrawal, Empire, that is, Conservative, officers took the place of the French officers, and the whole experiment came to nought.[4]

Maximilian had an excellent opportunity to make an appeal to this populous group. He was excellent linguist, and he could have made use of the Nahuatl tongue quickly enough to make it popular by his own example. Native art had waned, but there was enough left to reconstruct the throne of Montezuma and to capitalize on the rumors linking Maximilian with the legendary hero, Quetzalcoatl. Millions of

Indians would have acclaimed him and followed his standards with a fervor that the creoles could not have withstood. He could have surrounded himself with Indian cabinet officials—not Hispanicized Indians like Mejía or Lozada, or even Juárez or Díaz, who were only creoles with Indian parents—but real leaders from the Indian tribes, who were still a part of the Indian tradition. The Christian matrix would have made no difference because the Indian culture of 1864 was no longer that of 1519, and the Christian religion was an integral part of their life. Maximilian could have held his audiences on or in the shadow of the pyramids of Cholula or San Juan Teotihuacán— archaeological accuracy would not have been required. Thus he could have made himself a messiah of the people. In particular he could have made Nahuatl the official language of the court or at least could have put it on an equal basis with Spanish. The non-Nahuatl speaking Indians could not have found it more difficult than Spanish. When the Empire's stand became widespread, and when the Indians saw that their interest genuinely lay with the Empire, the accrual to the Empire forces would have left the Juarists with armies staffed only by officers.

The historic moment was at hand and crying out for embodiment. Both Maximilian and his French supporters had glimmerings of the problem, but neither was able to rise effectively to the occasion. Instead of invoking the legends of Montezuma and of Quetzalcoatl, the latest Hapsburgs tried briefly to awaken the shades of Charles V; he set himself up in the palace of the viceroys and spoke Spanish. He surrounded himself with an administration and with advisors whose training and political philosophy were those of 19th-century Western Europe. The time had not come for the leaders to realize, trust, nor appeal to the tremendous power of the Indian masses. Not until the next century were political leaders to learn to tap that source of political power.

The Interventionists tried to appeal to the stratagems of European politics and to the strata of society that they knew best. They predicated the new throne on political intrigues and tried to bring together Conservatives and the Liberals, both primarily creoles who only used the Europeans as tools and as weapons to fight each other. They thought in terms of diplomacy, of protocol, of guns, and of leaders who lived on the toil of the Indians. Their support was so ephemeral and fluctuating that there was no firm footing on which to build. Only by organizing it on the bedrock of a popular appeal to the subordinated peoples could the Europeans construct a lasting empire; and when the Interventionists defaulted on their chance to make that appeal, the empire had to fall.

NOTES

1. Drouyn de Lhuys to Marquis de Monthalon, 9 January 1866, in U.S., Congress, *Executive Documents*, 39th Cong., 1st sess. 1865–66, no. 93, pp. 17–20.

2. Ibid., Seward to Monthalon, 12 February 1866, esp. p. 29.

3. Jack A. Dabbs, "The Indian Policy of the Second Empire," in *Essays in Mexican History*, ed. Thomas E. Cotner and Carlos E. Castañeda (Austin: University of Texas Press, Institute of Latin American Studies, 1958), pp. 112–26.

4. Ibid. Aside from the battalions raised by the French, several moves made by Maximilian himself showed some concept of the need. He welcomed Indian leaders who presented themselves, primarily the Kickapoo visitors and Maya leaders. He passed laws aimed at relieving the virtual peonage of Indians on the haciendas, and he favored them when he could. But he was essentially the guest of the landowners and Conservatives who preferred the older status. He had difficulty finding real Indian leaders. The best example would have been Juan Álvarez in Guerrero State, an Indian leader of Indians; but the Emperor completely failed to attract Álvarez to the Empire's side.

PART IV
THE PORFIRIATO, 1876–1910

General Porfirio Díaz, a mestizo military commander who had fought in the wars of the Reform and the Intervention, became president in 1876. Díaz immediately began consolidating his power. Making use of the classic tactics of effective dictatorship, he practiced the politics of divide and conquer with the military, the Church, and even foreign powers like the United States and England. In addition, he added to the security of his regime by influencing the appointment of state governors, dispensing patronage to his friends, developing shifting commands for the military, controlling the courts, subsidizing the press, and cultivating the support of the Church. Taking for his political and economic creed the positivist slogan "Order and Progress," Díaz was determined to curb Mexico's tradition of anarchy so that economic development and modernization could occur. As Díaz reasoned, foreign and indigenous capital investments would lead to economic progress for Mexico, but to assure this development, the state would have to protect and promote the interests of that capital.

The Pax Porfiriano was maintained, in part, by a liberal use of the police powers of the state. Federal troops were used to pacify the frontier, protect the National Palace, guard the federal prisons, and, when needed, break labor strikes. In addition, Díaz had the services of the national guard, the *rurales* (a rural police force), and specially comissioned gendarmes, like those led by Colonel Emilio Kosterlitzky in Sonora. Díaz also established an elaborate spy system which consisted of consular agents on both sides of the U.S.-Mexican border, private informers in the pay of the state, U.S. and Mexican postal authorities, hired detectives (like the Furlong Detective Agency of St. Louis, Missouri), and diplomatic personnel in Mexico City. Political enemies were either shot on the spot (under the provisions of the infamous *Ley Fuga*, law of flight), sent to the federal prison at San Juan de Ulúa, or absorbed into an expanding bureaucracy.

Díaz succeeded all too well. Leaders of the industrial-creditor nations believed that Mexico was a model underdeveloped country (see Reading 17). Mexico's courts and laws protected and promoted the interests of the foreigner, especially the North American. Liberal land, mineral, and water concessions were an open invitation to foreign investors; the names of Doheny, Rockefeller, Guggenheim, Greene, Otis, and Hearst were as well known in Mexico as they were in the United States. Mixed companies and partnerships were often formed with domestic elites like the powerful hacendado of Chihuahua, Luis Terrazas (see Reading 19), or the local bankers, industrialists, and politicians in Mexico City known as *científicos* (see Reading 25). Like the social Darwinists in the United States at this time, the Mexican advocates of French positivism were able to rationalize the excesses of technocracy and capitalism, even going so far as to develop a secular, scientific Religion of Humanity (see Reading 21). The result was a society which was partially developed economically, but only in its extractive sector, and an aging president and government which could not or would not make room for social groups that had been politically mobilized by the limited modernization. These social groups included the agrarian workers, peones, industrial workers, railroad employees, miners, middle-class intellectuals, and, in a few instances, hacendados who had been excluded from the system. Thus, the same conditions which brought about order and progress in Mexico also set the stage for the Revolution of 1910.

Following the classic pattern of revolution, the countryside and the city joined together under the leadership of Francisco Madero to overthrow Porfirio Díaz after 1910. In the country the Indians' situation had worsened. Exploited by local bosses, their own chieftains *(caciques)*, and the Church, the peones displayed contradictory traits of obedience and anger, the result of years of repression (see Reading 20). As a result of the new commercial developments in agriculture, including the intrusion of foreign-owned railroads into Mexico—an event that was linked to widespread assaults on the property holdings of Indian free villages (see Reading 22)—the Indian lost his land to the neighboring hacendado (who was often the representative of a foreign owner) and, in some cases (like the Yaquis of Sonora or the Mayas of the Yucatán Peninsula), was reduced to a twentieth-century style of personal slavery (see Reading 18). All of this created a Porfirian tradition of agrarian disturbances that often resulted in protests and rebellions.

Industrial laborers in the factories and in the mines were also denied political rights and social justice in a system which protected only the rights of capital. Between 1905 and 1907 several strikes occurred in the textile and mining industries. Most, like that in Cananea in 1906, were suppressed and broken with the use of federal troops and rural police. After the Cananea strike, the grievances of both urban and rural labor were expressed by the revolutionary Liberal party in its July Manifesto of that year (see Reading 23). This kind of revolutionary nationalism, directed against domestic and foreign elites alike, finally swept through Mexico in 1910. The immediate antecedent of that revolution was Francisco Madero's Plan de San Luis Potosí, issued on October 5, 1910 (see Reading 24).

The Díaz age was over, but historians are still debating the true nature and meaning of the Porfiriato for Mexico (see Reading 26).

THE DÍAZ ERA: BACKGROUND TO THE REVOLUTION OF 1910

Robert Freeman Smith

Robert Smith, a professor of history at the University of Toledo, specializes in Cuban and Mexican history and United States foreign policy in those countries. His published works include The United States and Cuba, 1917–1960; What Happened in Cuba: A Documentary History; *and* Background to Revolution: The Development of Modern Cuba. *The following gives a general description of economic development during the Porfiriato and indicates most clearly the role of foreign capital in an underdeveloped nation. Note how the author shows the development of Porfirian and revolutionary nationalism and how this was a reaction to the presence of foreigners in Mexico. It is also interesting to try to distinguish any continuities between the radicalism of the early 1900s and the ideological content of Mexico's Constitution of 1917 and to compare the role of foreign capital in Mexico with the role of foreign capital in the United States after the War of 1812. Are there significant differences? Can foreign capital actually produce an underdeveloped economy? This question still faces the leaders of Latin America, Asia, and Africa today.*

> He [Porfirio Díaz] said that, so far as the ambassador was concerned, he was a Mexican, for whom mañana would do as well as today. As for the secretary of foreign affairs, he also could wait. But I, as one of his "collaborators in the development of Mexico," deserved instant admittance day or night, for "Mexico herself" waited on me.
>
> —John Hays Hammond

Reprinted from *The United States and Revolutionary Nationalism in Mexico, 1916–1932* by Robert Freeman Smith, pp. 1–14, by permission of The University of Chicago Press. Copyright © 1972 by the University of Chicago.

ECONOMIC BACKGROUND

THE FOREIGN OBSERVERS who came to Mexico City for the centennial of the Hidalgo rebellion of 1810 were impressed by the apparent serenity and opulence of this once turbulent country. The well-scrubbed streets and massive new buildings of the capital city seemed to symbolize the changed conditions which had taken place under the firm leadership of Porfirio Díaz. The leaders of the industrial-creditor nations now believed that Mexico was a model underdeveloped country. Peace, order, and stability were maintained, and foreign investments were protected. As a corollary, the legal system of Mexico had been reshaped to conform to the international legal order which the developed nations had constructed for the protection of trade and investment. The Mexican government not only accepted the industrial-creditor nations' rules for the "game" of international economic relations but also followed internal economic policies which opened Mexico to the full impact of foreign business expansion.

Changes had taken place under the auspices of the Porfirian peace. Political turbulence had ended, and older observers could contrast this with the situation in 1873 which had provoked the editor of the *Army and Navy Journal* to write: "We have stood enough from Mexico. . . . Come to order she must, or be punished."[1] The *rurales* (rural police) now maintained order in the country, and obstreperous elements such as Yaqui Indians and striking copper-miners were given bloody lessons from the catechism of law and order.

Economically, Mexico seemed to be fulfilling the prophecy of Cecil Rhodes: "Mexico is the treasure house from which will come the gold, silver, copper, and precious stones that will build the empire of tomorrow, and make the future cities of the world veritable Jerusalems."[2] Early in his presidential career Díaz had decided that the development of Mexico depended upon largescale foreign investments, and he instituted a variety of policies to make Mexico safe and attractive for foreign business. Low taxes; physical protection; legal guarantees, coupled with friendly courts; subsidies; governmental concessions to public lands and waters—all constituted important elements in the new economic order. The larger foreign companies also could depend upon the central government to handle any problems which arose with local and state authorities.

As a result, some development did take place. This generally was concentrated in the extractive industries and in satellite areas such as railroads and electric power. During the period 1891–1910 the production of copper rose from 5,650 to 48,160 metric tons; gold from 1,477 to 41,420 kilograms; and lead from 30,187 to 124,292 metric tons.[3] Railroad mileage increased from 416 miles in 1876 to 15,360 miles by 1910. This development produced attractive profits and such firms as American Smelting and Refining, Phelps-Dodge, and the Southern Pacific Railway developed extensive holdings. From the infant iron and steel industry of Monterrey to the sugar plantations of the south, U.S. capital was in a paramount position. By 1908, the *Wall Street Summary* could report that three-fourths of the dividend-paying mines in Mexico were owned by U.S. interests and that these "paid a sum 24 percent in excess of the aggregate net earnings of all the National Banks in the United States, or about $95,000,000."[4]

In 1901, Edward L. Doheny and his associates brought in the first oil well in Mexico, and by 1903 commercial production was underway. Until then the Waters-Pierce Oil Company (35 percent interest held by H. Clay Pierce and 65 percent by Standard Oil of New Jersey) had a monopoly on shipment of oil to Mexico by virtue of an import concession given by Díaz. After 1903, foreign capital poured into the Mexican oil industry. Two of the pioneer companies, the Huasteca Company (Doheny and Associates) and El Aguila (Mexican Eagle, controlled by Weetman Pearson and Sons of London), were paying substantial dividends by 1911.[5]

The developmental policies of the Díaz regime also were directed at the rural economy. Don Porfirio and his colleagues believed that the small *rancheros* and the Indians were unproductive. The government developed a systematic policy designed to redistribute the land to large holders. Theoretically these owners would either increase agricultural output or sell the land to colonies of productive foreigners. A law passed in 1883, and expanded in 1894, provided the legal basis which the government used to grant concessions to individuals and companies for the purpose of locating and surveying so-called empty lands. In effect these groups had the power to examine the land titles of any holder or village community. If the titles were questionable, or if the required pieces of paper could not be found, the land could be denounced, and the individual or company involved could retain one-third as a reward for "finding" lost national lands. In addition, the "finders" were allowed to purchase the remainder from the government at very low prices.

Political favorites obtained these concessions, and some became very large landowners. Many, however, transferred their concessions to foreign companies. Some colonization was effected as required by law, but most of the land was either held for speculation or became part of the expanding hacienda system. As a result a small number of individuals and companies obtained 72,335,907 hectares (one hectare equals 2.47 acres) of land during the Díaz era. This same element also gobbled lands under the pretext of enforcing the reform laws of the 1850s, which originally were designed to curb the corporate holdings of the Roman Catholic Church, and under the law of 1888 which allowed the president to grant monopoly concessions to water rights.

The enactment and utilization of these laws reflected the laissez-faire viewpoint of the ruling elite in Mexico and the foreign businessmen from the industrial-creditor nations. These groups operated on the simplistic belief that government cooperation with private enterprise would automatically lead to progress and modernization. The Mexican elite liked to call themselves *científicos* (scientific ones), since they utilized elements of Positivism to explain or rationalize their policies. They spoke in some detail about the future benefits which would "trickle down" to the rest of the population, but in the short run their actions were almost entirely designed to maximize private profits. The Díaz government did exert some national control over banks and railroads after 1900, but for most of this period regulation was minimal.

The dominant economic philosophy and the reinforcing legal framework of the industrial-creditor nations also were incorporated into the new mining legislation of Mexico. The mining code of 1884 eliminated all prior legislation and expressly removed the government's claim to ownership of bituminous and other mineral fuels and nonmetallic minerals. The ownership of these subsurface deposits was now given to those who owned the land. In spite of the new departures incorporated into the 1884 code, the old cultural-legal traditions of Mexico were not entirely eliminated. Fee simple titles were not granted and retention of titles was still subject to "regular workings" of the mine.[6]

The *científicos* were not completely satisfied with the 1884 code, and in 1892 a commission drafted a much more laissez-faire law. Its object was declared to be: "Facility to acquire, liberty to exploit, and security to retain." As Marvin Bernstein concisely notes, the mining code of 1892 reduced the state to a passive level, and "the mineowner and speculator in Mexico attained a position of almost complete liberty of action."[7] The legal framework of the Mexican economy had been substantially adjusted to the international legal order of the developed nations. This industrial-creditor nations' concept of order and stability went beyond the absence of violence to include the kind of protection which the laws and policies of underdeveloped nations provided for foreign enterprise. By this standard, foreign businessmen and government officials considered Porfirian Mexico to be one of the most well-behaved "backward" nations in the world. Indeed, in the light of the rising Populist movement some even believed that property rights were safer in Mexico than in the United States.

Elements of cultural conflict—as symbolized by the different legal traditions of the Anglo-American and Hispanic cultures—remained. The concept of a fee simple title to property did not appear in the mining code of 1892, and later legislation revealed that even the *científicos* had not been completely converted to the legal norms of the Anglo-American economic order. By 1900, some of them had even begun to realize that many of the legal and diplomatic doctrines of the industrial-creditor powers, such as "equality of opportunity" for investors and merchants and rights of aliens, had peculiar meanings when applied to the underdeveloped areas, meanings which primarily benefited the larger powers in their penetration of economically weak countries.

Control by foreign capital of large segments of the Mexican economy constituted an important facet of the distorted development of the Díaz period. While much of this control was a product of new enterprises, at least some of it was a result of foreign businesses absorbing smaller Mexican enterprises. Not only were the native enterprises overwhelmed by the size of foreign competitors but some also suffered from the favoritism which the Díaz government lavished upon foreign interests. One such example was the concession to an English cotton company of the Nazas River water rights. This action ruined the small Mexican farmers in the region. This is not to argue that Díaz and the *científicos* deliberately conspired to ruin their fellow countrymen, with the exception of the Indians. In fact, after 1900 the government tried to promote more Mexican economic activity, but, in their early haste to promote a "favorable climate" for foreign investments, Mexican officials did practice discrimination and rationalized it with the argument that some short-term sacrifice of indigenous interests would be more than compensated by rapid development. The *científicos* liked to talk about the necessity of "breaking eggs to make omelettes." There is a logic to this insofar as it is an expression of the necessity to force change under some circumstances. The *cien-tíficos'* problem, however, was their naive faith that broken eggs automatically become omelettes with little conscious direction.

There are various estimates concerning the exact extent of foreign control of the Mexican economy. All agree that foreign capital held a position of predominance in almost all areas of commerce and industry: approximately 97 percent of mining properties, 98 percent of the rubber and guayule industries, and 90, or more, percent of the petroleum industry. U.S. companies controlled approximately 70 percent of the total foreign investment. The henequen industry of Yucatan was one of the few to remain under Mexican control. Foreign ownership was not as heavy in the rural area, but Frank Tannenbaum notes that, as late as 1923, foreigners owned 20.1 percent of the privately owned lands in Mexico, a development concentrated largely in the northern and coastal states and affecting 42.7 percent of the land in Chihuahua and 41.9 percent in Nayarit. North Americans controlled 51.7 percent of all the foreign landholdings in Mexico in that year.[8]

The predominant role of foreign capital had a mixed effect upon the pre-1910 Mexican economy. Certainly it can be argued that development took place, jobs were created, and export earnings increased—and that all these factors were based on foreign investment. Yet the Mexicans did lose control of much of their economy, and as a result they lost much of their capacity to allocate reinvestment. This could be regained, but it would require extensive regulation of foreign business by the national government, since most of the power over allocation of profits was in foreign hands and Mexican business simply was not able to purchase a decisive share in the economy. Such action would produce conflict between the government and the foreign investors. The traditional private enterprise system did not recognize the legitimacy of the kind of extensive state action which would be required fundamentally to alter the status quo in economic relations between nations.

Unregulated foreign investment took back an ample share of the profits of development. Economists may argue whether this was a fair or distorted share. Mexico returned to the investing nations approximately 65 percent of her total export earnings (1910) in the form of profit remittances, service on the foreign debt, freight costs, insurance fees, and other charges. This did not include payment for imports.[9]

The Mexican economy was in a deep rut, and while foreign capital was not the only factor responsible, its predominance helped to deepen and limit the prevailing tendencies. In spite of oversimplified generalizations about underdeveloped countries, the early economic growth of Mexico and the United States cannot be compared. Domestic North American capital always retained sufficient control of the U.S. economy, often with government assistance, to be able to influence much of the allocation of profits, and the profit remittances of foreign investments did not divert very much capital from the domestic economy. Foreign investors made money in North America, but they did not dominate the productive enterprises.[10]

The impact of foreign investment in Mexico was conditioned in part by the physical, cultural, and socioeconomic aspects of the country. An archaic social structure, great concentration of wealth, a social value system which gave great prestige to the *hacendado*, and a limited resource base (especially arable land), all constituted important elements of the internal situation. Within this matrix foreign capital tended to reinforce, rather than solve, some of the basic socioeconomic problems of Mexico. As Frank Brandenburg has written: "The belief that foreign capital per se would become the panacea of Mexico's economic ills was disproven, for as long as the vicious circle of poverty shackled the economy, foreign capital tended to perpetuate the status quo."[11] By 1900 some of the *científicos* began to see certain implications of foreign capital predominance and advocated a policy of limited regulation.

PORFIRIAN NATIONALISM, 1898–1910

The intensification of nationalism, the growing concern over unregulated foreign enterprises, and the mounting agitation for reform in all areas of Mexican life characterized the decade from 1900 to 1910. All of these foreshadowed the developments of the revolutionary era. As the Porfirian epoch produced its most luxuriant by-products, the main feeder roots of revolution were reaching maturity.

Distrust of foreign capital and agitation for its regulation had never completely disappeared. The editor of *El Pacifico* lamented in 1881: "The invasion is pacific, and promises happy results for the American sowing his gold broadcast over the entire republic. Railroad enterprises, the purchase of mines and rural property are the means which are employed to cause the autonomy of Mexico to disappear."[12] This distrust of foreign enterprise increased, and its essence was expressed in the popular slogan that Mexico had become "the mother of foreigners and the stepmother of Mexicans."

The impact of foreign capital stimulated concern in the ranks of the governing elite. The *científicos* and their business and landowning compatriots did not necessarily desire foreign economic domination, and some of them began to consider regulatory measures. Under the leadership of the minister of finance, José Ives Limantour, the government, between 1903 and 1906, purchased controlling interests in the Interoceanic, Mexican National, and the Mexican Central Railways. By decrees in 1906 and 1907 the government combined these into the National Railways of Mexico. In 1908, the final agreement was signed with the seven foreign banking houses representing the other stockholders, and government ownership of the line was proclaimed. But it was ownership with a limitation. The agreement provided for two independent boards of directors—one in New York and one in Mexico City—with the former having the power to foreclose if the company did not meet the payments on its stock issues.[13]

Proponents of more stringent governmental regulation launched a campaign to change the mining laws. They particularly wanted to place all bitumens and petroleum under special national jurisdiction in order to control foreign corporations. Their arguments clearly indicated that the older legal definitions of ownership of the subsoil had not died. Instead they were gaining a renewed vitality as the proponents of strong regulation turned to them as instruments for the assertion of national control over Mexico's resources. This group demonstrated surprising strength in the vote on the mine law of 1910.[14] They lost this battle, but the stage was set for the regulatory measures of the revolutionary period. Foreign control of the Mexican economy had stimulated a new economic nationalism and a rising tide of anti-U.S. sentiment which even Díaz and the most laissez-faire *científicos* could not ignore.

There were further manifestations of these feelings in the post-1900 foreign policy of the Díaz government. The president and most of his advisers did not advocate an overt anti-U.S. position, or even a major break with past policies; they did indicate some desire to modify the role of U.S. influence in Mexico and to assert a greater degree of independent action in foreign policy matters. The growing predominance of North American capital in the Mexican economy and the expansion of U.S. economic and political power in the Caribbean and Central America stimulated these ideas.

In 1906 Díaz informed the German minister that Mexico was thinking about military reorganization and compulsory military training. The president also hinted strongly that German officers and equipment would be welcome. During 1906–7, the German government toyed with this subtle invitation, and several Mexican officials let it be known that the military reforms were aimed at U.S. influence. General Bernardo Reyes was considered the leading advocate of German-Mexican cooperation based upon opposition to the expanding power of the United States and its Monroe Doctrine. Most of the German officials—including the kaiser—had reservations about such a course of action, and after some initial enthusiasm the German government decided that it was unwise to provoke the United States over Mexico. Some Mexican officials also had mixed views of this kind of cooperation. Although nothing came of these overtures, the possibility of a German counterweight to the power of the United States did not completely disappear from the foreign policy calculations of some Mexicans.[15]

After 1903 the Mexican government began to play a more active role in Central American affairs. In part, this was due to the growing activity of the U.S. government in the area. Mexican officials hoped to protect what they considered to be Mexican interests and at the same time exercise some restraining influence on U.S. policy. Mexico and the United States generally cooperated in offering mediation and "good offices" in the settlement of disputes between the various countries. This cooperation vanished in 1909 when the U.S. government went beyond such limited tactics in a country which was friendly to Mexico. The increasingly hostile policy of the United States toward the government of José Santos Zelaya in Nicaragua disturbed the Mexicans, since Zelaya had sided with Mexico in her long-standing rivalry with Guatemala. The Mexicans tried to dissuade the United States from military intervention and offered to obtain the resignation of Zelaya. In this way, Mexican officials hoped that Zelaya's party would remain in power to continue its policy of friendship toward Mexico. U.S. officials did not want cooperation which was not subordinate to their objectives, and some even expressed fear of an independent Mexican influence in Central America. Mexican diplomacy failed as the United States pursued its own goals in Nicaragua, but as a final gesture of independence Mexico sent a warship to bring the deposed Zelaya to Mexico, where he was received by Díaz and other officials.[16]

Mexican officials also began to grant more favors to European businesses. One of the best examples of this was the concession-filled contract negotiated with the British oil company El Aguila in 1906.[17] This company received a number of privileges, including a three-kilometer buffer zone around all of its wells. Most tax obligations were eliminated for the life of the contract, and a fifty-year exemption from the export tax added frosting to the concession cake.

In 1910 Limantour made a special trip to Europe in order to obtain new loans and probably tried to bypass the New York banking firms which had handled most of the government's bond issues since 1899. The railway consolidation effort was partly designed to block plans of a U.S. group, sponsored by E. H. Harriman and H. Clay Pierce, to control and consolidate Mexican railroads. The finance minister also took steps prior to 1911 to acquire the largest meat packing concern in Mexico, a North American company which had a virtual monopoly over the industry. Thus, during this prerevolutionary decade, Mexico took the first halting steps to reduce the North American predominance over the economy of the country by means of government control and encouragement of European investment.

Latent anti-Yankee sentiment existed in several strata of Mexican society, and after 1900 it became particularly noticeable among the mining and railroad workers. Lower levels of the Mexican governmental system seemed to be particularly sensitive to the problem of foreign-owned railroads, and prior to 1906 the State Department protested a rising wave of incidents involving the arrest and imprisonment of North American railroad workers. Anti-Yankee feeling intensified after the *rurales* aided the North Americans in smashing the Cananea strike in 1906. Consular agents reported spreading antiforeign sentiment, and the State Department received many vivid rumors of antiforeign activity among miners and railroad workers. An incident in November 1910 provided a gauge to the kind of anti-Yankee sentiment which had been developing in the more urban and commercial areas. As word spread that a Mexican, Antonio Rodríguez, had been lynched at Rock Springs, Texas, violence flared spontaneously in Mexico City, Guadalajara, and other population centers. The mob in the former city trampled a U.S. flag and stoned the building of the *Mexican Herald*—the recognized voice of the North American investor and resident.

This type of antiforeign, and especially anti-U.S., feeling was more than a historical hangover from the conquest of the 1840s, or the border troubles of the 1870s. It was directed at property holders as well as other groups which were believed to be cooperating with the Mexican elite.

REVOLUTIONARY IDEAS

Between 1900 and 1910, the Díaz regime faced a growing opposition from diverse groups with varying interests and ambitions. For most of the period there was not much unity between the opposition groups in terms of either organization or agreement on desired reforms. Several organizations were formed for the purpose of building a coherent political opposition with national platforms which could unify these diverse groups. One of the more significant reform themes was that of asserting national control over natural resources.

A reform group especially important because of its later ideological influence developed under the leadership of Ricardo Flores Magón and his brothers. Ricardo began fighting against Díaz as a student in 1892, and in 1900 he and several others founded the newspaper *Regeneración*. The paper had a sporadic existence, but it was an articulate source for nationalist and reform ideas. As the Flores Magón brothers moved from a legalistic, anti-Díaz to a revolutionary, anticapitalistic position, the newspaper reflected this increasingly militant and anti-Yankee view.

In September 1905, Ricardo Flores Magón formed the organizing committee of the Mexican Liberal party in Saint Louis, and in July 1906 the committee issued a sweeping reform manifesto which foreshadowed many of the points later included in the constitution of 1917. Among other things, the manifesto demanded that Mexicans be given preference over foreigners in economic matters to establish equality of opportunity and that foreigners who acquired economic rights or concessions be treated as Mexican citizens. The eight-hour day for labor, the restriction of the church, and some type of land redistribution (especially of lands "illegally" acquired under Díaz) were also outlined in various parts of the program.[18]

Andrés Molina Enríquez was also one of the most influential and persuasive articulators of reform ideas. His book *Great National Problems*—published in 1909—contained a detailed analysis of the problems of Mexico and a prophetic discussion of the progression of revolution.[19] Molina Enríquez developed in great detail the concept that reform in Mexico had to be based upon the elaboration of an intensive Mexican nationalism and its enforcement upon all aspects of Mexican life. The economy and politics of Mexico were controlled by foreigners, especially North Americans, and their *criollo* allies in the Mexican upper class; Molina Enríquez believed that this power structure had to be broken in order for any real changes to take place in the living conditions of most of the people. His book constituted a significant step in the articulation of revolutionary nationalism in the underdeveloped world, for Molina Enríquez clearly saw that the economic and cultural presence of the developed nations was an integral part of the status quo and that foreign interests were part of the indigenous power structure. But within this system reform and more equitable distribution of wealth would be difficult, if not impossible, to achieve. Any real attempt to change the old order would produce conflict with foreign interests, since their power would be curtailed through the imposition of national controls. Molina Enríquez believed that revolutionary changes in Mexico would have international repercussions.

He also believed that in order for Mexico to achieve its true national independence it would have to expound a particularly self-conscious nationalism in all areas of its culture, from articles of everyday consumption to the arts. Only in this manner could Mexico resist the powerful influences from abroad and develop the cohesiveness needed for reform and development.

These views would be interesting but beside the point if they were simply the musings of one man. But Molina Enríquez articulated the ideas and feelings of those reform-minded intellectuals and professionals who would help to make the revolution and shape the policies of the government. Some seven years after writing *Great National Problems*, the author participated in the writing of another document—article 27 of the 1917 constitution.

REVOLUTION, 1910

Francisco I. Madero's campaign against the reelection of Porfirio Díaz provided the catalytic agent which drew together most of the opposition in a kind of nebulous unity. A sincere idealist, closely akin to many North American Progressives in his belief that "good government" solved most problems, Madero cut across ideological and group lines with his simple focus on the election issue. Díaz gave his unwitting cooperation by making Madero and the election issue an object of concentrated attack. The beauty of such a simple issue was that men could read into it a variety of reforms—or nothing except the issue of transfer of power within the elite.[20] The slogan "Effective Suffrage, No Re-election" became a temporary rallying cry for a wide variety of reformers, men on the make, and former supporters of Díaz who hoped they could use the movement to maintain their power after the president's demise. The ideas and rhetoric of reform were gaining momentum, and by 1911 all political factions had adopted parts of the paraphernalia of reform; for some, however, the hour was too late and the adoptions too limited.

NOTES

1. *Army and Navy Journal*, 31 May 1873, p. 668.
2. Quoted in P. Harvey Middleton, *Industrial Mexico: 1919 Facts and Figures* (New York: Dodd, Mead, 1919), as epigraph.
3. Marvin Bernstein, *The Mexican Mining Industry, 1890–1950: A Study of the Interaction of Politics, Economics, and Technology* (Albany, N.Y.: State University of New York, 1966), p. 51.
4. Ibid., p. 77.
5. Cleona Lewis, *America's Stake in International Investments* (New York: Brookings Institution, 1938), pp. 220–22; J. Vasquez Schiaffino, "Mexico," *Petroleum Magazine* (August 1919): 103–4.
6. Bernstein, *Mexican Mining Industry*, pp. 18–19.
7. Ibid., pp. 27–28.
8. Frank Tannenbaum, *Mexico: The Struggle for Peace and Bread* (New York: Alfred A. Knopf, 1960), pp. 140–41. See also Frank R. Brandenburg, *The Making of Modern Mexico* (Englewood Cliffs, N.J.: Prentice Hall, 1964), pp. 214–15; G. Butler Sherwell, *Mexico's Capacity to Pay: A General Analysis of the Present International Economic Position of Mexico* (Washington, D.C.: 1929), pp. 7–24; Bernstein, *Mexican Mining Industry*, pp. 72–77; War Department (Office of the Chief of Staff), "American and Foreign Capital Invested in Mexico," 14 March 1914, National Archives, Records of the Department of State, file number 812.503/19; hereafter cited as SD, followed by the file number.
9. Sherwell, *Mexico's Capacity to Pay*, pp. 7–24.
10. For the United States, the percentage of money earned through exports (including specie) that was returned to Europe as profit on investments, freight, and other costs, not including cost of goods imported, reached a peak of 25 percent in 1865. The percentage had been 12.5 in 1854 and 10.5 in 1860. It was 24 percent in 1872, 21 percent in 1874, and 13 percent in 1880. U.S. Department of Commerce, Bureau of the Census, *Historical Statistics of the United States: Colonial Times to 1957* (Washington, D.C.: Government Printing Office, 1960), pp. 562–64.
11. Brandenburg, *Making of Modern Mexico*, p. 214.

12. James M. Callahan, *American Foreign Policy in Mexican Relations* (New York: Macmillan Co., 1932), p. 500. See also Harvey O'Connor, *The Guggenheims: The Making of an American Dynasty* (New York: Couici, Friede, 1937), pp. 328–29; William Franklin Sands and Joseph M. Lalley, *Our Jungle Diplomacy* (Chapel Hill: University of North Carolina Press, 1944), pp. 143–44. Sands, a foreign service officer who served in Mexico during the latter part of the Díaz period, observed that many intellectuals, including some of the *científicos*, were talking about *el peligro yanqui* (the Yankee peril).

13. John H. McNeely, *The Railways of Mexico: A Study in Nationalization*, Southwestern Studies, vol. 2 (El Paso: Texas Western College Press, 1964) 1:16–19. The Mexican Southern Railroad was added in 1909.

14. Bernstein, *Mexican Mining Industry*, pp. 80–82.

15. Warren Schiff, "German Military Penetration into Mexico during the Late Díaz Period," *Hispanic American Historical Review* 39 (November 1959): 568–79.

16. Daniel Cosío Villegas, *La vida política exterior, parte primera*, vol. 5 of *Historia moderna de México: El Porfiriato* (Mexico: Editorial Hermes, 1960), pp. 620–92. Correspondence in the State Department files for December 1910 and the early part of 1911 reported a possible alliance between Guatemala and Mexico (and perhaps involving El Salvador) which would tend to offset U.S. influence not only in Guatemala but also in Honduras and El Salvador, SD 712.14/70.

17. Copy of this concession enclosed in Harold Walker (Huasteca Petroleum Co.) to Ira Patchin (J. P. Morgan & Co.), 4 April 1923, Thomas W. Lamont Manuscripts, Baker Library, Harvard Graduate School of Business Administration.

18. Manuel González Ramírez, *Planes políticos y otros documentos*, vol. 1 of *Fuentes para la historia de la Revolución Mexicana* (Mexico: Fondo de Cultura Económica, 1954), pp. 3–29. Antonio Díaz Soto y Gama collaborated in the writing and later became the leading adviser to Emiliano Zapata.

19. Andrés Molina Enríquez, *Los grandes problemas nacionales* (Mexico: A. Carranza, 1909), pp. 312–13, 338–40, 345–46, 356–60.

20. Francisco I. Madero, *La sucesión presidencial en 1910*, 3d ed. (Mexico: La Viuda de C. Bouret, 1911); see especially the conclusion.

THE DÍAZ SYSTEM

John Kenneth Turner

John Kenneth Turner (1879–1948) was a "muckraking" socialist journalist and writer who traveled and lived in Mexico during the last years of the Díaz era. In 1908 Turner, posing as a wealthy American businessman who wanted to invest in henequen and tobacco, was able to see the conditions of forced labor on the haciendas and plantations of Mexico. This experience enabled Turner to write an exposé of the Díaz government, in the form of a series of articles that appeared in American Magazine. *These writings later were published as a book entitled* Barbarous Mexico, *from which the following selection was taken.*

In this essay, Turner alleges that slavery and peonage were reestablished by Díaz as a necessary part of a political machine which was designed to exploit labor and protect capital. According to Turner, an obvious critic of the regime, Díaz's land policies encouraged the confiscation and denouncement of the lands of the native peoples and reduced to slavery the Indians of Yucatán and Sonora. Barbarous Mexico, *which has been compared to* Uncle Tom's Cabin, *circulated throughout the United States and undoubtedly shaped the attitudes of many North Americans concerning the wretchedness of the Díaz regime.*

When the Revolution began, Turner helped to purchase weapons that were smuggled into Baja California for the conquest of Mexicali. Later he wrote articles on Pancho Villa (in which he opposed the Pershing expedition), the American intervention at Veracruz, and a book entitled Hands Off Mexico, *a critical and polemical study of foreign and American interference in Mexican affairs. His wife, Ethel Duffy Turner, is also well known as an author and a student of Mexican affairs.*

THE SLAVERY AND PEONAGE of Mexico, the poverty and illiteracy, the general prostration of the people, are due, in my humble judgment, to the financial and political organization that at present rules that country—in a word, to what I shall call the "system" of General Porfirio Díaz.

That these conditions can be traced in a measure to the history of Mexico during past generations, is true. I do not wish to be unfair to General Díaz in the least degree. The Spanish Dons made slaves and peons of the Mexican people. Yet never did they grind the people as they are ground today. In Spanish times the peon at least had his own little patch of ground, his own humble shelter; today he has nothing. Moreover, the Declaration of Independence, proclaimed just one hundred years ago, in 1810, proclaimed also the abolition of chattel slavery. Slavery was abolished, though not entirely. Succeeding Mexican governments of class and of church and of the individual held the people in bondage little less severe. But finally came a democratic movement which broke the back of the church, which overthrew the rule of caste, which adopted a form of government as modern as our own, which freed the slave in fact as well as in name, which gave the lands of the people back to the people, which wiped the slate clean of the blood of the past.

It was at this juncture that General Porfirio Díaz, without any valid excuse and apparently for no other reason than personal ambition, stirred up a series of revolutions which finally ended in his capture of the governmental powers of the land. While professing to respect the progressive institutions which Juarez and Lerdo had established before him, he built up a system all his own, a system in which he personally was the central and all-controlling figure, in which his individual caprice was the constitution and the law, in which all circumstances and all men, big and little, were bent or broken at his will. Like Louis XIV, The State—Porfirio Díaz was The State!

It was under Porfirio Díaz that slavery and peonage were reestablished in Mexico, and on a more merciless basis than they had existed even under the Spanish Dons. Therefore, I can see no injustice in charging at least a preponderance of the blame for these conditions upon the system of Díaz.

I say the "system of Díaz" rather than Díaz personally because, though he is the keystone of the arch, though he is the government of Mexico more completely than is any other individual the government of any large country on the planet, yet no one man can stand alone in his iniquity. Díaz is the central prop of the slavery, but there are other props without which the system could not continue upright for a single day. For example, there is the collection of commercial interests which profits by the Díaz system of slavery and autocracy, and which

puts no insignificant part of its tremendous powers to holding the
central prop upright in exchange for the special privileges that it
receives. Not the least among these commercial interests are American, which, I blush to say, are quite as aggressive defenders of the
Díaz citadel as any. Indeed, as I shall show in future chapters, these
American interests undoubtedly form the determining force in the
continuation of Mexican slavery. Thus does Mexican slavery come
home to us in the full sense of the term. For the horrors of Yucatan and
Valle Nacional, Díaz is to blame, but so are we; we are to blame insofar
as governmental powers over which we are conceded to have some
control are employed under our very eyes for the perpetuation of a
regime of which slavery and peonage are an integral part.

In order that the reader may understand the Díaz system and its
responsibility in the degradation of the Mexican people, it will be well
to go back and trace briefly the beginnings of that system. Mexico is
spoken of throughout the world as a Republic. That is because it was
once a Republic and still pretends to be one. Mexico has a constitution
which has never been repealed, a constitution said to be modeled after
our own, and one which is, indeed, like ours in the main. Like ours, it
provides for a national congress, state legislatures and municipal
aldermen to make the laws, federal, state and local judges to interpret
them, and a president, governors and local executives to administer
them. Like ours, it provides for manhood suffrage, freedom of the
press and of speech, equality before the law, and the other guarantees
of life, liberty and the pursuit of happiness which we ourselves enjoy,
in a degree, as a matter of course.

Such was Mexico forty years ago. Forty years ago Mexico was at
peace with the world. She had just overthrown, after a heroic war, the
foreign prince, Maximilian, who had been seated as emperor by the
armies of Napoleon Third of France. Her president, Benito Juarez, is
today recognized in Mexico and out of Mexico as one of the most able
as well as unselfish patriots of Mexican history. Never since Cortez
fired his ships there on the gulf coast had Mexico enjoyed such prospects of political freedom, industrial prosperity and general advancement.

But in spite of these facts and the additional fact that he was
deeply indebted to Juarez, all his military promotions having been
received at the hands of the latter, General Porfirio Díaz stirred up a
series of rebellions for the purpose of securing for himself the supreme
power of the land. Díaz not only led one armed rebellion against a

peaceable, constitutional and popularly approved government, but he led three of them. For nine years he plotted as a common rebel. The support that he received came chiefly from bandits, criminals and professional soldiers who were disgruntled at the anti-militarist policy which Juarez had inaugurated and which, if he could have carried it out a little farther, would have been effective in preventing military revolutions in the future—and from the Catholic church.

Repeatedly it was proved that the people did not want Díaz at the head of their government. Three times during his first five years of plotting he was an unsuccessful candidate at the polls. In 1867 he received a little more than one-third the votes counted for Juarez. In 1871 he received about three-fifths as many votes as Juarez. In 1872, after the death of Juarez, he ran against Lerdo de Tejada and received only one-fifteenth as many votes as his opponent. While in arms he was looked upon as a common rebel at home and abroad and when he marched into the national capital at the head of a victorious army and proclaimed himself president hardly a European nation would at first recognize the upstart government, while the United States for a time threatened complications.

In defiance of the will of the majority of the people of Mexico, General Díaz, thirty-four years ago, came to the head of government. In defiance of the will of the majority of the people he has remained there ever since—except for four years, from 1880 to 1884, when he turned the palace over to an intimate friend, Manuel Gonzalez, on the distinct understanding that at the end of the four years Gonzalez would turn it back to him again.

Since no man can rule an unwilling people without taking away the liberties of that people, it can be very easily understood what sort of regime General Díaz found it necessary to establish in order to make his power secure. By the use of the army and the police powers generally, he controlled elections, the press and public speech and made of popular government a farce. By distributing the public offices among his generals and granting them free rein to plunder at will, he assured himself of the continued use of the army. By making political combinations with men high in the esteem of the Catholic church and permitting it to be whispered about that the church was to regain some of its former powers, he gained the silent support of the priests and the Pope. By promising full payment of all foreign debts and launching at once upon a policy of distributing favors among citizens of other countries, he made his peace with the world at large.

In other words, General Díaz, with a skill that none can deny, annexed to himself all the elements of power in the country except the nation at large. On the one hand, he had a military dictatorship. On the other, he had a financial camarilla. Himself was the center of the arch and he was compelled to pay the price. The price was the nation at large. He created a machine and oiled the machine with the flesh and blood of a people. He rewarded all except the people; the people were the sacrifice. Inevitable as the blackness of night, in contrast to the sun-glory of the dictator, came the degradation of the people—the slavery, the peonage and every misery that walks with poverty, the abolition of democracy and the personal security that breeds providence, self-respect and worthy ambition; in a word, general demoralization, depravity.

Take, for example, Díaz's method of rewarding his military chiefs, the men who helped him overthrow the government of Lerdo. As quickly as possible after assuming the power, he installed his generals as governors of the various states and organized them and other influential figures in the nation into a national plunderbund. Thus he assured himself of the continued loyalty of the generals, on the one hand, and put them where he could most effectively use them for keeping down the people, on the other. One variety of rich plum which he handed out in those early days to his governors came in the form of charters giving his governors the right, as individuals, to organize companies and build railroads, each charter carrying with it a huge sum as a railroad subsidy.

The national government paid for the road and then the governor and his most influential friends owned it. Usually the railroads were ridiculous affairs, were of narrow-gauge and of the very cheapest materials, but the subsidy was very large, sufficient to build the road and probably equip it besides. During his first term of four years in office Díaz passed sixty-one railroad subsidy acts containing appropriations aggregating $40,000,000, and all but two or three of these acts were in favor of governors of states. In a number of cases not a mile of railroad was actually built, but the subsidies are supposed to have been paid, anyhow. In nearly every case the subsidy was the same $12,880 per mile in Mexican silver, and in those days Mexican silver was nearly on a par with gold.

This huge sum was taken out of the national treasury and was supposedly paid to the governors, although Mexican politicians of the old times have assured me that it was divided, a part going out as actual subsidies and a part going directly into the hands of Díaz to be used in building up his machine in other quarters.

Certainly something more than mere loyalty, however invaluable it was, was required of the governors in exchange for such rich financial plums. It is a well authenticated fact that governors were required to pay a fixed sum annually for the privilege of exploiting to the limit the graft possibilities of their offices. For a long time Manuel Romero Rubio, father-in-law of Díaz, was the collector of these perquisites, the offices bringing in anywhere from $10,000 to $50,000 per year.

The largest single perquisite whereby Díaz enriched himself, the members of his immediate family, his friends, his governors, his financial ring and his foreign favorites, was found for a long time in the confiscation of the lands of the common people—a confiscation, in fact, which is going on to this day. Note that this land robbery was the first direct step in the path of the Mexican people back to their bondage as slaves and peons.

In a previous chapter I showed how the lands of the Yaquis of Sonora were taken from them and given to political favorites of the ruler. The lands of the Mayas of Yucatan, now enslaved by the *henequen* planters, were taken from them in almost the same manner. The final act in this confiscation was accomplished in the year 1904, when the national government set aside the last of their lands into a territory called Quintana Roo. This territory contains 43,000 square kilometers or 27,000 square miles. It is larger than the present state of Yucatan by 8,000 square kilometers, and moreover is the most promising land of the entire peninsula. Separated from the island of Cuba by a narrow strait, its soil and climate are strikingly similar to those of Cuba and experts have declared that there is no reason why Quintana Roo should not one day become as great a tobacco-growing country as Cuba. Further than that, its hillsides are thickly covered with the most valuable cabinet and dyewoods in the world. It is this magnificent country which, as the last chapter in the life of the Mayas as a nation, the Díaz government took and handed over to eight Mexican politicians.

In like manner have the Mayos of Sonora, the Papagos, the Tomosachics—in fact, practically all the native peoples of Mexico—been reduced to peonage, if not to slavery. Small holders of every tribe and nation have gradually been expropriated until today their number as property holders is almost down to zero. Their lands are in the hands of members of the governmental machine, or persons to whom the members of the machine have sold for profit—or in the hands of foreigners.

This is why the typical Mexican farm is the million-acre farm, why it has been so easy for such Americans as William Randolph Hearst, Harrison Gray Otis, E. H. Harriman, the Rockefellers, the Guggenheims and numerous others each to have obtained possession of millions of Mexican acres. This is why Secretary of Fomento Molina holds more than 15,000,000 acres of the soil of Mexico, why ex-Governor Terrazas, of Chihuahua, owns 15,000,000 acres of the soil of that state, why Finance Minister Limantour, Mrs. Porfirio Díaz, Vice-President Corral, Governor Pimentel, of Chiaspas, Governor Landa y Escandon of the Federal District, Governor Pablo Escandon of Morelos, Governor Ahumada of Jalisco, Governor Cosio of Queretaro, Governor Mercado of Michoacan, Governor Canedo of Sinaloa, Governor Cahuantzi of Tlaxcala, and many other members of the Díaz machine are not only millionaires, but they are millionaires in Mexican real estate.

Chief among the methods used in getting the lands away from the people in general was through a land registration law which Díaz fathered. This law permitted any person to go out and claim any lands to which the possessor could not prove a recorded title. Since up to the time the law was enacted it was not the custom to record titles, this meant all the lands in Mexico. When a man possessed a home which his father had possessed before him, and which his grandfather had possessed, which his great-grandfather had possessed, and which had been in the family as far back as history knew, then he considered that he owned that home, all of his neighbors considered that he owned it, and all governments up to that of Díaz recognized his right to that home.

Supposing that a strict registration law became necessary in the course of evolution, had this law been enacted for the purpose of protecting the land owners instead of plundering them the government would, naturally, have sent agents through the country to appraise the people of the new law and to help them register their property and keep their homes. But this was not done and the conclusion is inevitable that the law was passed for the purpose of plundering.

At all events, the result of the law was a plundering. No sooner had it been passed than the aforesaid members of the government machine, headed by the father-in-law of Díaz, and Díaz himself, formed land companies and sent out agents, not to help the people keep their lands, but to select the most desirable lands in the country, register them, and evict the owners. This they did on a most tremendous scale. Thus hundreds of thousands of small farmers lost their property. Thus small farmers are still losing their property. In order to cite an example, I reprint a dispatch dated Merida, Yucatan, April 11, 1909, and published April 12 in the Mexican Herald, an American daily newspaper printed in Mexico City:

> Merida, April 11.—Minister Olegario Molina, of the Department of Fomento, Colonization and Industry, has made a denouncement before the agency here of extensive territory lying adjacent to his lands in Tizimin *partido*. The denouncement was made through Esteban Rejon Garcia, his *administrador* at that place.
>
> The section was taken on the ground that those now occupying them have no documents or titles of ownership.
>
> They measure 2,700 hectares (about 6,000 acres, or over nine square miles), and *include perfectly organized towns*, some fine ranches, including those of Laureano Breseno and Rafael Aguilar, and other properties. The *jefe politico* of Tizimin has notified the population of the town, the owners and laborers on the ranches, and others on the lands, that they will be obliged to vacate within two months *or become subject to the new owner*.
>
> The present occupants have lived for years upon the land and have cultivated and improved much of it. Some have lived there from generation to generation, and have thought themselves the rightful owners, having inherited it from the original 'squatters.'
>
> *Mr. Rejon Garcia has also denounced other similar public lands in the Espita partido.*

Another favorite means of confiscating the homes of small owners is found in the juggling of state taxes. State taxes in Mexico are fearfully and wonderfully made. Especially in the less populous districts owners are taxed inversely as they stand in favor with the personality who represents the government in their particular district. No court, board or other responsible body sits to review unjust assessments. The *jefe politico* may charge one farmer five times as much per acre as he charges the farmer across the fence, and yet Farmer No. 1 has no redress unless he is rich and powerful. He must pay, and if he cannot, the farm is a little later listed among the properties of the *jefe politico*, or one of the members of his family, or among the properties of the governor of the state or one of the members of his family. But if he is rich and powerful he is often not taxed at all. American promoters in Mexico escape taxation so nearly invariably that the impression has got abroad in this country that land pays no taxes in Mexico. Even Frederick Palmer made a statement to this effect in his recent writings about that country.

Of course such bandit methods as were employed and are still employed were certain to meet with resistance, and so we find numerous instances of regiments of soldiers being called out to enforce collection of taxes or the eviction of time-honored land-holders. Mexican history of the past generation is blotched with stories of massacres having their cause in this thing. Among the most noted of these massacres are those of Papantla and Tomosachic. Manuel Romero Rubio, the late father-in-law of General Díaz, denounced the lands of several thousand farmers in the vicinity of Papantla, Veracruz. Díaz backed him up with several regiments of regulars and before the farmers were all evicted four hundred, or some such number, were killed. In the year 1892, General Lauro Carrillo, who was then governor of Chihuahua, laid a tax on the town of Tomosachic, center of the Tomosachic settlement, which it was impossible for the people to pay. The immediate cause of the exorbitant tax, so the story goes, was that the authorities of the town had refused Carrillo some paintings which adorned the walls of their church and which he desired for his own home. Carrillo carried away some leading men of the town as hostages, and when the people still refused to pay, he sent soldiers for more hostages. The soldiers were driven away, after which Carrillo laid siege to the town with eight regiments. In the end the town was burned and a churchful of women and children were burned, too. Accounts of the Tomosachic massacre place the number of killed variously at from 800 to 2,000.

Cases of more recent blood spillings in the same cause are numerous. Hardly a month passes today without there being one or more reports in Mexican papers of disturbances, the result of confiscation of homes, either through the denunciation method or the excuse of nonpayment of taxes. Notable among these was the case of San Andreas, State of Chihuahua, which was exploited in the Mexican press in April, 1909. According to those press reports, the state authorities confiscated lands of several score of farmers, the excuse being that the owners were delinquent in their taxes. The farmers resisted eviction in a body and two carloads of troops, hurried to the scene from the capital of the state, promptly cleaned them out, shooting some and chasing half a hundred of them into the mountains. Here they stayed until starved out, when they straggled back, begging for mercy. As they came they were thrown into jail, men, women and children. The government carefully concealed the truth as to the number killed in the skirmish with the troops, but reports place it at from five to twenty-five.

An incident of the same class was that of San Carlos, also in the State of Chihuahua, which occurred in August, 1909. At San Carlos, center of a farming district, the misuse of the taxing power became so unbearable that four hundred small farmers banded together, defied a force of fifty *rurales*, forcibly deposed the *jefe politico*, and elected another in his place, then went back to their plows. It was a little revolution which the newspaper reports of the time declared was the first of its kind to which the present government of Mexico ever yielded. Whether the popularly constituted local government was permitted to remain or whether it was later overthrown by a regiment of soldiers is not recorded, though the latter seems most likely.

Graft is an established institution in the public offices of Mexico. It is a right vested in the office itself, is recognized as such, and is respectable. There are two main functions attached to each public office, one a privilege, the other a duty. The privilege is that of using the special powers of the office for the amassing of a personal fortune; the duty is that of preventing the people from entering into any activities that may endanger the stability of the existing regime. Theoretically, the fulfillment of the duty is judged as balancing the harvest of the privilege, but with all offices and all places this is not so, and so we find offices of particularly rosy possibilities selling for a fixed price. Examples are those of the *jefes politicos* in districts where the slave trade is peculiarly remunerative, as at Pachuca, Oaxaca, Veracruz, Orizaba, Cordoba and Rio Blanco; of the districts in which the drafting of soldiers for the army is especially let to the *jefes politicos;* of the towns in which the gambling privileges are let as a monopoly to the mayors thereof; of the states in which there exist opportunities extraordinary for governors to graft off the army supply contracts.

Monopolies called "concessions," which are nothing more nor less than trusts created by governmental decree, are dealt in openly by the Mexican government. Some of these concessions are sold for cash, but the rule is to give them away gratis or for a nominal price, the real price being collected in political support. The public domain is sold in huge tracts for a nominal price or for nothing at all, the money price, when paid at all, averaging about fifty Mexican *centavos* an acre. But never does the government sell to any individual or company not of its own special choice; that is, the public domain is by no means open to all comers on equal terms. Public concessions worth millions of dollars—to use the water of a river for irrigation purposes, or for power, to engage in this or that monopoly, have been given away, but not indiscriminately. These things are the coin with which political support is bought and as such are grafts, pure and simple.

Public action of any sort is never taken for the sake of improving the condition of the common people. It is taken with a view to making the government more secure in its position. Mexico is a land of special privileges extraordinary, though frequently special privileges are provided for in the name of the common people. An instance is that of the "Agricultural Bank," which was created in 1908. To read the press reports concerning the purpose of this bank one would imagine that the government had launched into a gigantic and benevolent scheme to re-establish its expropriated people in agriculture. The purpose, it was said, was to loan money to needy farmers. But nothing could be farther from the truth, for the purpose is to help out the rich farmer, and only the richest in the land. The bank has now been loaning money for two years, but so far not a single case has been recorded in which aid was given to help a farm that comprised less than thousands of acres. Millions have been loaned on private irrigation projects, but never in lumps of less than several tens of thousands. In the United States the farmer class is an humble class indeed; in Mexico the typical farmer is the king of millionaires, a little potentate. In Mexico, because of the special privileges given by the government, medievalism still prevails outside the cities. The barons are richer and more powerful than were the landed aristocrats before the French Revolution, and the canaille poorer, more miserable.

And the special financial privileges centering in the cities are no less remarkable than the special privileges given to the exploiters of the *hacienda* slave. There is a financial ring consisting of members of the Díaz machine and their close associates, who pluck all the financial plums of the "republic," who get the contracts, the franchises and the concessions, and whom the large aggregations of foreign capital which secure a footing in the country find it necessary to take as coupon-clipping partners. The "Banco Nacional," an institution having some fifty-four branches and which has been compared flatteringly to the Bank of England, is the special financial vehicle of the government camarilla. It monopolizes the major portion of the banking business of the country and is a convenient cloak for the larger grafts, such as the railway merger, the true significance of which I shall present in a future chapter.

Díaz encourages foreign capital, for foreign capital means the support of foreign governments. American capital has a smoother time with Díaz than it has even with its own government, which is very fine from the point of view of American capital, but not so good from the point of view of the Mexican people. Díaz has even entered into direct partnership with certain aggregations of foreign capital, granting these aggregations special privileges in some lines which he has refused to his own millionaires. These foreign partnerships which Díaz has formed have made his government international insofar as the props which support his system are concerned. The certainty of foreign intervention in his favor has been one of the powerful forces which have prevented the Mexican people from using arms to remove a ruler who imposed himself upon them by the use of arms.

When I come to deal with the American partners of Díaz I mention those of no other nationality in the same breath, but it will be well to bear in mind that England, especially, is nearly as heavily as interested in Mexico as is the United States. While this country has $900,000,000 (these are the figures given by Consul General Shanklin about the first of the year 1910) invested in Mexico, England (according to the South American Journal) has $750,000,000. However, these figures by no means represent the ratio between the degree of political influence exerted by the two countries. There the United States bests all the other countries combined.

Yet there are two English corporations so closely identified with the Mexican financial ring as to deserve special mention. They are the combination represented by Dr. F. S. Pearson, of Canada and London, and the other corporation distinct from the first, S. Pearson & Son, Limited. Of Dr. F. S. Pearson it is boasted that he can get any concession that he wants in Mexico, barring alone such a one as would antagonize other foreign interests equally powerful. Dr. Pearson owns the electric railway system of the Federal District and furnishes the vast quantity of electric light and power used in that political division of Mexico. Among other things, he is also a strong power along the American border, where he and his associates own the Mexico Northwestern Railway and several smaller lines, as well as vast tracts of lands and huge lumber interests. In Chihuahua he is establishing a large steel plant and in El Paso, just across the line, he is building a half-million-dollar sawmill as a part of his Mexican projects.

S. Pearson & Son have been given so many valuable concessions in Mexico that they were responsible for the invention of the term, "the partners of Díaz." Through concessions given them by the government they are in possession of vast oil lands, most of which are unexploited, yet so many of which are producing that the company recently gave out a statement that it would hereafter be in a position to supply its entire trade with Mexican oil. Its distributing company, "El Aguila," contains on its directorate a number of Díaz's closest friends. Pearson & Son, also, have monopolized the contracts for deepening and improving the harbors of Mexico. Since their advent into the country some fourteen years ago the government treasury has paid to this concern $200,000,000 for work on the harbors of Salina Cruz and Coatzacoalcos, and the Isthmus railroad. This amount, a government engineer told me personally, is an even double the price that should have been paid for the work. In 1908 Díaz's congress appropriated $50,000,000 to install an extensive irrigation project on the Rio Nasus, for the benefit of the cotton barons of the Laguna district in the State of Durango. Immediately afterwards the Pearson company organized a subsidiary irrigation concern with a capital of one million. The new company drew up plans for a dam, whereupon the Díaz congress promptly voted $10,000,000 out of the $50,000,000 to be paid to the Pearsons for their dam.

In this chapter I have attempted to give the reader an idea of the means which General Díaz employed to attract support to his government. To sum up, by means of a careful placing of public offices, public contracts and special privileges of multitudinous sorts, Díaz absorbed all of the more powerful men and interests within his sphere and made them a part of his machine. Gradually the country passed into the hands of his officeholders, their friends, and foreigners. And for this the people paid, not only with their lands, but with their flesh and blood. They paid in peonage and slavery. For this they forfeited liberty, democracy and the blessings of progress. And because human beings do not forfeit these things without a struggle, there was necessarily another function of the Díaz machine than that of distributing gifts, another material that went into the structure of his government than favors. Privilege–repression; they go hand in hand.

CHIHUAHUA IN THE DÍAZ ERA

William H. Beezley

William H. Beezley teaches Mexican history at North Carolina State University. He has written several articles on the Mexican Revolution, caudillismo, and U.S. consular activities in nineteenth-century Latin America. This selection, an excellent example of regional history, was taken from his Insurgent Governor: Abraham González and the Mexican Revolution in Chihuahua. *It is Beezley's contention that regional aristocrats represented the Porfiriato as surely as the dictator. In this study, he describes the various family factions in Chihuahua City and Guerrero City and shows how they struggled for political and economic power. Beezley pays especial attention to Luis Terrazas and his son-in-law, Enrique C. Creel. It is of particular interest to see how a kind of power triad developed between Díaz, foreign investors, and the Terrazas family. The reader should also note how developments in the national economy affected regional politics and economics. Finally, a study of the Terrazas provides the reader with a representative example of the role of extended family units in Latin America.*

FOR THIRTY-FIVE YEARS, from 1876 to 1911, Porfirio Díaz dominated the social, economic, and political life of Mexico. Ruthless in rooting out his opponents, he alternately bribed and prodded, alternately offering prominent Mexicans political and economic opportunities and threatening imprisonment, even death. Political challengers, rural bandits, churchmen, all received the choice of preferment or persecution. With *pan o palo*, the carrot or the stick, Díaz secured his dictatorial regime and simultaneously established peace and order as prerequisites for progress. Many Mexicans, grateful for an end to the half century of turmoil that had followed independence from Spain, eagerly traded political and civil rights for a stable society that could

Reprinted from William H. Beezley, *Insurgent Governor: Abraham González and the Mexican Revolution in Chihuahua* (Lincoln: University of Nebraska Press, 1973), pp. 1–12.

lure investment and technology from industrial nations. As Díaz's reign wore on, this general from Oaxaca ensured his authority by increased control of elections and appointments. All political power emanated from the Presidential Palace overlooking the Zócalo: his cronies gathered in the halls of Congress to provide conventional forms for legislation he had already approved; state governors held office at his will, and their success in maintaining order determined their reelection; even local officials felt his heavy hand in the appointment of prefects, the *jefes politicos*, to displace locally elected administrators. Business and society both worked within the boundaries marked by Díaz. Franchises, tax exemptions, corporate organization, and bank credit, without which a business failed, required governmental sanction. Foreigners received favored treatment as Díaz promoted development with external capital and enterprise. Only in arranging a second marriage did he seem typically Mexican as he bore witness to the adage *A gato viejo, ratón tierno* (For the old tomcat, a tender mouse). Even then his nuptial contract with Carmen Romero Rubio, several decades his junior, served the practical purpose of allying him with an old, established family; and the new Señora Díaz assisted in arranging a reconciliation between Díaz and the Catholic Church and in gathering support for him from the Mexico City aristocracy.

Members of the Mexican gentry who stood in the dictator's shadow succeeded in business and politics. His favor brought concessions and property which regional leaders parlayed into land and commercial empires that only the foolish dared challenge. Men such as Ramón Corral in Sonora and Luis Terrazas in Chihuahua dominated local society and state politics while sharing economic benefits with North American and European developers. These regional aristocrats represented the Porfiriato as surely as the dictator. Thus, the porfirian government created a closed society, allowing only those who remained within Díaz's limits to compete for profits and positions. Nowhere were the privileges extended to favorites and the rivalry among the gentry for political and business preference more clearly evident than in the state of Chihuahua.

I

Located on the northern border, Chihuahua before the completion of the railroad in 1884 was free to some extent from national interference because of its isolation. Its desert wastes and rugged mountains discouraged settlement, as did sporadic raids by Apaches from the southwestern United States. The opportunities for mining and ranching attracted only a sparse population. The scattered residents, numbering 180,758 in 1877, adopted provincial, or *patria chica*, attitudes in the administrative and commercial centers of Chihuahua City, Guerrero City, and similar towns.[1] Political groups represented little more than cliques of self-seeking patricians—merchants, mine owners, and military officers—whose position as landowners provided both time and ambition to direct state affairs and to set social conventions. Family ties and local residence formed the basis for enduring loyalties; political parties were temporary factions lacking common ideals and long-range programs. In Chihuahua City, for example, Luis Terrazas, a wealthy, experienced politician, led one faction, while the Trías family, an old political power, formed the center of another. The extended Casavantes and González families forged a powerful group in Guerrero City, a service and shipping center for the rich mineral district in the Sierra Madre. Other state aristocrats headed similar loose alliances.[2]

Since most of the factions managed to hold at least one of the fifteen seats in the state legislature and to dominate their district governments, the political prize was the governorship. Although campaign rhetoric appealed to national issues, elections merely provided opportunities to advance local rivalries. In the gubernatorial election of 1873, for example, the candidates offered indistinguishable programs in support of national policies; the slate presented no choice except among the personalities of members of the state's oligarchy.[3]

The revolt and victory of Porfirio Díaz in 1876 brought political opportunity to the dissenting gentry in Chihuahua. Angel Trías, Jr., joined the Díaz rebellion in order to challenge Governor Luis Terrazas. With official support from Mexico City, he won the gubernatorial election of 1876, but he could neither destroy Terrazas's political influence nor impair his economic activities. Díaz's usurpation of national authority forced a new alignment of the state's upper class as the *terracistas* allied with their usual antagonists from Guerrero City to win about half of the seats in the legislature. Despite the national backing for Trías, the rival deputies attacked his program in the assembly chamber and in the newspapers. At the same time, they remained within the limits established by the dictator and seized every opportunity to obtain the concessions he offered. All the gentry

benefited from the development programs of the porfirian government. Rivals in the legislature shared concessions for tax-exempt
companies and divided vast tracts of land. The major land companies
were the Ignacio Gómez del Campo Company of Luis Terrazas and his
relatives and associates and the Jesús E. Valenzuela Company formed
by prominent politicians from Guerrero City.[4]

Among the gentry, Terrazas was the most adroit at seizing both
political and economic advantages. A middle-class native of
Chihuahua, he had escaped from his small butchering business and
minor civil service posts through the Wars of the Reform and the
French Intervention. He had served Benito Juárez and been rewarded
with military command. His part in minor but well-publicized military actions gave him widespread popularity that led to his election as
governor in 1860. From that time his power in the state increased, but
the vicissitudes of national politics—Maximilian's Empire, Juárez's
Restoration, revolts against Juárez, and the seizure of power by
Díaz—complicated Terrazas's efforts to establish political domination
of Chihuahua.

During the porfirian years Terrazas was the prototype of the
entrepreneur who prompted the extraordinary growth of the Mexican
economy. His main wealth was in land, which in the arid North was
used primarily for cattle raising. His latifundio stretched over some
two and a half million hectares (one hectare = 2.47 acres), or about
one-tenth of the surface area of Mexico's largest state. Terrazas stocked
his haciendas with cattle and his herds grew to huge numbers. He
shipped thousands of cattle to the United States through the El Paso
port of entry, and according to popular stories he was willing to supply
any number of cattle in matching colors to American importers. In
Chihuahua City, he held a virtual monopoly over the supply, butchering, and distribution of beef.[5]

But in Chihuahua state, Terrazas could dominate neither politics
nor the economy in the first decades after the porfirian takeover. Other
families contested his every move. When the legislature increased the
number of banking houses with the privilege of issuing currency, for
example, the Terrazas clan obtained only two of the six new franchises, while the Guerrero faction received one and other groups in the
state got the remaining three. The factional rivalry became more
intense in the mid-1880s as the old restraints on the state's
economy—Chihuahua's isolation and susceptibility to Indian
raids—were removed. The combined campaigns of the state militia

and the United States Army broke the power of the Apaches and soon the telegraph linked Chihuahua with the rest of the nation. But the most significant event was the completion in 1884 of the Mexican Central Railroad running from El Paso, Texas, to Mexico City.[6]

The railroad connected Chihuahua with the southwestern United States and North Americans began to treat the Mexican borderland as an extension of their own territory. In the 1880s a small but growing number of foreigners drifted into the state to exploit its minerals, grazing land, and timber and to secure railroad concessions. El Paso merchants tried their luck in Chihuahua City. Typical was the Krakauer, Zork and Moye Hardware Company, which opened a general merchandise store in 1887 but soon expanded into banking, railroads, and mining. These entrepreneurs presaged a rush of foreign speculators at the end of the century.[7]

The telegraph, the railroad, and the elimination of the Indian threat made Chihuahua a frontier of unusual appeal which the federal government accentuated by promulgating new surveying and mining laws to facilitate the exploitation of land and minerals. By the end of the 1880s land companies had obtained over four million hectares for the competing Terrazas and Guerrero factions. Both sides sponsored corporations ranging from telephone to trolley companies, dealing in goods from textiles to cigarettes, and obtained exemptions from state and local taxes as well as a monopoly of the market for periods of up to twenty years.[8]

The Guerrero party dominated state politics until 1892, but the Terrazas family, often in association with foreign investors, consolidated profitable agricultural and commercial enterprises. With increasing financial strength, the *terracistas* became restive under the Guerrero-dominated political administration. After unsuccessful local revolts in 1887 and 1889, they launched a determined effort to win the gubernatorial election of 1892. An incident in one of the mountain settlements provided them with an issue. Opposition to local officials had crystallized around an old couple in Tomochic who possessed a holy image reputed to have miraculous powers. The townspeople challenged the district prefect with intense religious fervor. For over a year, they resisted the authorities and ignored assurances of an investigation of their grievances by the *jefe político*. Just before the elections they defeated a detachment of troops sent to suppress their rebellion.

In its publication, *El Norte*, the Terrazas party attacked the state government. The ensuing newspaper war received a gruesome touch after an article in *El Norte* charged that the editor of the administration's newspaper, *El Diario de Chihuahua*, had offered to defect to the Terrazas side. Luis Díaz Couder, *El Diario's* editor, printed a challenge to the author. Although the editor of *El Norte* attempted to protect his anonymous contributor, Díaz Couder shot to death his opponent, Pablo Ochoa.[9] Reports of the duel and the mismanagement of the Tomochic rebellion soon reached Mexico City. Because the incumbent regime had failed to maintain peace and order, Díaz intervened in Chihuahua. He removed the governor and refused to consider a local candidate, least of all Luis Terrazas, for office, deciding instead to appoint a regent who could control the state's intraclass struggle.

Under the watchful eye of the new governor, Miguel Ahumada of Jalisco, who ruled from 1892 to 1903, the legislature turned its attention almost exclusively to the distribution of economic favors. In eleven years the Ahumada government issued more than twice the number of concessions granted from 1876 to 1892. Since Díaz had made it evident that he would not accept Terrazas in a major political office, the old patriarch concentrated all his efforts on multiplying his financial and agricultural empire.[10] The Terrazas latifundium grew to be the largest in Mexico. Cattle exporting and local marketing through his own slaughter houses provided Terrazas with capital for investment in other commercial and manufacturing projects. He obtained concessions for such varied enterprises as a sugar beet refinery, a meat-packing plant, and a candle factory, while his relatives invested in beer production and streetcar lines, among other businesses. The clan also acquired a virtual monopoly of the state's finance and banking by merging rival banks, managing branches of national institutions, and controlling local pawn shops.[11]

During the Ahumada years developments resulting from the arrival of the railroad laid the basis for a Díaz-Terrazas rapprochement in 1903. As a railway division and shipping point, Chihuahua City experienced a boom in both population and business that accentuated its importance as the state capital. Guerrero City, which was not on the main line, declined until a spur joined it to the transportation network. Juárez, a railhead and port of entry, suddenly emerged as the state's second city.[12] The Terrazas family benefited from the growth of the state capital, long its headquarters, and from the developments in Juárez, where the family had provided most of the capital for commerce, utilities, and recreation facilities.[13]

An alteration of state politics occurred as the allocation of electoral and legislative districts mirrored the shifts of population. Chihuahua City received two additional seats in the legislature for a total of three, and the district that included Juárez was divided as a result of that city's growth.[14] Luis Terrazas could not personally take advantage of the situation because of Díaz's hostility toward him, but his sons and relatives obtained a number of district and legislative offices during the Ahumada administration. The family patriarch also gained an advantage as the Guerrero group dispersed. Some of its members went into graceful inactivity in the national Congress, but most were old men in the 1890s who either retired or died. Luis, of the same generation, proved longer-lived and moreover could rely on his son-in-law, Enrique C. Creel, under whose direction the family's economic and political fortunes prospered.

Creel began building carefully about 1892 to dominate the state. He perceived opportunities in a far different manner than his patron. Terrazas had built an agrarian empire without porfirian assistance, but Creel saw the possibilities of corporate enterprise. He arranged close association between foreign, especially North American, businesses and the Terrazas interests to obtain increased control of the state economy. Acquisition of complementary political authority required a rapprochement between his father-in-law and the dictator, and by 1903 Creel achieved an alliance of Díaz, Terrazas, and foreigners to monopolize politics as well as business in Chihuahua.[15]

With the encouragement of both state and national governments, foreigners surged into Chihuahua to obtain concessions for mining, ranching, and lumbering. A few came as individual speculators, but most were corporate representatives. Guggenheim's mining and smelting cartel dominated mining, and other international firms such as the Sierra Madre Land and Timber Company of William C. Greene, the Madera Lumbering Company of Lord Pearson, and the Palomas Land and Cattle Company joined in the exploitation of the state.[16] Industry was thrice favored with tariff protection, tax exemptions, and cheap labor. The Mexican Central played a major part in the economic growth as it shuttled agricultural goods, cattle, and ore from Chihuahua south to domestic markets or north to the United States.[17]

Only those thus favored by the legislature benefited from the boom economy, however. The rest of the nation suffered economically. Business expansion brought inflation that meager salary increases could not match, and the buying power of wage earners declined by as much as half during the Díaz years. In central Mexico some nine out of ten Mexicans lived on someone else's property, working for credit or coupons redeemable at a company store or utilizing spare lots as sharecroppers. In Chihuahua the situation was slightly better, but land concentration was taking place there and by the end of the Díaz regime, nineteen hacendados owned estates of more than one hundred thousand hectares each in the state.[18] One observer reported that the state's workers lived under deplorable conditions, "with no alternative but to work for what they can get, and they get only what is necessary to support existence." A more callous writer added, ". . . the common laborer earning only one dollar per day, unless assisted by other members of the family has a hard struggle, but with his few and simple needs manages to make ends meet."[19]

Centralization of political power in the state coincided with the concentration of commercial and manufacturing enterprises. Using a national law of 1887, politicians attempted to synchronize local and state governments by making the *jefe político* the major administrator in local districts. Appointed by and responsible to the governor, the *jefes* had executive and judicial authority over minor criminal cases and in public health and economic affairs. In 1904 they were authorized to preside at meetings of local town councils.[20] Opponents of the system began to look to more extreme measures than the ballot to alter the status quo: the triad of Terrazas, Díaz, and the foreigners did not triumph without opposition in Chihuahua.

II

During the last years of the nineteenth century, intermittent insurrections stemming from local grievances marred the porfirian peace of Chihuahua: revolts followed unsatisfactory election returns, the imposition of *jefes políticos*, abuses by surveying companies, and the expansion of large estates. Guerrero earned a reputation as a particularly recalcitrant canton as violence erupted there in 1879, 1887, 1892, and 1899. From 1900 to 1911, Guerrero's citizens regularly petitioned state governors protesting the arbitrary administration by prefects.[21] Located on the margin of the established settlements of the plateau, Guerrero was a transition zone between the ranching country and the sierra district of Indian villages, mining settlements, and logging camps. The region had been the scene of incessant struggles between the indigenous population and Spanish, later Mexican, settlers. Its inhabitants often reacted forcefully to unpopular decisions by the state government; many would later enlist in the Revolution of 1910. Guerrero City was the most prominent settlement in the transition zone. Astride the 107th meridian that paralleled the axis of the Sierra Madre Occidental, the city was located on "the longitude of war."[22]

The alliance between Díaz and the Terrazas clan meant that local recourse to violence could not succeed, but as authority was tightened in Chihuahua, a newly organized political party rose to challenge the national government. The Mexican Liberal Party (PLM) called for a national revolt against the established order.[23] Exiled to the United States, its leaders in 1905 and 1906 launched a militant campaign against the dictatorship. They distributed a newspaper, La regeneración, and promoted the organization of Liberal clubs throughout Mexico in anticipation of a national insurrection. At the end of 1905, they drafted a program calling for the overthrow of the porfirian government and the securing of social justice for all Mexicans. Although they distributed propaganda and started clubs throughout Mexico, they encountered their greatest success in the states along the northern border. In Chihuahua La regeneración had a large circulation and several affiliated groups met regularly to plan cooperative action with the exiled leaders.[24]

In response to the PLM's activity, Creel, now governor of Chihuahua, coordinated efforts to extirpate the radical menace. He prepared border defenses to deter guerrilla attacks from the United States, placed informers among the Liberals, censored mail, and circulated pictures of prominent members of the PLM among district chiefs to prevent their infiltration into the state. Adding teeth to his program, he ordered troops to Cusihuiriáchic to maintain the peace in that potential danger zone, enlarged the police force in Juárez, and requested an additional army regiment from the national government.[25] The Mexican government enlisted the services of the United States, particularly the Post Office and Justice departments, to investigate violations of neutrality legislation. The Ministry of Foreign Relations retained American detectives, including the famous Pinkertons, to complement the surveillance of informers located in border towns with the hope of having the PLM leaders arrested and extradited for trial in Mexico. Creel relied on the Thomas Furlong Agency of St. Louis, Missouri, for his calculated pursuit of the Liberals.[26]

The widespread circulation of its newspaper and the successful organization of Liberal affiliates emboldened the PLM, despite harassment in both Mexico and the United States, to attack the government directly. Twice they invaded border states attempting to incite a general revolution. In late 1906 they struck at Jiménez, Coahuila, and tried to launch a simultaneous expedition from El Paso into Juárez. Their efforts failed completely because of the well-prepared border defenses. Before another attempt could be made in 1907, Thomas Furlong apprehended the PLM leaders in Los Angeles, California, and turned them over to a federal court, which eventually sentenced them to prison. A small contingent captured Las Vacas, Chihuahua, for the PLM in late 1907, but federal troops forced them to retreat back across the border within a matter of hours.[27] Chihuahua's PLM members protested the arbitrary persecution of their leaders and even petitioned the president of the United States to intervene in behalf of the Liberals arrested there,[28] but their efforts came to nothing.

The PLM's failure to instigate a general uprising did not deter disillusioned railroad workers from striking in 1906 and 1908 in Chihuahua. The first action was in support of workers' demands in the central part of the nation, and the second concerned a state question. Trouble developed on the Chihuahua section of the Mexican Central in the fall of 1908 when the management began discharging illiterate Mexican trainmen and replacing them with North American workers. Most of the Mexicans who held posts as brakemen or firemen were forced into unskilled jobs at lower pay. The National Railroad Brotherhood (La Gran Liga Mexicana de Empleados de Ferrocarril) supported the workers' protest and halted rail service for a short time in the North before the Díaz administration resolved the issue by promising some concessions.[29]

The failure of the Liberals and the railroad strikers resulted from the systematic suppression organized by Creel in Chihuahua. The PLM suffered from a lack of finances and its exile in the United States, where it was harassed by agents directed from Mexico, while the workers were easily coerced by the national government. The ease with which Creel eliminated threats to the established authority made the state government complacent and overconfident of its ability to crush opposition if it should reach serious proportions. That official attitude predominated in Chihuahua and throughout Mexico in the critical years preceding the Revolution of 1910, while for the future, the PLM left a legacy of resistance that could be utilized by a skillful organizer.

Meanwhile, the alliance between the federal dictator and the state oligarch, between Díaz and Terrazas, had made the government increasingly repressive and the economic monopoly even more grinding. Although some Chihuahuans had joined the Liberals and others had flirted with their conspiracy, most of the state's residents were not ready to overturn local and national governments until after the heated presidential campaign and election of 1910.

NOTES

1. Chihuahua City, with eighteen thousand residents in 1879, was the only town in the state with a population over ten thousand. See Moisés González Navarro, *Estadísticas sociales del porfiriato, 1877–1910* (Mexico: Talleres Gráficos de la Nación, 1956), p. 7, table 1.

2. Information on Chihuahua during this period is contained in José Fuentes Mares, . . . *Y México se refugió en el desierto: Luis Terrazas, historia y destino* (Mexico: Editorial Jus, 1954), pp. 1–128, 181–98.

3. See two studies by Francisco R. Almada, *Gobernadores del estado de Chihuahua* (Mexico: Imprenta de la H. Cámara de Diputados, 1950), pp. 219–448, and *La revolución en el estado de Chihuahua*, 2 vols. (Mexico: Talleres Gráficos de la Nación, 1964), 1:37–42 (hereafter cited as *Revolución en Chihuahua*).

4. These statements are based on a collation of information in Almada's *Gobernadores*, pp. 336, 383, 405, with the concessions reported in Almada, *Revolución en Chihuahua*, 1:57, 63–64. For a detailed examination of Díaz's efforts to centralize government and to strengthen his authority during his first presidential administration, see Daniel Cosío Villegas, *El Porfiriato: La vida política interior*, vol. 9 of *Historia moderna de México*, ed. Daniel Cosío Villegas, 9 vols. (Mexico: Editorial Hermes, 1955–70).

5. There is no dispassionate account of Luis Terrazas and his influence in Chihuahua, but the following is serviceable: Francisco R. Almada, *Juárez y Terrazas (alaraciones históricas)* (Mexico: Libro Mex, 1958); for the development of Terraza's landholdings, see Moisés González Navarro, *El Porfiriato: La vida social*, vol. 4 of *Historia moderna de México*, pp. 215–16; for his cattle herds, see Fernando Rosenzweig, et al., *El Porfiriato: La vida económica* vols. 7 and 8 of *Historia moderna de México*, 7:152–53.

6. Fernando Jordán, *Crónica de un país bárbaro*, 3d ed. (Mexico: B. Costa-Amic, editor, 1967), pp. 229–41; Clarence C. Clendenen, *Blood on the Border: The United States Army and the Mexican Irregulars* (New York: Macmillan Co., 1969), pp. 85–86, 95–112.

7. Daniel Cosío Villegas, *El Porfiriato: La vida political exterior*, vols. 5 and 6 of *Historia Moderna de Mexico*, 2:xxi, 37–38; U.S. Senate, Committee on

Foreign Relations, *Revolutions in Mexico*, 62d Cong., 2d sess., 1913 (Washington, D.C.: Government Printing Office, 1913), testimony of Charles M. Newman, pp. 113–17 (hereafter cited as *Hearings, 1913*). The entire volume is a catalog of North American investment in Mexico, particularly the northern states.

8. Almada, *Gobernadores*, p. 409; González Navarro, *Porfiriato: Vida social*, p. 191, note citing *Memoría que presentó el C. Gobernador del estado de Chihuahua, Lauro Carrillo en el año 1888*.

9. Francisco R. Almada, *Resumén de historia del estado de Chihuahua* (Mexico: Libros Mexicanos, 1955), p. 350.

10. Terrazas did serve one term in the national Congress, but it appears to have been the exception to his elimination from politics; see Almada, *Gobernadores*, p. 266.

11. Almada, *Revolución en Chihuahua*, 1:64–70, 89; Fuentes Mares, . . . *Y México se refugió en el desierto*, pp. 155–77; Rosenzweig, *Porfiriato: Vida económica*, 1:152–53; Reports by the U.S. consuls at Ciudad Juárez regularly recorded the exportation of Mexican cattle; see Charles W. Kindrick, U.S. consul, Juárez, to Secretary of State, 12 January 1898, National Archives, Record Group 59, Consular Dispatches, Ciudad Juárez, vol. 1, passim.

12. González Navarro, *Estadisticas*, pp. 67, 69. The capital city's population more than doubled, while the state's grew by only 81 percent in the years from 1877 to 1910. In 1900, Chihuahua City had slightly over 9 percent of the state's population. The growth of the city was as follows: 1877, 12,000; 1895, 18,279; 1900, 30,405.

13. Terraza's investment in Juárez can be traced in the list of concessions granted by the legislature in Almada, *Revolución en Chihuahua*, 1:64–80. The Terrazas activities reached a climax in 1909 when Luis's son Alberto established the Juárez Jockey Club, with a membership almost exclusively of New York financiers, to sponsor an annual race meeting and to promote business interests; see *El Paso Morning Times*, 26 and 27 November 1909 (hereafter cited as *EPMT*).

14. Almada, *Revolución en Chihuahua*, 1:41; Almada, *Resumén*, p. 344.

15. Almada, *Gobernadores*, pp. 266, 426–34; Harold D. Sims, "Espejo de caciques: Los Terrazas de Chihuahua," *Historia mexicana* 18 (January–March 1969): 379–99.

16. A detailed, although at times overstated, record of foreign investment is contained in the testimony in *Hearings, 1913*, passim; Luther T. Ellsworth, U.S. Consul, Porfirio Díaz, to Secretary of State, 11 June 1907, National Archives, Records of the Department of State, Numerical Files, 1906–10, Record Group 59, case 69/15–20 (hereafter cited as NF). Charles M. Leonard, U.S. vice-consul, Chihuahua City, to Secretary of State, 26 September 1905, National Archives, Dispatches from U.S. Consuls in Chihuahua, 1830–1906 (microcopy 289, reel 2) includes a four-page list of American citizens and corporations engaged in business in the Chihuahua district; Enrique C. Creel prepared a list of Europeans who had contributed to the state's economic growth in *El estado de Chihuahua: Su historia, geografía, y riquezas naturales* (Mexico: Tip. el progreso, 1928), p. 27.

17. Leonard to Secretary of State, 7 September 1908, NF, case 13911/70–71.

18. Manuel González Ramírez, *Las ideas, la violencia*, vol. 1 of *La revolución social de México* (Mexico: Fondo de Cultura Económica, 1960), pp. 20–21; Almada, *Revolución en Chihuahua*, 1:59–60.

19. Thomas D. Edwards, U.S. Consul, Juárez, to Secretary of State, 28 August 1908, NF, case 13911/83–84; Leonard to Secretary of State, 7 September 1908, NF, case 13911/70–71.

20. Robert L. Sandels, "Silvestre Terrazas, the Press, and the Origins of the Mexican Revolution in Chihuahua" (Ph.D. diss., University of Oregon, 1967), citing Chihuahua's constitution of 1887; Alberto Calzadíaz Barrera, *Hechos reales de la revolucion*, 3 vols., 2d ed. (Mexico: Editorial Patría, 1961), 1:29.

21. Almada, *Revolución en Chihuahua*, 1:93–94; Michael C. Meyer, *Mexican Rebel: Pascual Orozco and the Mexican Revolution, 1910–1915* (Lincoln: University of Nebraska Press, 1967), pp. 14–15.

22. Jordán, *Crónica*, chap. 27, passim; Moreno, *Hombres de la revolución*, p. 62; Florence and Robert H. Lister, *Chihuahua, Storehouse of Storms* (Albuquerque: University of New Mexico Press, 1966), 183–86.

23. Ward Sloan Albro III, "Ricardo Flores Magón and the Liberal Party: An Inquiry into the Origins of the Mexican Revolution of 1910" (Ph.D. diss., University of Arizona, 1967); James D. Cockcroft, *Intellectual Precursors of the Mexican Revolution, 1900–1913* (Austin: University of Texas Press, 1968), pp. 91–156.

24. Albro, "Flores Magón," p. 76, estimates that fifteen hundred copies of the newspaper were regularly sent into Mexico, largely to the northern tier of states. For the development of the PLM in Chihuahua, see Silvestre Terrazas Collection, Correspondence and Papers, Bancroft Library, University of California, Berkeley (hereafter cited as STC). Box 27, folder 11b, contains a list of subscribers to *Regeneración* compiled by the state government.

25. Creel to Ramón Corral, 27 October and 6 November 1906, STC, box 26, folder 7a.

26. See letters from Creel to Corral, October and November 1906, STC, box 26, folder 7a. Reports of the Furlong Agency to Creel are included in [José C. Valades?], ed., "siguiendo la pista a políticos mexicanos," *La opinión* (Los Angeles) weekly from 16 April to 11 June 1939. Reports from Furlong and other detective agencies are also scattered throughout the Archivo de Relaciones Exteriores de México, Mexico City, file series H/13–1910–1920/1.

27. [Ricardo Flores Magón] to José de la L. Soto, 22 June 1906, STC, box 26, folder 1; Albro, "Flores Magón," pp. 23–30. Furlong described his arrest of the PLM leaders in his *Fifty Years a Detective* (St. Louis: C. E. Barnett, 1912), pp. 137–48.

28. "Liberals of Chihuahua" to President [Theodore Roosevelt] of the United States, 23 September 1906, NF, case 100/100.

29. Cockcroft, *Precursors*, pp. 141–43; William F. Sands, U.S. Consul, Chihuahua City, to Secretary of State, 20 October 1908, NF, case 3289/15–16; González Navarro, *Porfiriato: Vida social*, p. 339.

MEXICAN TRAITS

Charles Macomb Flandrau

Charles Macomb Flandrau (1871–1938) is the author of Viva Mexico!, *a classic of travel literature that first appeared in 1908. Flandrau, a wealthy bachelor and writer for the* Saturday Evening Post, *lived on his brother's coffee plantation in Veracruz for five years, from 1903 to 1908. His book, filled with amusing anecdotes and delightful humor, describes the character of Mexico. Unlike most travel literature, Flandrau's work focused on the rural landscape of a limited zone north of Jalapa. He preferred the company of rural hacendados and peones to that of the powerful in Mexico City. And, in spite of the colorful language, his descriptions were usually objective. In this excerpt he describes the many traits of the Mexican peon, traits which were the result of a long history of repression by local caudillos and the Church alike.*

WHY PEOPLE ARE WHAT THEY ARE is always an interesting subject on which to exert one's talents, however slight, for observation and inference. On an isolated Mexican farm one spends many odd moments in considering and attempting to explain the traits of the people who condescend to work for one. For most of the problems of one's daily life there arise from those traits, and by them, all are complicated. The amicable relations between employer and employed everywhere is one that necessitates on the former's part considerable tact to preserve, but in Mexico both the nation's history and the people's temperament combine to render the situation one of unusual delicacy.

In 1519 Spain and the Roman Catholic Church affixed themselves to Mexico's throat and were with extreme difficulty detached from it

From Charles Macomb Flandrau, *Viva Mexico!* (1908; reprint ed., Urbana: University of Illinois, 1964), pp. 59–76. Reprinted by permission of Hawthorn Properties (Elsevier-Dutton Publishing Co., Inc.).

only after three hundred years. During most of that time, in addition to the fact that the Church got possession actually of something more than a third of the country's entire property, "real, personal, and mixed," the metaphorical expression, "he could not call his soul his own," was true of the inhabitants in its baldest, its most literal sense. To call one's soul one's own in Mexico between the years 1527 and 1820 was to be tried in secret by the Holy Office of the Inquisition and then turned over to the secular authorities—a formality that deceived no one—to be either publicly strangled and then burned, or burned without even the preliminary solace of strangulation. "The principal crimes of which the Holy Office took cognizance," we read, "were heresy, sorcery, witchcraft, polygamy, seduction, imposture, and personation"—a tolerably elastic category. Without the slightest difficulty it could be stretched to cover anyone "not in sympathy with the work," and during the period in which the Holy Office was exercised it covered many.

It is true the royal order by which the Inquisition was formally established in Mexico exempted Indians from its jurisdiction, but when the clause was observed—which it was not in the case of Indians who displayed a capacity for thought—it was almost the only form of oppression from which, under the bigoted and avaricious rule of Spain, they were exempt. Until the advent of the conquerors this part of the new world had been, for no one knows how long, a slaughterhouse of the gods. Spain and the Church continued a carnage of their own in the name of God.

The limited scope of these impressions permits of scarcely a reference to Mexico's history. I can only assert that almost every phase of it is imbedded in layer upon layer of the rottenest type of ecclesiastical politics and that the great mass of the people to-day reflects—in a fashion curiously modified at unexpected moments by the national awakening—its generations of mental and physical subjection. For whatever, from time to time, has happened to be the form of government, the people have never enjoyed any large measure of freedom. Even now, with an acute, patriotic, and enlightened president at the head of the nation, Mexico—and quite inevitably—is not a republic, but a military Diazpotism.

In the name of gods and of God, of kings, dictators, popes, generals, emperors, and presidents, the people of Mexico have been treated, one would be inclined to say, like so many head of irresponsible cattle, if cattle, as a rule, were not treated more solicitously. And this general tendency of the governor toward the governed has accentuated certain traits easy enough to isolate and describe, if they were not complicated by the facts that: First, the Mexican of to-day naturally has many characteristics in common with the Spaniard who begat him and whom he still hates; second, that the nation is becoming more and more conscious of itself as a nation, and, third, that in a multitude of petty ways a kind of mediæval tyranny is still often exercised by the very persons who, as officials of a theoretically excellent republic, ought to stand for all that is liberal and just.

Now, if the attitude of a Mexican peon were always consistently that of the oppressed and patient creature who looks upon his patrón as omnipotent and omniscient, or if it were always that of the high-falutin Spaniard whom at times he so much resembles—or, if it were always that of Young Mexico, conscious of at least his theoretical independence and in theory "as good as anybody," there would be little difficulty in getting along with him; one would know at any given moment how to treat him. But as a matter of fact it is a rather intricate combination of all three, and one can rarely predict which he will choose to exhibit. Add to this an incredible depth of superstition that is both innate and very carefully encouraged by the Church, and it is not difficult to see why an employer in certain parts of Mexico is compelled to treat his laborers much as one has to treat nervous and unreasonable children.

Although they are hired and receive wages on various terms of agreement, the normal relation between the proprietor of, say, a café finca of moderate size and the people who work for him, suggests in many respects the relation that existed before the Civil War between our Southerners of the better type and their slaves. Some of the people have small farms of their own in the neighborhood, but when they go to work for any length of time they usually close their houses and live on the ranch of their employer in one-roomed huts built by the patrón at a cost—if they are made of bamboo—of from six to ten dollars an edifice. Closing their houses for the coffee-picking season consists of gathering up four or five primitive pottery cooking utensils, several babies, a pair of thin and faded sarapes, calling to the dogs and strolling out of the door. Under ordinary amicable circumstances they are disposed to look up to the patrón, to be flattered by his notice of them—to regard him, in fact, as of different and finer clay than themselves. And when this lowly and dependent mood is upon them there is not only nothing the señor cannot, in their opinion, accomplish if he desires to—there are no demands upon his time, his money, his implements, and his sympathies that they hesitate to make. The proprietor of a far-away ranch acquires a certain proficiency in the performance of almost every kindly office, from obstetrics to closing the eyes of the dead.

One Agapito, whose baby died on our place, informed us—after we had sufficiently condoled and he had cheerfully assured us that the baby was "better off with God"—that it would give him and his wife great pleasure to pay us the compliment of having the wake in our sala! There, of course, was a delicate situation at once. Agapito yearned for the prestige that would be his if we permitted him to suspend his dead baby—dressed in mosquito netting and orange blossoms—against the sala wall and leave it there to the edification of the countryside for a day and a night. To refuse was, without doubt, to offend him; but to consent was to establish a somewhat ghastly precedent impossible in subsequent cases of affliction to ignore. As my brother declared, when we withdrew to discuss the matter, one had to choose between hurting Agapito's feelings and turning the sala into a perpetual morgue. Agapito was in several respects an efficient and valuable person. He could even persuade the machine for dispulping coffee-berries to work smoothly when—as they express it—"it does not wish to." But, nevertheless, with much regret we decided to hurt Agapito's feelings. Like children they do not shrink from making naïvely preposterous demands upon one, and like children their sense of obligation is almost entirely lacking. They are given to bringing one presents of oranges and bananas, or inedible blood puddings and cakes when they kill a pig or have a party, but they are rarely incited to display appreciation of kindness—even when it would be easy for them to do so—in a way that counts.

One afternoon, during the busiest season of the year on a coffee ranch, all the coffee-pickers—men, women, and children—with the exception of one family, suddenly struck. When asked what the trouble was, the spokesman in a florid and pompous address declared that they were "all brothers and must pick together or not at all." It came out during the interview that the father of the family who had not struck had received permission for himself, his wife, and six small children to pick in a block of coffee by themselves, and to this the others had been induced to object. Why they objected they could not say, because they did not know. It was explained to them that the man had wished his family to work apart for the sole and sensible reason that, first, he and his wife could take better care of the children when they were not scattered among the crowd, and, secondly, that as the trees of the particular block he had asked to be allowed to pick in were younger and smaller than the others, the children had less difficulty in reaching the branches. He not only derived no financial advantage from the change, he was voluntarily making some sacrifice by going to pick where the coffee, owing to the youth of the trees, was less abundant.

"Don't you see that this is the truth and all there is to it?" the strikers were asked.

"Yes."

"And now that it has been explained, won't you go back to work?"

"No."

"But why not?"

"Because."

"Because what?"

"Because we must all pick together."

A strike for higher wages or shorter hours or more and better food is usual and always comprehensible anywhere, but one has to go to Mexico, I imagine, to experience a strike that involves neither a question of material advantage nor of abstract principle. It was recalled to them that the fact of their being "all brothers" did not operate against their eloping with one another's wives and slashing one another with machetes in the mazy dance whenever they felt so inclined—a reflection that produced much merriment, especially among the ladies. But upon the point at issue it had no effect whatever, and irritating as it was to be forced into submitting to this sort of thing, before work could be resumed the family of eight had to be sent for and told to pick with the others. All these people were indebted to their employer for loans, for medicines—for assistance of various kinds too numerous to mention or to remember, and, in their way, they liked him and liked the ranch. I can account for such inconsiderate imbecility only by supposing that after generations of oppression the desire among an ignorant and emotional people to assert their independence in small matters becomes irresistible from time to time, even when they cannot discover that their rights have been in any way infringed upon.

However, their rights *are* constantly infringed upon in the most obvious and brazen manner, and knowledge of this undoubtedly contributes to their uncomfortable habit of vibrating between an attitude of doglike trust and one of the most exaggerated suspicion. Last year, for example, a stone bridge was being built in a small town some six or eight miles away from our ranch. As the heavy summer rains were but a few months off, it was desirable that the bridge should be completed. Labor, however, was exceedingly scarce, and for a long time the work made no visible progress. At first the authorities resorted to the usual plan of making arrests for drunkenness and obliging the victims to haul stones and mortar, but as this immediately resulted in the exercise of unusual self-restraint on the part of the populace, the jefe político evolved the quaint conceit of detaining every able-bodied man who appeared in town without trousers! The Indians in that part of the country, and many of the people who are not pure Indian, wear, instead of the skin-tight Mexican trousers, a pair of long, loose white cotton drawers resembling in cut and fit the lower part of a suit of pajamas. They are not only a perfectly respectable garment, they are vastly more practical and comfortable than the pantalones, inasmuch as they can be rolled above the knee and, in a land of mud and streams, kept clean and dry. But until the jefe had acquired a force sufficient to complete the bridge, he arrested everybody who wore them. A law had been passed, he said, declaring them to be indecent. Just when the law had been passed and by whom he did not trouble to explain. Among the small rancheros of the neighborhood who did not own a pair of trousers, the edict caused not only inconvenience but now and then positive hardship. Many of them who had not heard of it and innocently attended church or market were sent to bridge-building for indefinite periods when they ought to have been at home harvesting their corn. Their crops were either spoiled or stolen. The Indians on our place did not dare venture into town for supplies until we bought a pair of trousers for lending purposes. "Trinidad (or Lucio, or Jesús) is going to town and begs that you will do him the favor of lending him the pants," was an almost daily request for weeks.

I remember one jefe político to whom it occurred that he might start a butcher shop and ruin the business of the only other butcher shop in town, which was kept by a man he happened to dislike. When he had completed his arrangements for the sale of meat, he caused a rumor to circulate among the lower classes to the effect that life would be a gladder, sweeter thing for all concerned if the meat he was now prepared to dispense should find a market both ready and sustained. To the American and English rancheros of the neighborhood he had letters written by various friends of his who happened to know them; courteous not to say punctilious letters that, however, contained somewhere between the lines an ominous rumble. "I thought it might interest you to learn that H——, the jefe, has opened a butcher shop and would consider it an honor if you were to favor him with your patronage, instead of bestowing it upon his competitor," the letters ran in part. Though somewhat more rhetorical, it all sounded to the unattuned ear as innocent as any of the numerous advertisements one receives by post in the course of a week at home. But it wasn't. In a "republic," where the governors of the various states must be without question the political friends of the president, and the jefes are usually, with no more question, the political friends of the governors, the suggestion that a jefe would not object to one's purchasing beefsteaks from him is not lightly to be ignored. The local jefe can, in a hundred subtle ways, make one's residence in Mexico extremely difficult and disagreeable. Every foreigner who received one of the inspired epistles changed his butcher the next day. Another jefe of my acquaintance—a rather charming man—decided to pave a certain country road chiefly because it went through some land owned by his brother. As most of the able-bodied convicts of that district were engaged in paving a much more important highway and he could not very well draw upon their forces, he magnificently sent out a messenger who floundered through the mud from ranch to ranch, announcing to the countryside that henceforth every man would have to labor, without compensation, one day in eight upon the road. Now, to most of the people who received the message, this particular road was of no importance; they rarely used it and they owned no land through which it ran. And yet—whether from the habit of submitting to tyranny, or from guilty consciences, I don't know—many responded with their time and their toil. When asked, as we frequently were, for advice on the subject, we refrained from giving any.

The habit of suspicion and the impulse to make, for no very definite reason, little displays of personal independence would tax one's patience and amiability to the utmost if one did not keep on hand a reserve fund of these qualities with which to fortify oneself against frequent exhibitions of Mexican honor. In referring to this somewhat rococo subject, it is perhaps but fair for me to admit that even so comparatively simple a matter as the Anglo-Saxon sense of honor presents certain difficulties to my understanding. Explain and expound as many intelligent gentlemen have to me, for instance, I have never been able to grasp why it is so much more dishonorable to evade one's gambling debts than it is to evade one's laundress. Therefore I do not feel competent to throw a great light upon the kind of honor that obtains in Mexico. I can only observe that, like politeness, smallpox, and fine weather, it is very prevalent, and record an example or two of the many that arise in my memory, by way of illustrating one of the obstacles in the employer's path.

A few winters ago we hired a youth to bring our letters and fresh meat every day from the town to the ranch. He performed this monotonous service with commendable regularity, and with a regularity not so commendable always cut off at least a quarter of the meat after leaving the butcher shop and gave it to his mother who lived in town. Furthermore, when the workmen on the place intrusted him with letters to post on his return, he posted them if they were stamped, but scattered them in fragments if they were not, and pocketed the money. We knew he did both these things because we found and identified some of the epistolary fragments, and his mother had the monumental brass to complain to the butcher when the meat was tough! But even so, he was a convenience—none of the laborers could be regularly spared at the time—and we made no moan. One day, however, it was impossible to ignore the matter; he arrived with a bit of beefsteak about as large as a mutton chop and had the effrontery, as we thought, to deliver it without a word of explanation. So, as the imposition had been going on for at least six weeks, he was as kindly as possible, most unfortunately, accused. Then followed an exhibition of outraged innocence such as I have never before seen. He turned a kind of Nile green; he clenched his fist and beat upon his chest. He made an impassioned address in which he declared that, although his family was poor and needed the twenty-five centavos a day we paid him, he could not continue to work for anyone who had sought to cast a reflection upon his spotless honor; and he ended by bursting into tears and sobbing for ten minutes with his head on a bag of coffee.

The tragic, humorous, and altogether grotesque part of the affair was that on this particular day for the first time, no doubt, since we had employed him, he *hadn't* stolen the meat! We learned from the butcher a few hours afterwards that there had been scarcely any beefsteak in the shop when the boy had called, but that he had sent a few ounces, thinking it was better than nothing at all. We lost our messenger; his mother would not allow him to work for persons who doubted his honesty.

A friend of mine had in his employ an old man—an ex-bullfighter—who took care of the horses and accompanied the various members of the family when they went for a ride. He was given to gambling, and on one occasion when he had lost all his money but could not bring himself to leave the game, he gambled away a saddle and bridle of his employer. Shortly afterwards my friend recognized them in the window of a harness shop and bought them back, without, however, mentioning the fact to old Preciliano, who, when casually asked where they were, replied quite as casually that at the public stable where the horses were kept they had become mixed with some other equipment and taken away by mistake. He explained that he knew the distant ranchero who had inadvertently done this and that steps had been taken to have them returned. For several weeks my friend amused himself by asking for—and getting—minute details of the saddle's whereabouts and the probable date of its arrival, and then one day he abruptly accused Preciliano of having lost it in a game of cards.

This was followed by almost exactly a repetition of the performance we had been given by the meat-and-letter boy. Preciliano was not only astonished that the señor could for a moment imagine such a thing, he was hurt—wounded—cruelly smitten in his old age by the hand he had never seen raised except in kindness. All was lost save honor. That, thank God, he could still retain—but not there; not under that roof. He could not remain covered with shame in the shadow of so hideous a suspicion. Honor demanded that he should "separate" himself at once—honor demanded all sorts of things in this vein until my friend, who said he was positively beginning to believe Preciliano very much as Preciliano believed himself, suddenly stooped down and pulled the saddle and bridle from under the table. Collapse. Tears. Forgiveness. Tableau.

Preciliano subsequently left this family—gave up an agreeable and lucrative position—because the wife of the employer thoughtfully suggested that, on account of his advancing years, it would be wiser of him not to exercise a certain imperfectly broken horse. He was "covered with shame" and sorrowfully bade them farewell.

AGUSTÍN ARAGÓN AND MEXICO'S RELIGION OF HUMANITY

W. Dirk Raat

W. Dirk Raat teaches Mexican history at the State University of New York at Fredonia. He is the author of several articles, in English and Spanish, on positivism, Mexican intellectual history, Mexican historiography, and the Mexican Revolution. His books include El positivismo durante el Porfiriato and Revoltosos. Mexico's Rebels in the United States, 1903–1923.

In the following essay Professor Raat describes the beliefs and activities of Mexico's orthodox positivists. Their type of Comtean or French positivism included a science of ethics, social sacraments, religious rituals, and a positivist calendar; it is interesting to note the parallels and similarities between Mexico's Religion of Humanity and Mexico's religion of Catholicism. As a movement, positivism influenced, and was influenced by, other developments of Díaz's Mexico, such as industrialization, material growth, technology and science, and the decline of traditional liberalism. Did orthodox positivism complement the capitalist ethic and científico rule of Díaz's government?

In 1817, Henri de Saint-Simon won the nineteen-year-old Auguste Comte over to his views concerning the lamentable condition of post-revolutionary French society and the necessity for a radical scheme of reform, and it was during the political turmoil of the second quarter of the nineteenth century that Comte, intending to reorder society through the application of scientific knowledge to social ills, presented his philosophy of positivism. Comte's project was nothing less than a blueprint for universal reform that would not only save

"Agustín Aragón and Mexico's Religion of Humanity" by William D. Raat is reprinted from the Journal of InterAmerican Studies and World Affairs, vol. 11, no. 3 (July 1969): 441–57, by permission of the publisher, Sage Publications, Inc.

France from ruin but would also, hopefully, rescue all of humanity. In its entirety the Comtean doctrine included a philosophy of history, a theory of knowledge and pedagogy, a method or logic of science, a positivist ethic (the so-called "subjective synthesis"), a socioeconomic plan, a theory of government, and a type of secular faith which he called the Religion of Humanity.[1]

Comte's view of secular religion envisioned a state in which political power would be shared between temporal leaders (industrial titans, bankers, merchants, etc.) and the intellectual elites, i.e., the positivist philosophers who were also considered priests of learning and wisdom. The role of the clergy was basically an educational one. They were to advise the capitalists and public functionaries on the fine art of scientific management in economy and politics. Through friendly persuasion and the force of example they would act as a check upon tyranny and misgovernment. The power of the clergy also reached into the individual household where women and children were instructed in the truths of scientific morality. The spiritual leaders not only served society in particular, but also dedicated themselves to the Grand Being or Humanity itself. Within the ranks of the spiritual authority there was to be a single High Priest of Humanity (akin to the pope of Catholicism) who would have total control over the rest of the clergy and whose prime intellect would be used for the general good. At least to the orthodox disciples of Comte this High Priest of Humanity was obviously Comte himself.

It was left to the followers of Comte to put into practice that which the master had only theorized. His disciples soon split into two camps. The heterodox desired to modify Comte and restrict themselves to his ideas of scientific method and logic, while the orthodox were willing to follow both the scientific and religious writings of Comte. After the death of Comte in 1857 the leadership of the heterodox group fell to Emile Littré. The French orthodox followed Pierre Laffitte and Emile Corra and established a ceremonial cult of worship in honor of the Supreme Being of Humanity. The more radical even promoted the deification of Comte himself. Organized positivism and the Positivist Church of England were founded by Richard Congreve. Although Congreve's dogmatic approach alienated many intellectuals, his influence as a teacher led to the conversion of three leading English positivists, E. S. Beesley, J. H. Bridges, and Frederick Harrison. The Religion of Humanity was also carried to South America where it met with particular success in Brazil under the skillful leadership of Miguel Lamos, head of the Positivist Church of Brazil.[2]

Proponents of both the Littré and Laffitte schools of thought were active in propagandizing positivism in Mexico. The scientific emphasis of Littré in logic and education was promoted by Gabino Barreda who became the founder and director of the *Escuela Nacional Prepa-ratoria* after 1868.[3] In 1877 Barreda helped to establish the *Sociedad Metodófila* which published several works on Darwinism and positivism. These publications evidently converted several intellectuals to the cause of Comte, including the young engineering student, Agustín Aragón. From 1888 to 1914 Aragón's energy would be directed towards propagating the "good news" or gospel of Comte and the "truths" of the Religion of Humanity.[4]

This Religion of Humanity, while of limited political significance, forms an important and interesting page in the social and intellectual history of late nineteenth-century and early twentieth-century Mexico. As a humanistic religion it contributed to the secularization of Mexican life, so noticeable in the days of Don Porfirio. And more important, orthodox positivism aided in the transformation of Mexican liberalism from an atomistic to an organic definition of society. Although Leopoldo Zea's works on positivism in Mexico remain the classic studies, no historian (including Zea himself, but excluding Aragón who, prior to his death in 1954 wrote a semihistorical survey of the "porfiriato" entitled *Porfirio Díaz: Estudio Histórico-Filosófico*) has given serious attention to Mexico's Religion of Humanity.[5]

It was not until after 1890 that Agustín Aragón and a small group of faithful became vividly aware of Laffitte and his movement in France, and started to develop the vehicles of positivist diffusion for Mexico. In 1898, Aragón was honored by being selected to represent Mexico's positivists at the centennial celebration held in Paris in honor of Comte's "living spirit." It was on this occasion that Aragón, standing inside Comte's old apartment on Monsieur-le-Prince street, delivered aloud his essay on positivism in Mexico before the famous Pierre Laffitte and other French coreligionists. After speaking in an optimistic vein about the past successes of Mexican positivism, Aragón concluded his address by calling for a larger, more efficient, missionary program in Mexico that would continue the work which the master Comte and the prophet Barreda had started. He acknowledged his own humble position as a third generation positivist (even though his contemporaries, both friendly and unfriendly, soon gave him the more exalted title of the "Positivist Pope of Mexico"), and with religious zeal promised to fulfill Mexico's historical destiny of arriving at a pure positivist state of evolution.[6]

Evidently the cry from Paris was heard, for while Aragón was busy in Paris his brethen in Mexico were instrumental in soliciting funds so that a monument could be erected to Comte in Paris.[7] These same believers also initiated and attended a ceremony to honor Comte on the date of his death (September 5). From this group came the nucleus of the first orthodox positivist organization in Mexico. This organization, affiliated with the Laffitte-Corra tradition in France and the Beesly-Harrison group in England, as well as certain Central American organizations, was called the "Sociedad Positivist." By 1900 the Positivist Society would be directed by Aragón's companion and friend, the positivist logician and teacher Porfirio Parra. Parra would be aided in his work by Horacio Barreda, the son of the prophet Gabino Barreda. From 1900 until the revolutionary period this society met annually in commemoration of Comte, Laffitte, and Barreda.

In order to spread the gospel, Aragón founded and became editor of the official journal of positivism in Mexico, the *Revista Positiva*. This periodical took as its slogan the Comtean motto of "Orden y Progreso" which was printed on each title page. The *Revista* discussed all of the central aspects of positivism including the "law of three stages," the positive polity, positivist ethics, the "subjective synthesis," and of course, the Religion of Humanity. The orthodox Laffitte, not the heterodox Littré, became one of its patron saints. This orthodox position of the *Revista* was maintained throughout its years of publication from 1901 to 1914.[8]

As early as 1901 the *Revista* took as its position that the essential aspect of positivism was Comte's Religion of Humanity. The Mexican positivists subscribed to E. S. Beesly's outline of religious positivism. The thirteen points of the outline can be paraphrased as follows.:[9]

1. Humanity in the total is an organism that lives and develops.
2. The progress of humanity is indicated by the development of different religions from earliest times to the present.
3. All religions have been good and useful during their epochs, but have been invalidated by the new knowledge of science and by the development of different social necessities.
4. The last religion, Christianity, when judged in the aggregate, was superior to the older religions, not in the credibility of its assertions but in its personal and social utility.

5. The development of positivist knowledge (or science) has discredited Christian doctrine and Christianity is now at the stage of its dissolution.
6. No religion can have any influence or utility in the future unless it is based upon scientific knowledge.
7. There is no way of demonstrating the existence of God or the immortality of the soul, therefore the positivist neither affirms nor negates these doctrines.
8. The Being of the great nature and of the most benefit to mankind is Humanity (although it is neither omnipotent nor perfect). This Being consists of all that man has contributed in the past, is contributing presently, and will contribute in the future.
9. To this Being we offer our Love, Service, and Veneration. This Being is not a god but takes the place of God. Each one can serve this Being by following the maxim: "Live for others."
10. In the service of Humanity we find all that was useful in the service of God.
11. The accepted rules of morality which man has practiced have generally been believed to have been revealed or dictated by God to man. In reality the rules of morality have been the result of good and wise men who have speculated on man's condition in all ages.
12. We accept these moral rules as a result of the work of Humanity, not God, and shall strive to perfect them in the future.
13. The necessity most immediate and urgent of our times is the formation of a universal religious society founded upon the above mentioned principles in which men and women of all nations, without respect to political or national differences, will be united morally and intellectually just as the people of western Europe were during the middle ages under the Church.

These, then, were the thirteen articles of faith that would guide the religious positivists of Mexico in their task of merging the Mexican nation into the Oversoul of Humanity.

Agustín Aragón, as editor of the *Revista*, subscribed to the principles of the Religion of Humanity. Accepting, like Beesly, the necessary role of conventional religion for the progress of humanity, he argued that the Religion of Humanity was not an enemy of any faith, but rather a friend that promoted the final realization of any religion for man. Thus the object of the *Revista*, as defined by Aragón, was one of fulfilling all in life which was useful, beautiful, and truthful. Aragón readily proclaimed that "We of the Revista are soldiers of culture and our love is the Religion of Humanity."[10]

Although Comte's Religion of Humanity was obviously not foreign to the mind of the prophet Barreda, still Barreda's major concern was that of promoting the Classification of the Sciences as a philosophy of education. In asserting Barreda's relationship with the Religion of Humanity, Aragón went further than most positivist adherents or later historians, including Leopoldo Zea, were willing to go. Aragón taught that Barreda was not satisfied with scientific culture alone; that he, Barreda, wanted to satisfy all the aspirations of man. Therefore, according to Aragón, Barreda practiced with his disciples the Religion of Love and Responsibility, a religion purified of all theological superstitions. Aragón asserted that Barreda taught in his lectures at the Preparatory of the most sublime of all beings known to man, the collective being known as Humanity. Barreda not only taught the ideal of Humanity but he, like all great men of history, was a living example of the maxim of positivist ethics: "To live for the family, the country, and for Humanity." Thus Aragón, rightly or wrongly, brought the authority of Barreda to his own campaign of religious positivism.[11]

The writings of the Orthodox Chilean positivist, Juan Enrique Lagarrigue, were used by the *Revista* in propagandizing the Religion of Humanity. In several articles Lagarrigue advanced the doctrine of Humanity. From his writings the central aspects of the Religion of Humanity as taught in Mexico can be constructed.[12] It will be noted that the message was orthodox in that there was little divergence from the teachings of the master Comte. Comte's utopian ideal of a universal brotherhood, brought together through the common knowledge of science (the universal language) that would end the traditional conflict between religion and science and result in the new synthesis of Humanity, was accepted by the orthodox positivists of Mexico.

The Religion of Humanity, in Comte's thinking, was the logical extension of his entire system. The priests of science, like all great men in the history of progress, would influence the behavior of both the temporal leaders of society and the moral leaders (mothers and wives) of the family through ethical instruction and example. These positivist priests or philosophers possessed ethical wisdom as a result of the "subjective synthesis"—i.e., a synthesis derived from an overview of all the sciences—which was a moral scheme believed to be akin to scientific knowledge in that it was universally valid for all men. With this special knowledge of morality the positivist clergy, including the coreligionists of Mexico, would usher in the "millennium" of Humanity, the last and purely positivist stage of history. The Comtean slogan implied that the principle of Love would be pursued by mankind (this type of love being a sort of fellow-feeling) operating upon a base of social order so as to achieve the ultimate state of progress: "El amor por principio y el orden por base; el progreso por fin"[13]

The positivist ethic of Love was considered to be a part of the physical and organic functioning of the human being, and was therefore a rule of morality scientifically derived through an examination of the operations of the human organism. Love itself was divided into three organic categories—sentiment, intelligence, and activity. Sentiment inspired and motivated mankind. Intelligence, operating with scientific knowledge, would act as a guide for the sentiments in inducing proper activity. There were further subdivisions under sentiment, intelligence, and activity. Sentiment consisted of seven egoistic functions (such as sex or vanity) and three altruistic functions (like veneration). There were five intellectual operations (concrete contemplation, abstract contemplation, inductive reasoning, deductive reasoning, and language) and three areas of activity (valor, prudence, and perseverance). Thus Love consisted of eighteen functions, seven of which were egoistic and in opposition to altruism. Yet it was believed that in the total activity of humanity the egoism of each individual would reinforce the altruism of others. Thus this type of positivistic love was not only a principle of morality, but a physiological reality. Morality, according to Comte's *Système de Politique Positive*, was the science of sciences.[14]

In order to establish a cult of worship to the secular God of Humanity and to its self-appointed savior Comte, the coreligionists of Mexico pursued the practice of the social sacraments. The purpose of the sacraments was to develop within the members of the private cult the spirit of altruism and to lead them away from egoism. The sacraments were seven in number, with an additional rite celebrated sixty years after death, and were akin in many respects to the sacraments of the Roman Catholic church. (It should be noted that Comte admired many aspects of Catholicism and, like Beesly, considered it superior to the earlier religions.)

The first social sacrament was called presentation (baptism) and this took place when the individual received birth into the Religion of Humanity. The exercise of this sacrament occurred with the education of children by the mother. During the next stage of life, from age fourteen to twenty-one, the child was educated by the spiritual authorities in the basic sciences, including morality. This was the social sacrament of initiation and admission (confirmation). From twenty-one to thirty-one the individual went through redemption and penance and started to practice his life vocation. This decade was the sacrament of destination. When women arrived at age twenty-eight and men at thirty-five, the sacrament of matrimony took place. All previous education was designed to develop a perfect reciprocity between man and wife. At forty-two man arrived at the period of wisdom and received his holy orders or the sacrament of maturity. It was now his full responsibility to aid in the task of ushering mankind into Humanity. At sixty-four he received the sacrament of retirement in which his role was one of rest and counsel. At death, extreme unction or transformation occurred. And sixty years after death, incorporation occurred in which the individual achieved union with Humanity.[15]

It will be observed that the positivist rites of sacrament were usually not formal occasions, but rather periods of human growth and development. These rites were social sacraments, i.e., organic processes of life which were imbued with a religious significance. Yet it would be incorrect to leave the impression that no formal rituals accompanied the sacraments of life. The mother, in educating her children in the positivist ethic, was actually performing the sacrament of presentation. And this was also true for the positivist clergy, who, in educating the individual, were administering the sacrament of initiation. Marriage involved a formal ritual and was considered to be the prerogative of the state, not the Christian church. And finally, in many instances in which members of a positivist church or society met to honor the death of Comte, they would prematurely grant to Comte the immortality of the sacrament of incorporation. In Mexico this occurred in 1902 (technically fifteen years too early since Comte had died in 1857) when Parra, speaking before the Positivist Society of Mexico, argued for Comte's spiritual immortality and noted that the Great Being of Humanity does not die with the individual, but lives on in a secular sense with the thought, art, and poetry of great men.[16]

Comte's veneration of the great men of history also received formal acceptance in Mexico with the publication of a Spanish version of the positivist calendar by the *Revista Positiva* in 1902.[17] Like the men of the French Revolution, Comte held that a new theory of history necessitated the creation of a new calendar. One of his attempts in this direction was called the Calendar of Great Men. For Comte the Calendar had both an educational and religious purpose. The youth of his new order could derive lessons of history from this Calendar in that the thirteen stages of mental development in the history of human progress were represented in this Calendar. Further, morality lessons could be derived from a study of the Calendar by noting the great men represented and then through a conscious imitation of their behavior. And finally, the Calendar itself was a religious tribute to some 558 individuals who were agents of the general march of civilization. In this sense the Calendar was symbolic for Comte's general theory of historical development.

Unlike the Gregorian Calendar, positivism divided the year into thirteen months each consisting of four seven-day weeks. Each month was named after a great man: Moses, Homer, Aristotle, Archimedes, Caesar, Saint Paul, Charlemagne, Dante, Gutenberg, Shakespeare, Descartes, Frederick the Great, and Bichat (an early nineteenth-century biologist). The days of the week were also given the names of great servants of Humanity such as the Buddha or Confucius. Comte's intention was to picture the preparatory period of the history of Humanity through the most noted people who were active in the various areas of life (religion, poetry, philosophy, war, politics, industry, and science). To make his Calendar complete in its correlation to the Gregorian Calendar, Comte had to do something about the one day left over each year and the extra day on a leap year. His solution was to make these extra days holy days, the first being called the Fiesta of Death and the second the Fiesta of the Holy Virgin. On the former occasion Comte was to be worshiped while on the latter the sacred symbol of femininity was to be an object of honor. In dating its various issues of publication the *Revista Positiva* actually utilized the positivist Calendar.[18]

Apart from its journal, the Positivist Society of Mexico was active from 1900 until the outbreak of the revolution in meeting annually in commemoration of Comte. Within these meetings a cult of worship was being developed around not only the personality of Comte, but Barreda, Bichat, Laffitte, and Mill as well. These sessions were usually characterized by an invocation, chamber music, readings of literary and poetic works, and at least one major discourse in honor of the person being eulogized.

Typical of these meetings were the solemn services in honor of John Stuart Mill in 1906 and of Comte in 1908 by the Positivist Society. The eulogies for Mill were held by the Positivist Society in conjunction with the National Law School. On May 19 the Society met at the house of the director of the Preparatory School, Don José Terrés. The meeting opened with a violin quartet from Weber. Then Agustín Aragón delivered a major discourse in honor of Mill, followed by two musical works, one by Mozart and the other a piece for the piano written by Weber. After the music an unknown member read a eulogy of Mill written by the Englishman, John Morley. After another selection from Mozart, a poem was read in honor of Mill. The meeting finally closed with a Mozart quintet written for clarinet and violin. On the next day another session took place at the School of Jurisprudence in which Aragón was again featured, this time in the company of Antonio Caso and Beethoven. This program had been arranged by Miguel Macedo and the president of Mexico, Porfirio Díaz, was in attendance and had, of course, the seat of honor.[19]

The eulogy for Comte was similar to that of Mill, except that in 1908 Horacio Barreda had replaced Aragón and Schubert's music with that of Mozart and Weber. This session was opened with an invocation delivered by Horacio Barreda. A major part of Barreda's invocation was taken from Comte's *Catechism*. In this invocation Barreda declared that a group of Humanity's servants had come together in the name of the past and the present in order to realize their providential end, that of instituting the true intellectual and moral realm of Humanity. With more music and more "humble discourses" in honor of Comte's immortality, the meeting closed with a scherzo from Schubert.[20] The intellectual atmosphere and prim piety of this session and others, not unlike a group of Unitarian ministers meeting at Gethsemane in order to debate whether or not Jesus was praying to himself, was obviously too cold a climate for the majority of Mexico's Catholic people.

In addition to the formal activities of the Society, Aragón and Parra were active in promoting positivism through personal pursuits. These men were responsible for the successful fund raising drive of the late 1890's which provided a Mexican contribution for the building of a statute of Comte in Paris. According to Aragón, Mexico was responsible for a contribution which covered one fourth of the total cost of erection. This was considered by Aragón to be ample testimony of the impact of positivist ideas in Mexico.[21] Speaking in honor of Comte on two occasions in Paris, the first in 1902 and the second in 1907, Aragón testified that not only was Comte's dream of positivist education realized only in Mexico, but that the successes of Mexican positivism were vindicated by the great esteem in which both Comte and Barreda were held in Mexico.[22] Prior to 1908 Aragón had been certain that his missionary program of positivist diffusion would eventually be successful. His optimism had been aided by the fact that his efforts, along with those of López de Llergo, were rewarded by legislation in 1907 authorizing the erection of a statue in honor of Barreda.[23]

Not only were the Mexican positivists concerned with maintaining a working relationship with the Laffitte and Harrison branches of European positivism, but they were also active in promoting positivism throughout the Americas. As early as 1902 the Positivist Society of Mexico had allied itself with the *Sociedad Positivist a de Centro-América*. The latter Society, founded in Guatemala, merged its efforts with Mexican positivists in order to realize their ultimate ideal of a common American community in Humanity.[24] And although there was no significant positivist organization in the United States with which the Mexicans could ally themselves, the *Revista Positiva* was more than willing to feature articles by William G. Sumner (not, by the way, those on Social Darwinism but rather his critiques of imperialism) and to identify Andrew Carnegie's "gospel of wealth" with Comte's theory of altruism.[25]

The positivists of Mexico after 1900, like Barreda in 1867, were concerned with the primary role of eduction in the diffusion of their ideas. Both informal and formal means were employed in this process. From 1899 to 1901 a public lecture series was instituted in Mexico City to teach adults and those untouched by the public school system the philosophy of Comte and Laffitte. By 1903 Aragón had established seminary study of positivist doctrines in Zacatecas. These scholarly conferences were under the direction of José Manuel Villa and were held in the *Teatro Calderón*.[26] Earlier, in 1902, Aragón was able to report the successful initiation of a positivist curriculum in the Michoacán School of Law.[27] And if Aragón's testimony is correct, that positivist curriculum was still intact by 1907.[28] The following year Aragón had not only opened a new lecture series in Mexico City, but was active in promoting the translation of Laffitte's works from French to Spanish.[29]

The traditional question of the nature of logic to be taught in the public schools was still an issue to the positivists of the 1900's. For Aragón, like Barreda, the primacy of logic was essential for any scientific education. Logic, especially inductive logic, was considered to be the essence of the scientific approach to knowledge. And an understanding of logic could not be achieved without a thorough grounding in the sciences, i.e., the deductive method of mathematics, the induction of physics, and the comparative method of sociology. In other words, logic and science were interdependent studies.[30] For these reasons Aragón and other positivists constantly promoted the use of Alexander Bain's text of empirical logic both in the National Preparatory Schools and the institutes of Toluca and Zacatecas.[31]

Both Aragón and Parra were in very good positions to promote the use of the latter's text at the National Preparatory School. Parra's text was entitled *Nuevo sistema de lógica inductiva y deductiva* and was published after 1902. Aragón not only had many associates at the Preparatory School, but he was also able to give the text highly favorable publicity through his speeches and writings, most of which appeared in the *Revista Positiva*. This journal constantly promoted Parra's text as being in the best of empirical traditions, and in this respect, as valid as Bain and Mill.[32] Not only was Parra's examination of the syllogism supposed to be more sophisticated than Mill's, but Parra was believed to have analyzed inductive logic with a greater intensity.[33] Parra himself had not only been a teacher of logic at the Preparatory School, but after 1902 he became secretary of the Superior Council of Education and in that capacity was able to make educational recommendations to the public schools.[34]

Yet when Parra's text is compared with Gabino Barreda's earlier work of logic, *Examen del cálculo infinitesimal bajo el punto de vista lógico*, it becomes obvious that Parra, probably because of his orthodox positivist position, had abandoned Barreda's objective and descriptive style for the more normative approach in which the dogma of science and scientific methodology was being promoted. No longer was the role of logic content with examining the operations of the scientific method, but rather Parra's logic was nothing other than a listing of rules, dogmatic in tone, stating what the operations of science *ought* to be.[35]

The Mexican positivists were not overtly active in the political arena. Many times, especially after 1910, they were often apologetic in mood, attempting to disassociate themselves from those conditions which made for the revolution and assuring their audiences that positivism was a true heir of liberalism. Yet it was in this last respect that positivism made a genuine contribution to the political traditions of Mexico. Like Barreda, *La Libertad*, and the científicos, orthodox positivism redefined traditional liberalism away from the earlier atomistic emphasis upon the individual towards an organic definition of state. Thus the transformation of liberalism which Barreda began was made more complete by the later positivists.[36]

All of the later positivists were willing to associate themselves with what they called the liberal tradition of Juárez. Yet their idolization of Juárez was due to one fact, i.e., his relationship with Barreda. Both Aragón and Parra lauded Juárez because it was he, Juárez, who secured the evolutionary progress of Mexico by promoting scientific education through Barreda.[37] The liberal tradition was defined around Barreda, and Barreda was in that mainstream of Mexican liberalism that included Cuauhtemoc, Hidalgo, Morelos, Juárez, and Porfirio Díaz.[38] Yet the liberalism of which they spoke was of a different sort than the traditional type. This was a liberal tradition which was enriched and made more "progressive" by Barreda. Sabino M. Olea waxed poetic on this point, noting that in 1907 Mexico no longer needed bayonets, but laws; not egoism but altruism; not guerrilla fighters but scientists. In fact, for Olea, liberalism meant scientific liberalism and as such he equated it with political order.[39] Thus the positivist emphasis upon an organic State correlated to the rise of powerful centralized government in an industrial age.

Another positivist who reinforced the Barreda tradition through his writings was the son of Gabino Barreda, Horacio Barreda. In several essays written in 1908 he attempted to defend his father's reforms at the National Preparatory School.[40] In answer to the Catholic and liberal critics of his day, Horacio Barreda attempted to demonstrate the constitutionality of his father's educational changes of Mexico's public school system. Although he originally asserted that these reforms were in harmony with the Constitution of 1857 and the ideals of the reforma, he went further to accept and develop the organic theory of liberalism. He held that the "liberty" of the Constitution was in agreement with the thesis of positivism, i.e., an orderly and limited liberty. While conscience may be free in the individual areas (such as theology or metaphysics), this type of freedom would only lead to anarchy in the social realm. The founders of the Constitution, Horacio asserted, would never create a type of liberty that would lead to chaos and therefore defeat their own ends. The mission of government was nothing other than to reconcile individual independence within a context of social order. And in the realm of thought, positivist education was necessary to eliminate the spiritual and mental forms of anarchy. Justice could not be considered as an unchanging abstraction. For Horacio "progressive" justice implied responsibility: a type of justice that made human behavior responsible to the conditions of order. Thus not only did Horacio Barreda aid in the general redefinition of liberalism, but he went further to assert that the Constitution of 1857 was in itself a corporate and organic document.

Whether or not it can be demonstrated that positivism affected the course of Mexican liberalism, it can be stated that at least a few individuals outside of the positivist clique proper did adhere to the position that positivism, more than any other intellectual "current," directly influenced the political conditions of Mexico. In a speech delivered by Pedro González to the National Committee of the Universal Scientific Alliance in 1910, on an occasion celebrating the centennial of Mexican independence, Comte's philosophy was declared to be the major revolutionary force of recent Mexican history. And the revolution of which González spoke was not only an intellectual revolution. Positivism had literally transformed Mexico's political life, the major characteristic of this transformation being the "extension of the powers of the State." For González, positivism had redefined liberalism, but he, like many Mexicans immediately prior to the Revolution, was uncertain whether this change had been a "positive" good or bad.[41]

At that same conference, Agustín Aragón reaffirmed his faith in positivism as the only ideological solution for the present and future problems of Latin America. And even though he had publicly admitted at an earlier date that the diffusion of positivism in Mexico was very limited and suffered from a lack of "real" influence,[42] he still insisted that positivism was the best hope for the social and political future of Mexico. Aragón believed that the most important problem facing Latin America's future was the incorporation of the Indian into society. For Aragón, nothing from Comte's system was more important than the positivist concern with the problem of the alienated proletariat. And the proletariat of Latin America, at least for Aragón, was the Indian. Another problem confronting Latin America was its political chaos. Only, asserted Aragón, by following Lafitte's maxim "that man ought to be, above everything, a citizen," could Latin America solve her political problems. Aragón's mood in this year, pessimistic about past successes, hopeful for the future of positivism, was to follow him throughout the chaotic years of the revolution.[43] That hope was based upon his sincere and even religious convictions embodied in a Religion of Humanity.

In the period from 1910 to 1913, Aragón attempted to adjust his positivist faith to the new social problems created by the disruption caused by revolution. When the Madero government came to power, he cautioned its leadership that to be successful its administration would have to be originally based on and derived from society.[44] Writing in 1911, he argued that in these days of revolution, only the principles of positivism and the Religion of Humanity could provide the necessary doctrines that would place in harmony the two contrasting trends of order and progress.[45] As an evolutionist, he was not able to accept in total the principal of revolution. Yet by 1912 he admitted that some revolutions, including the Mexican one, were inevitable. Yet he was saddened by the prospect and faithfully asserted that if all people would only practice the Religion of Humanity there would be no need for revolution.[46] By 1913 he had accepted many of the revolutionaries' goals, or at least the justice of their grievances, and had disassociated Mexican positivism from any past connections with the Díaz government. Díaz, Aragón said, had actively opposed positivism. And if the Díaz government had lived up to positivist desires the *Revista* would have been the first to defend his government against the charges of the revolutionaries. Nothing other than an abandonment of positivism by Mexico accounted for revolutionary sorrows.[47]

Because of the force of revolution and the economic dislocations of 1914, the *Revista* was forced to cease publication. But in this last year of life the positivist organ wholeheartedly threw its support behind the revolution and against the Díaz tradition. The Díaz government, Aragón said, was based upon the principle of militarism and as such was opposed to the principles of republican institutions. His government had been beneficial only to those who were dedicated to the making of money.[48] Justice and liberty should be the common property of everyone. Therefore the Mexican people were justified in overthrowing the tyranny of Díaz.[49] Not only did Aragón join the liberals in their accusations against Díaz, but he went further to assert that the new reordering of society which the Revolution was realizing would usher in the age of the Religion of Humanity.[50] In the last statement that Aragón published in the *Revista* he still idealistically, and perhaps naively, held to his faith in positivism for Mexico,[51] but for all practical purposes his small group of rational believers had been swallowed up in the tide of Revolution.

Yet if the chaos of the early twentieth century disrupted the formal structure of Aragon's movement, much of the content remained. Aragón himself continued to write until his death in 1954; and, although it is difficult to measure the impact of Mexico's experiment in secular religion upon the thinking of contemporary Mexicans, certain tentative observations can be suggested.

Mexico's current push towards modernization and industrialization has been accompanied by an ideology of technocracy and faith in science. The last fifty years of Mexico's history have witnessed a scientific revolution in which Mexican theorists and educators have participated. This revolution has been broadly based, embracing such areas as atomic theory, relativity, quantitative physics, biochemistry, astronomy, and cybernetics.[52] A way of thinking that shares many of the premises of a Religion of Humanity is the almost inevitable by-product of such a revolution.

The intellectual milieu of Don Porfirio's Mexico is still apparent today. Ideas of linear progress, the positive state, liberalism, atomism, technocracy, and scientism do have their defenders. Secular religion of the Comtean mold is no longer existent, but a more diffuse type of religious and scientific humanism remains. It is part of the modern mood of Mexico.

NOTES

1. Between 1830 and 1842 Comte published a series of public lectures that were designed to acquaint men of science with the "positive philosophy." These lectures, representing Comte's philosophy of science, were collectively entitled *Course in Positive Philosophy* and appeared in six volumes. His Religion of Humanity can be found in several works, including the four-volume *Positive Polity* (1851–54), *Positive Catechism* (1854), and *Subjective Synthesis or Universal System of Ideas Concerning the Normal State of Humanity* (1856). An informative and critical account of the Religion of Humanity can be found in John Stuart Mill, *Auguste Comte and Positivism* (Ann Arbor: University of Michigan Press, 1961), pp. 125–200. For a brief treatment of Comte's general philosophy see Leszek Kolakowski, *The Alienation of Reason: A History of Positivist Thought* (Garden City, N.Y.: Doubleday & Co., 1968), pp. 47–72.

2. See both Walter M. Simon, *European Positivism in the Nineteenth Century* (Ithaca: Cornell University Press, 1963) and João Cruz Costa, *A History of Ideas in Brazil*, trans. Suzette Macedo (Berkeley and Los Angeles: University of California Press, 1964), pp. 82–175. For reproductions of letters written by Brazilian positivists see Ivan Lins, "Primeriors contactos brasileiros com Augusto Comte," *Revista Brasileira de Filosofia*, 2 (January–March 1952): 77–83.

3. This does not imply that Barreda was formally a member of any

corporate group of Littréists, or that he was unaware of or unsympathetic to Laffitte. It only means that his own temperament and interests were more akin to those of Littré than of Laffitte. Moisés González Navarro has demonstrated that Barreda only met Comte through the good offices of Laffitte's companion and friend, Pedro Contreras Elizalde. González Navarro also notes that Barreda planned a series of conferences aimed especially at Mexican women, in order to teach them the lessons of Humanity. In this role Barreda would be acting in a manner consistent with Comte's teachings concerning the duties of positivist priests. See González Navarro, "Los positivistas mexicanos en Francia," *Historia mexicana*, 9 (July–September 1959): 119–29.

4. For biographical data on Aragón, see Miguel Angel Peral, *Diccionario biográfico mexicano* (Mexico: Editorial P.A.C., n.d.), p. 59. Pierre Laffitte tells of Aragón's conversion in an introduction to Aragón's history of positivism entitled *Essai sur l'histoire du positivisme au Mexique* (Mexico and Paris: Chez l'Auteur, 1898), pp. vii–xii.

5. The two most important works by Zea on positivism in Mexico are *El positivismo en México* (Mexico: El Colegio de México, 1943) and *Apogeo y decadencia del positivismo en México* (Mexico: El Colegio de México, 1944). For my own critique of Zea's thought and writings, see William Raat, "Leopoldo Zea and Mexican Positivism: a Reappraisal," *Hispanic American Historical Review* 48 (February 1968): 1–18.

6. Aragon, *Essai*, p. 46.

7. González Navarro, "Los positivistas mexicanos en Francia," 123–25.

8. The *Revista Positiva* is not only a primary source for the ideology of orthodox Mexican positivism, but also an important guide to the activities of the Positivist Society of Mexico as well. The original magazine can be found in the Nettie Lee Benson Latin American Collection of the University of Texas at Austin. See *Revista Positiva: filosófica, literaria, social y política*, 14 vols. (Mexico: 1901–14). Hereafter *Revista Positiva* will be cited as *RP*.

9. E. S. Beesly, "Lo esencial en el positivismo," *RP* 1 (December 1901): 502–6. Beesly's outline has also been reproduced by Elí de Gortari, *La ciencia en la historia de México* (Mexico and Buenos Aires: Fondo de Cultura Económica, 1963), p. 307.

10. Aragón, "El positivismo," *RP* 5 (January 1905): 90–92.

11. Aragón, "El Sr. Dr. Don Gabino Barreda," *RP* 6 (April 1906): 240–42.

12. See both Lagarrigue, "La Religión de la Humanidid," *RP* 2 (July 1902): 209–302, and Lagarrigue, "Lo sobrenatural ante el positivismo," *RP* 7 (October 1907): 617–47.

13. Lagarrigue, "La Religión de la Humanidad," p. 222.

14. Ibid., pp. 217–24.

15. Ibid., pp. 252–54.

16. Porfirio Parra, "Oración leída en conmemoración de Augusto Comte," *RP* 2 (October 1902): 424–34.

17. The Spanish translation of the positivist Calendar has been fully reproduced in *RP* 2 (1 July 1902): 303–15.

18. For a discussion of the positivist Calendar, see both Frederic Harrison, "Nuevo calendario de los grandes hombres," *RP* 3 (1 January 1903): 7–12, and Aragón, "El calendario positivista," *RP* 14 (January 1914): 26–30.

19. Aragón, "El centenario de John Stuart Mill en México," *RP* 6 (May 1906): 315–17.

20. Horacio Barreda, "Oración en honor de Augusto Comte," *RP* 8 (October 1908): 581–98.

21. Aragón, "Párrafos," *RP* 7 (April 1907): 344.

22. Aragón, "Inauguración de la estatua de Augusto Comte en París," *RP* 2 (August 1902): 352–55; Aragón, "Discurso . . . celebrado en París, en representación de los positivistas mexicanos," *RP* 7 (November 1907): 711–16.

23. Reproductions of the legislation of the Chamber of Deputies and the Senate concerning the authorization of Barreda's statute can be found in López de Llergo, "Monumento al Dr. D. Gabino Barreda," *RP* 7 (June 1907): 469–76.

24. Aragón, "La Sociedad Positivista de Centro-America," *RP* 2 (December 1902): 522–24.

25. See both William G. Sumner, "La conquista de los Estados Unidos por España," *RP* 2 (1 January 1902): 1–29, and Aragón, "Párrafos," *RP* 3 (May 1903): 278.

26. Aragón, "El positivismo en Zacatecas," *RP* 3 (November 1903): 515–19.

27. Aragón, "Párrafos," *RP* 2 (August 1902): 376.

28. Ibid., 7 (29 January 1907): 133–34.

29. Ibid., 8 (1 January 1908): 21–22.

30. Aragón, "El estudio de la lógica," *RP* 6 (29 January 1906): 80–82.

31. Aragón, "El Dr. Alejando Bain," *RP* 3 (November 1903): 481–87.

32. See Aragón, "Nuevo sistema de lógica," *RP* 2 (December 1902): 514–16) idem, "El Sr. Dr. D. Porfirio Parra," *RP* 12 (September 1912): 433–46.

33. Aragón, "Una grande obra mexicana de filosofía," *RP* 4 (March 1904): 271–94.

34. Aragón, "Párrafos," *RP* 2 (August 1902): 375–76.

35. Gortari, *La ciencia*, 311–13.

36. An excellent study of the continuity of nineteenth-century liberalism can be found in Charles A. Hale, "José María Luis Mora and the Structure of Mexican Liberalism," *Hispanic American Historical Review* 45 (May 1965): 196–227.

37. For the relationship of positivism to Juárez, see Parra, "Juárez," *RP* 1 (August 1901): 341–49; Aragón, "Juárez," *RP* 6 (March 1906): 191–99; Aragón, "Juárez: su obra y su tiempo," *RP* 6 (March 1906): 187–91.

38. Aragón, "Discurso . . . celebrado en París," *RP* 7 (November 1907): 711.

39. Sabino M. Olea, "La constitución mexicana," *RP* 7 (February 1907): 221–26.

40. Horacio Barreda, "La Escuela Nacional Preparatoria," *RP* 8 (April, May, June, and July 1908): 232–86, 305–381, 385–437, 449–506, respectively.

41. Pedro González, "El desarrollo de las ideas científicas y su influencia social y política," in *Concurso Científico y Artístico del Centenario* (Mexico: Tip. de la Viuda de F. Díaz de León, Sucs., 1911), pp. 10–13.

42. Aragón, "Párrafos," *RP* 8 (1 January 1908): 22.

43. Aragón, "La obra civilizadora de México y de las demas naciones de la

América Latina," in *Concurso Científico y Artístico del Centenario*, pp. 31–32.

44. Aragón, "Notas politicas," *RP* 11 (December 1911): 637–39.
45. Ibid., 11 (September 1911): 540–43.
46. "La *Revista positiva*," *RP* 12 (1 January 1912): 44–47.
47. Ibid., 13 (1 January 1913): 41–45.
48. "Notas políticas," *RP*, 14 (March 1914): 140–43.
49. Ibid., 14 (August 1914): 408–13.
50. Ibid., 14 (January 1914): 17–24.
51. "A los lectores de la *Revista positiva*," *RP* 14 (December 1914): 517–22.
52. Gortari, *La ciencia en la historia*, p. 338.

RAILROADS, LANDHOLDING, AND AGRARIAN PROTEST

John Coatsworth

John Coatsworth, an associate professor of history at the University of Chicago, is a specialist on the economic history of the Porfiriato. He has written a two-volume study on the railroads in Mexico, entitled El impacto económico de los ferrocarriles en el Porfiriato. *In the following essay Coatsworth reviews the research on agrarian conflict in the nineteenth century and suggests that most of the Indian communities of central Mexico managed to retain their lands until sometime after 1876. His analysis of fifty-five incidents of rural protest and rebellion between 1877 and 1884 indicates a connection between these incidents and actual or projected railroad routes. In other words, Porfirian economic development led to land-grabbing, an increase in the size and numbers of private estates, a decline in Indian communal properties, an alienation of public lands, and increasing agrarian protest and rebellion.*

UNDER CONDITIONS OF rigid social and political hierarchy, and especially where rural cultivators form a distinct and subordinate ethnic group, marked improvement in the profitability of agricultural enterprise tends to be associated with regressive movements in the distribution of property (land, livestock, implements, and the like) as well as direct assaults on the political liberties and other rights of peasants. While there has been some recognition that such a process accompanied the large scale penetration of foreign capital and technology into much of Indo-Latin America in the last decades of the nineteenth century, the process has not received the attention it deserves.[1]

Perhaps the most visible and costly byproduct of nineteenth-

From John H. Coatsworth, "Railroads, Landholding, and Agrarian Protest in the Early *Porfiriato*" (*Hispanic American Historical Review* 54:48–71). Reprinted by permission of the publisher. Copyright 1974, Duke University Press (Durham, N.C.).

century foreign intrusion were the railroads. Hundreds, even thousands, of miles of railroads often were built even before substantial direct investments were made in other kinds of enterprise. In fact railroads accounted for more than half of all British and United States investments in Latin America until well after the turn of the century.[2]

The close relationship between transport innovation and export sector development has been very evident to historians.[3] However, much less is known of the impact of railroads on agrarian conditions except where the new transport system formed part of the agricultural export system. Yet railroads often induced profound transformations in more or less traditional patterns of rural social and economic life, even where agricultural exports did not predominate.

In the mountainous plateaus of Indo-Latin America particularly, railroads radically altered supply and demand schedules for agricultural products.[4] By reducing transport costs dramatically and by connecting distant (domestic and international) markets with previously isolated rural areas, railroads made landowning more profitable than ever before.[5] Of course, some landowners were disadvantaged when the location of transport facilities favored competitors or when the natural protection of local markets disappeared. A simultaneous process of integration and marginalization occurred, with some regions adjusting to new opportunities while others declined into more or less permanent backwaters. In either case, transport innovation was the cause of important shifts in crop structure, estate management, labor arrangements, land tenure patterns and rural welfare. Rural populations shared few of the benefits of this modernization and frequently suffered as a result. Often the only benefit the railroad brought was increased mobility, the opportunity to escape the railroad's effects on rural social life.

It is the purpose of this paper to explore one aspect of this process in nineteenth-century Mexico, namely the link between railroad construction and the new concentration of landownership in the early Porfiriato. The argument is advanced that railroad construction between 1877 and 1884 was closely linked to widespread assaults on the property holdings of Indian free villages. Evidence is also introduced to suggest a possible link between transport innovation and the wholesale alienation of public domain associated with this period.

The hypothesis explored here is not entirely new. A half century ago, George McBride suggested that the effect of nineteenth-century railroad development in Mexico, as in the United States, was "to increase the value of lands already under cultivation rather than to relieve the demand by opening up new areas of development. Hence real estate now became of great prospective value. As a consequence, there followed an era of land grabbing."[6] The land-grabbing, according to McBride, included seizure of communal property from Indian villages as well as more "speculative" acquisition of public domain in the sparsely settled North and South. McBride did not pursue this concept further, and it does not appear to have been repeated in any subsequent accounts of Mexico's nineteenth-century land systems.

To both Mexican and foreign entrepreneurs, the construction of railroads presented very real opportunities for personal advantage. As railroads reached productive areas formerly isolated or poorly connected to external markets, land values and production possibilities increased markedly.[7] To maximize appropriation of these external benefits of railroads, entrepreneurs had to anticipate railroad construction and move quickly to secure additional property in the path of new lines. For such land acquisition to be fully profitable, the new properties had to be acquired at something near the prevailing prerailroad prices. Two methods were in fact employed to gain control of additional lands. The first method, usurpation, sometimes involved the Reform Laws which required alienation of Indian communal landholdings and the distribution of such lands in individual parcels. Once the formerly inalienable property had been distributed, the individual holdings were acquired at relatively low cost through artful combinations of legal sale and illegal acquisition.[8] The second method involved purchase from the government at a low fixed price of "vacant" public lands. Both of these methods required permissive legislation and sympathetic intervention of public authorities, but neither can be explained on legal or political grounds alone.

The first eight years of the Porfirian era (1877–1884) provide the focus of this investigation for two reasons. First, these years witnessed a marked increase both in assaults on Indian communal landholding and in sales of public domain (the so-called *terrenos baldíos*).[9] Historians have usually attributed this phenomenon to the application of Liberal land laws and to the social bias, economic goals and military capacity of the Porfirian regime.[10] However, application of the Reform laws seems to account for only a small portion of early Porfirian concentration of landownership, while the characteristics of the Porfirian regime usually advanced to explain the phenomenon did not become evident until the process was well under way. Second, the

effects of the worldwide depression of the mid-1880s, and other factors affecting "commercialization" and land tenure patterns thereafter
make it more difficult to isolate a specific railroad impetus to land-
grabbing after 1884.[11] While the distribution of public domain continued to increase *after* the period studied here, agrarian protests as
well as railroad concessions (and mileage constructed) reached a peak
in the late 1870s and early 1880s.

Reliable historical statistics on land tenure patterns in Mexico do
not exist.[12] Historians therefore have had to rely on a confusing and
often contradictory array of qualitative evidence from which to make
judgements about the timing, location, magnitude and direction of
changes in the agrarian system. The most ample body of qualitative
evidence used for this purpose is that produced by conflict between
the opposing land hunger of *hacendado* and Indian villager. Despite
the pioneering work of a few scholars, including Jean Meyer most
recently, considerable basic research on this important topic remains
to be done.[13] What follows is a tentative discussion of some of the
known characteristics of this conflict as it evolved in the period between Independence and the *Porfiriato*. In the process two possible
viewpoints are challenged: (1) that rural violence was usually, or even
frequently caused by the usurpation of village lands before the
Porfiriato, and (2) that application of the Reform laws between 1856
and the late 1870s resulted in widespread destruction of Indian communal landholding.[14]

Conflict between Indian villager and *hacendado* took many forms.
Evidence from early in the Colonial period demonstrates the capacity
or tendency of villagers for prolonged litigation over real estate, water
rights, pasturage, and the like.[15] Petitions to officials, including the
Viceroy, apparently were not unusual.[16] There is little evidence of
land seizures or occupations by villagers until after Independence.
Violence was endemic on the northern frontier between colonists and
nomadic tribes, but much less common in the Center and South.[17]
Much of the violence which did occur pitted Spanish authority against
Indian groups which had never been successfully integrated into the
colonial social and economic structure.

After Independence, the locus of rural violence shifted steadily to
the Center and South. While Indian warfare continued sporadically in
the far North, widespread violence erupted repeatedly within Mexican society in the Center of the Republic as well as throughout the less
assimilated regions of the extreme South and Yucatán.[18] From the

Hidalgo revolt to the Porfirian coup d'etat, agrarian violence appears to have been roughly correlated with periods of political instability. According to Meyer's "Chronology," Indian disturbances clustered in the years 1844, 1849, 1856–57, 1869, 1873 and 1877.[19] In some cases, Indian villagers capitalized on the political struggles which preoccupied mestizo and criollo elites and resulted in the breakdown of local and national authority. In others, disturbances and revolts appear to have been deliberately mobilized, or at least encouraged and manipulated, by parties to national political disputes.[20]

The evidence which has been uncovered on the nature of agrarian disturbances suggests that until the late 1870s most of them did not erupt in response to usurpations of village lands by the haciendas. Instead, the little research which has been done suggests that (1) where land was an issue, it usually involved Indians seizing hacienda lands rather than the reverse; (2) where land was not clearly an issue, the uprising often appears attributable more to the behavior of politicians rather than of *hacendados* directly; and (3) where Indian disturbances appeared based on political or religious issues, agrarian complaints were sometimes voiced, but almost always in general terms.[21]

Whatever the immediate cause of the Indian uprising, the "restoration" of village lands, or legislation granting land to the villages, was usually included among the rallying slogans and avowed objectives. Accusations of usurpation are frequently encountered, but seldom is any distinction made between the usurpation of lands which recently had belonged to the villages and "usurpations" perpetrated in the distant past. In most cases for which any evidence has been adduced, charges of usurpation involved lands that the Indians used or coveted and to which they believed themselves morally entitled, but which they never had legally owned or could claim to have owned only "long ago."[22]

It is my belief that until the late 1870s Mexico's political instability together with the miserable state of the economy inhibited wholesale absorption of village lands by the haciendas. True, ownership of estates could confer social status and probably involved less risk than investments in trade, industry or finance. It also provided access to Church credit at a low fixed rate of interest. Nonetheless, it is not certain that latifundist agriculture had been highly profitable even before economic and political conditions deteriorated after 1810.[23] Hacienda ownership may then have become even less stable than it had been in colonial times. Indeed, there is some basis to suggest that the landed estate may have been contracting, rather than expanding, during the first half century of Independence. The *Hacienda de Cojumatlan*, for example, was subdivided in 1861 and sold to *arrendatarios* in the municipality of San José de Gracia (Michoacán) because the owner could apparently find no one to rent the whole estate for the customary $4,700 per year.[24]

Long before passage of the Reform Laws, a number of states passed legislation requiring the breaking up of communal property holdings. Only rarely was the legislation enforced.[25] Encroachment on village lands probably did take place, in a variety of forms, but what evidence exists does not suggest that this encroachment was widespread, systematic, or increasing in frequency.[26] Jean Meyer is certainly right in stating that "the Reform law of 1856 appears at the end of a long process more than at the inauguration of a new one."[27]

The Reform Laws did make alienation and division of communal lands a matter of *national* policy. But evidence concerning enforcement is needed before historians can accept the assumption that widespread destruction of communities occurred. In the Central District of Oaxaca, Charles Berry found prospective buyers reluctant to purchase disamortized real estate because of the region's unsettled political and military conditions after 1857.[28] Village lands were disamortized and sold, but at least in this part of Oaxaca Berry concluded that they were sold "freely," by delegations of villagers who appeared before the authorities "to state that in a village meeting, a decision had been reached to sell the lands as required by law."[29] Implementation of the Reform Laws to favor the haciendas against the villages depended both on official capacity and private initiative. In most of Mexico, not just Oaxaca, neither condition existed to a sufficient degree to render this assumption plausible, at least not until the *Porfiriato*. Until more research has been carried out, McBride's conclusion that by 1876 "few [Indian] communities had . . . been broken up" should stand.[30]

The first three years of Porfirian rule probably witnessed the most widespread agrarian disturbances in nineteenth-century Mexico. Agrarian rebellions began or erupted anew in at least fourteen states and the Federal District between 1877 and 1879. Many occurred in areas which had previously experienced such conflict. In nearly every case, the new military regime and its local authorities proved capable of suppressing the rebels. During the presidency of Manuel González, agrarian conditions slowly stabilized again.[31]

A survey of contemporary newspaper accounts in the capital and a quantity of published material produced a list of fifty-five incidents of agrarian protest between 1877 and 1884, ranging from attempts to institute law suits on behalf of villages to uprisings which required federal troops to suppress. Nearly all of the incidents involved alleged usurpations of village lands and most of the usurpations referred to had only just occurred. To test the hypothesis of a significant link between railroad construction and usurpation of village lands, the location of each of the fifty-five incidents was plotted on a map of the actual and *projected* railroad network in each year. The results are suggestive. Of the fifty-five incidents reported, only five (9.1 percent) took place more than 40 kilometers from a railway line or the route of a projected railroad for which the federal government's concession was still active. Nearly 60 percent (thirty-two of the fifty-five) of the incidents took place within 20 kilometers of an actual or projected rail line. Most of the incidents took place some time before the actual construction of the nearby rail line. Of the fifty incidents within 40 kilometers of a railroad route, twelve were reported after a concession had been issued, but before any construction had begun, while thirty-two occurred after construction had begun, but before the line had reached the immediate area. Two occurred in areas where the projected line was never built.

Despite obstacles to easy communication, there is no question that news of railroad concessions and even of the exact routes ran far ahead of actual construction. Landowners could read the texts of each concession in the *Diario Oficial*. Newspapers in the capital as well as those in the provinces reported fully on every detail of progress in construction and financing. State governors in 1876 and 1877 applied for local concessions and attempted to form private companies based on provincial as well as national and foreign capital to build newly authorized lines.[32] Lotteries were created in several states as a device to tap the income of the poorer classes for new railroads.[33] In San Luis Potosí, the state government issued new paper currency in 1878 in denominations of one centavo to five pesos which had to be used for payment of a special ten percent capitation tax surcharge imposed on all male citizens. New paper issues were printed in 1879 and 1880. The purpose of the tax was inscribed on each note: "*Ferrocarril de San Luis a Tampico.*"[34]

Of the fifty-five incidents, seven which took place in 1877 occurred along the route of a projected Mexico City to León railroad line, the concession for which had been issued in 1874 and revoked two years later. In this case, the concession was cancelled only after an initial survey for the route had been completed and a considerable sum of money had been spent on preparation and construction of the roadway. While seven of the incidents reported here took place after the revocation of the concession, the government had already indicated that it assigned a high priority to finding a new concessionaire, and Mexico City newspapers had optimistically expressed the view that the government would be successful. A number of promoters reportedly were seeking the concession, which was finally issued to the Mexican National Construction Company as part of its line from Mexico City to the northern border in late 1880.[35] Because of the special circumstances surrounding this line, the map for 1877 includes the México-León line, despite the revocation of that concession the previous year.

Of the fifty-five incidents, ten involved violent Indian uprisings, and another four reported attempts at reoccupation of hacienda lands by Indian villagers. The remaining forty-one cases involved various forms of peaceful protest ranging from petitions to President Díaz to "agitation" accompanying legal proceedings. Looked at from the other side, the protests alleged nineteen cases of physical dispossession by violence on the part of *hacendados*, and thirty-six cases of usurpation in which violence appears as terror tactics in the form of assassinations and kidnapping (four cases) or involves the use of state or federal troops to retake lands seized by Indians (twelve cases). In fifteen cases allegations of violence do not appear at all in the reports.

With the exception of cases involving railroad companies directly, all these conflicts over land engaged traditional antagonists. Conflicts between estate owners and villagers, as well as those between neighboring villages, occurred in the colonial era. Even conflicts with railroad companies have a familiar counterpart in disputes over the taking of village (or hacienda) lands by public authority exercising the right of eminent domain. Legal controversies over land form an important source of data for historians of colonial society. Invasions of haciendas by villagers and usurpations of village lands by *hacendados* became a familiar aspect of the Mexican rural scene long before railroad building and continued in many places long afterwards. This continuity in the nature of disputes over land, and in the social types who appear as opponents, has probably obscured significant shifts in the intensity, magnitude and spatial distribution of agrarian conflict. This has certainly been true for the early *Porfiriato*, although the extent of the shifts in this period cannot be measured with any precision until more systematic research is available for the pre-Porfirian era. At least as important as the changing *pattern* of conflict, however, was the changing *balance* of winners and losers. Here the evidence speaks more clearly. While the level and frequency of protest and conflict may be more symptomatic than explanatory of land tenure shifts, the villagers probably lost more, and more rapidly, during the *Porfiriato* than ever before.[36]

The process of usurpation and concentration of landowning was more widespread and continuous than the incidents of protest or the land sales data reveal. The peaceful transformation of Naranja, a Tarascan Indian village near Pátzcuaro, illustrates this quite well. In Paul Friedrich's account, the transformation begins when surveyors arrived in 1881 and discovered beneath the Zacapu swamp "a black soil of rare fertility."[37] In 1883, "two Spanish brothers named Noriega . . . managed to acquire the ancient legal titles through collusion with the mestizos of the village, notably the mayor. . . ." In 1886, the Noriegas "formed a commercial company with eight other Spanish and mestizo parties . . ." to drain the swamp. The Naranjeños did not resist the usurpation of their swamplands "mainly because they lacked competent leaders." By 1900, five haciendas, including the Zacapu Hacienda de Cantabria, surrounded the village, encroaching on its lands. "Thus," concludes Friedrich, "did the villagers pass through a classic sequence . . . Naranja had become a village of hired men and migrant plantation hands, a sort of rural semi-proletariat."[38]

The history of Naranja in this period can be read as a testimony to the greed and influence of Spanish outsiders and mestizo collaborators. But it can also be read as a response to North American investment in Mexican railroads. The surveyors arrived in Naranja less than a year after the Mexican government granted a railroad concession to the Mexican National Construction Company for a line through Pátzcuaro to Uruapan.[39] The Noriegas acquired title to the swamp in 1883, just after the National's line reached Acámbaro and work on the branch to Uruapan had begun. The commercial company was formed in 1886 just as the railroad reached Pátzcuaro.[40] By the time the swamp was drained, a small private railroad linked the Zacapu with Irapuato on the Mexican Central's main line to the north.[41] Until much more research is done, it will be impossible to know how many leaderless villages peacefully lost their lands to greedy outsiders seizing properties in anticipation of railroad construction. It is conceivable that Naranja's experience was repeated in countless local dramas throughout the Porfirian railroad era.

If the results of this study may be extended somewhat, they suggest that foreign enterprise in the form of major railroad construction projects significantly altered the shape and balance of Mexico's agrarian system in the last quarter of the nineteenth century. The *Porfiriato* saw a considerable expansion and consolidation of the hacienda at the expense of competing rural institutions, notably the Indian free village. Until further research brings new evidence to light, the full dimensions of this process are difficult to specify. Regional variations, consistent with variations in natural conditions, local agrarian institutions, and the penetration of new transport and industrial technologies may prove to have been quite complex. It does seem possible to conclude, however, that Mexico's developing international economic connections will provide a list of variables quite critical to explaining the evolution of agrarian institutions during the *Porfiriato*.

Some historians and social scientists, including Barrington Moore in a recent work, have stressed the importance of agrarian social change during periods of rapid "commercialization" at the beginning of the industrial era.[42] Some of the crucial parameters of institutional behavior in the contemporary period, it is argued, have their origins in these earlier agrarian transformations. The Mexican Revolution makes it impossible to draw lines as straight as those Moore seems able to identify through the modern history of several European and Asian nations. Still, the development of modern authoritarian political rule in Mexico may well be linked as much to the socially regressive commercialization of agriculture in the *Porfiriato* as to the defeat of the agrarian movements of the 1910s and 1920s.

In nineteenth-century Mexico, as perhaps was true in other parts of Latin America, many contemporary social and political institutions and behavior patterns developed at least in part through response to the penetration of foreign enterprise and technology. Nevertheless, billiard ball models of external dependence, in which discrete units of foreign influence bounce into equally self-contained Latin American economic, social and political variables, are not likely to prove useful in the analysis of the impact of modern imperialism. What can be assumed is that when the Mexican official of today greets the visiting North American entrepreneur, or casts him a suspicious glance, he is looking at his own history.

NOTES

1. Sidney W. Mintz describes a familiar case in the pre-railroad era in "Labor and Sugar in Puerto Rico and Jamaica, 1800–1850," in *Slavery in the New World: A Reader in Comparative History*, ed. Laura Foner and Eugene Genovese (Englewood Cliffs, N.J.: Prentice Hall, 1969), pp. 170–71. See Sanford Mosk, "Latin America and the World Economy, 1850–1914," *Inter-American Economic Affairs* 2 (Winter 1948): 53–82.

2. William Glade, *The Latin American Economies: A Study of Their Institutional Evolution* (New York: American Book, 1969), pp. 218–19, 221–22; Cleona Lewis, *America's Stake in International Investments* (Washington, D.C.: Brookings Institution, 1938), pp. 612–16.

3. Glade, *Latin American Economies*, pp. 265–66.

4. This may be inferred from a voluminous literature. For an estimate of social savings due to railroad freight services in Porfirian Mexico see John H. Coatsworth, "The Impact of Railroads on the Economic Development of Mexico, 1877–1910," (Ph.D. diss., University of Wisconsin, 1972), chap. 4.

5. Leopoldo Solis, *La realidad económica mexicana* (Mexico: Siglo XXI, 1970), pp. 54–55.

6. George McCutchen McBride, *The Land Systems of Mexico* (New York: American Geographical Society, 1923), p. 72.

7. On the connection between railroads and land values, opinion is unanimous even though systematic data are lacking. See Eugene Viollet, *Le problème de l'argent et l'étalon d'or au Mexique* (Paris: V. Giard y E. Briére, 1907), pp. 62–63; Fernando González Roa, *El problema ferrocarrilero y la Compañia de los Ferrocarriles Nacionales de México* (Mexico: Carranza e Hijos, 1915), pp. 75–88; Jesús Silva Herzog, *El agrarismo mexicano y la Reforma Agraria: exposición y crítica* (Mexico: Fondo de Cultura Económica, 1959), pp. 125–26.

8. Moisés González Navarro, "El Porifirato. La vida social" in *Historia moderna de México*, ed. Daniel Cosio Villegas, 10 vols. (Mexico: Editorial Hermes, 1955–72), 5:187–216.

9. See Coatsworth, "Railroads, Landholding, and Agrarian Protest in the Early *Porfiriato*," *Hispanic American Historical Review* 54 (February 1974): 67–68.

10. McBride, *Land Systems*, pp. 133–36; José Valadés, *El porfirismo: historia de un régimen (1877–1884)*, 2 vols. (Mexico: José Porrúa e Hijos, 1941) 1:237–60.

11. After the recession of the mid-1880s a number of factors related only indirectly to the railroad diffused the incentives to acquire rural properties so that the pattern of concentration of landownership became somewhat more complex. These factors included the depreciation of the nation's silver cur-

rency, a high rate of inflation, changes in the prices of agricultural output due to world market conditions, land acquisition for speculative purposes or mineral surveys, the entry of considerable foreign capital into the land market, the development of new urban centers linked to expanding export production, and the like.

12. A useful summary of the existing data and their limitations is Moisés González Navarro, "Tenencia de la tierra y población agrícola, 1877–1960," in *México: El capitalismo nacionalista* (Mexico: B. Costa-Amic, 1970), pp. 273–95.

13. Jean Meyer, *Problemas campesinos y revueltas agrarias, 1821–1910* (Mexico: SepSetentas, 1973).

14. Ibid., pp. 28–32; Donald J. Fraser, "La política de desamortización en las comunidades indígenas, 1856–1872," *Historia mexicana* 18 (April–June 1972): 615–52.

15. E.g., William B. Taylor, *Landlord and Peasant in Colonial Oaxaca* (Stanford, Calif.: Stanford University Press, 1972), pp. 89–109.

16. Enrique Semo, *Historia del capitalismo en México: Los orígenes, 1521–1763* (Mexico: Ediciones Era, 1973), p. 79.

17. Silvio Zavala and José Miranda, "Instituciones indígenas en la Colonia," in *Métodos y resultados de la política indigenista en México*, Memorias del Instituto Nacional Indigenista, 6 (1954): 82. On the Yucatecan peninsula, however, conflicts similar to those in the far North occurred during the colonial period.

18. Meyer, *Problemas*, pp. 8–16.

19. Ibid.

20. Ibid., pp. 8–25; Moisés González Navarro, "Instituciones indígenas en México independiente," in *Métodos y resultados de la política indigenista en México*, Memorias del Instituto Nacional Indigenista, 6 (1954): 147–49.

21. In addition to sources cited in n. 20, see T. G. Powell, "Liberalism and the Peasantry in Central Mexico, 1850–1876" (Ph.D. diss., University of Indiana, 1972), passim. Roland Mousnier suggests an interesting comparison with nineteenth-century Mexico in *Peasant Uprisings in Seventeenth Century France, Russia and China*, trans. Brian Pearce (New York: Harper & Row, 1970).

22. David Brading, *Miners and merchants in Bourbon Mexico* (Cambridge: Cambridge University Press, 1971), pp. 215–19.

24. Luis González, *Pueblo en vilo: microhistoria de San José de Gracia* (Mexico: El Colegio de Mexico, 1968), pp. 91–100. David Brading speaks of a "perceptible trend toward subdivision of some haciendas which operated in the years before the Reform," in "Creole Nationalism and Mexican Liberalism," *Journal of Inter-American Studies and World Affairs* 15 (May 1973): 148.

25. Meyer, *Problemas*, pp. 116–19; Manuel Aguilera Gómez, *La Reforma Agraria en el desarrollo económico de México* (Mexico: Instituto Mexicano de Investigaciones Económicas, 1969), p. 50.

26. It is to be noted, however, that this question has not yet been adequately researched.

27. Meyer, *Problemas*, p. 118.

28. Charles Berry, "The Fiction and Fact of the Reform: The Case of the Central District of Oaxaca, 1856–1867," *Americas* 26 (January 1970): 281–83.

29. Ibid., p. 280.

30. McBride, *Land Systems*, p. 92.

31. Meyer, *Problemas*, pp. 21–24.

32. Francisco Calderón, "Los ferrocarriles," in *El Porfiriato. La vida económica*, pt. 2, in *Historia Moderna de México*, ed. Cosío Villegas, 7:491–502.

33. On the lottery established to support the Mexico-Toluca-Cuautitlan concession, see ibid., 690–91.

34. Antonio Kalixto Espinosa, "Emisíon de Billetes del Ferrocarril San Luis Potosí-Tampico, Años 1878–1880," *Archivos de Historia Potosina* 1 (April–June 1970): 219–23.

35. Matías Romero, *Report of the Secretary of Finance of the United States of Mexico . . . Rectifying the Report of the Hon. John W. Foster . . . to Mr. Carlisle Mason* (New York: G. Putnam, 1880), pp. 54–62; David M. Pletcher, *Rails, Mines and Progress: Seven American Promoters in Mexico, 1867–1911* (Ithaca: Cornell University Press, 1958), pp. 35–105.

36. Spread over the thirty-four years from 1877 to 1910, the process of concentrating landownership involves an almost impenetrable pattern of cumulative dispossession. Clearly, the marked political stability of the *Porfiriato* made the process all the more easy. And Porfirian stability itself was reinforced by the extension and consolidation of the hacienda as well as by the economic stimulus of Mexico's growing links to the world economy.

37. Paul Friedrich, *Agrarian Revolt in a Mexican Village* (Englewood Cliffs, N.J.: Prentice Hall, 1970), pp. 43–44.

38. Ibid., p. 46.

39. The concession was authorized by Congress on June 1, and issued to the company by the Fomento ministry on September 13, 1880. The concession specified the construction of a narrow gauge railroad from Mexico City to Laredo on the U.S. border. The company was also authorized to construct a line from a point between Maravatío and Morelia through Zamora and La Piedad to the Pacific Coast port of Manzanillo. On July 15, 1880, the company acquired a concession previously issued to the government of the state of Michoacán in 1877 for a branch line from Pátzcuaro to Morelia and Salamanca. See *Memoria (1877–1882)*, 4 vols. (Mexico: Secretaría de Fomento, 1885), 3:348–49.

40. For a report of construction towards Pátzcuaro from Acambaro, see *Memoria (1883–1885)*, 5 vols. (Mexico: Secretaría de Fomento, 1887), 3:276.

41. Freidrich, *Agrarian Revolt*, p. 44.

42. Barrington Moore, Jr., *Social Origins of Dictatorship and Democracy: Lord and Peasant in the Making of the Modern World* (Boston: Beacon Press, 1966), passim.

LIBERAL PARTY
PROGRAM, 1906

In 1900 the first significant stirrings of revolt began to agitate Mexico. During that year a middle-class liberal, Camilo Arriaga, formed the Liberal Club of San Luis Potosí. The original concern of the members was to restore nineteenth-century liberalism. Thus they criticized the regime for abandoning democracy and free enterprise and for allowing a resurgence of clericalism. Soon liberal clubs were forming in other parts of the country and intellectuals were agitating for reform. By 1905 one of the more radical intellectuals, Ricardo Flores Magón, had established the revolutionary Partido Liberal Mexicano (PLM) and was instigating rebellion from his exile in St. Louis, Missouri. After the Cananea strike on June 1, 1906, his organization issued a public manifesto and program outlining their plan for revolution and reform. The program called for the elimination of militarism, attacked the properties of the Church and foreigners, declared certain rights of labor, and promised confiscation of unproductive lands and restoration of the ejido. *The document is of special interest because it signaled the start of serious revolt and because portions of it were incorporated into the Constitution of 1917.*

The notes accompanying this document were prepared by James D. Cockcroft, a professor of sociology at Livingston College, Rutgers University. Professor Cockcroft is a specialist in comparative revolution and comparative sociology.

PROGRAM[1] OF THE LIBERAL PARTY (PLM), 1906

Constitutional Reforms

1. Reduction of the Presidential term to four years.*
2. No re-election for President and state governors.* These

Reprinted from James D. Cockcroft, *Intellectual Precursors of the Mexican Revolution*, pp. 239–45, by permission of The University of Texas Press. Copyright © James D. Cockcroft, 1968.

public officials can be newly elected only after the elapse of two terms following the ones in which they have served.

3. The Vice President shall not carry out legislative functions or any other duty resulting from popular election, but he shall be allowed to perform duties assigned by the Executive.

4. Elimination of obligatory military service and the establishment of a National Guard. Those who serve in the standing Army will do so freely and voluntarily. Military ordinance will be reviewed in order to remove from it anything considered oppressive or humiliating to the dignity of man, and the incomes of those who serve in the national militia will be increased.**

5. Reform and regulation of Articles 6 and 7 of the Constitution, removing restrictions that private life and public safety impose upon the freedom of speech and press, but declaring that falsehoods involving fraud, blackmail, and lawless immorality will be punished.*[2]

6. Abolition of the death penalty except for those who are traitors to their country.**[3]

7. Increase in the responsibility of public officials, imposing severe prison sentences on offenders.*

8. Restoration of the territory of Quintana Roo to Yucatán.**

9. Elimination of military tribunals in time of peace.*

Improvement and Development of Education

10. Multiplication of elementary schools,** on such a scale that educational institutions closed down because they belong to the Clergy can be advantageously replaced.*

11. Obligation to provide completely secular education in all schools of the Republic, be they public or private; those directors who do not comply shall be held responsible.*

12. Compulsory education to the age of fourteen; the government shall be responsible for providing protection in whatever form possible to poor children who, because of their poverty, might lose out on the benefits of an education.*

13. Good salaries for elementary schoolteachers.**

14. Obligatory instruction in the rudiments of arts and crafts and military instruction for all schools of the Republic, with special attention to civic instruction, which today receives so little notice.*

Foreigners

15. Prescribe that foreigners, by the sole act of acquiring real estate, lose their former nationality and become Mexican citizens.**

16. Prohibit Chinese immigration.**4

Restrictions on Abuses by the Catholic Clergy

17. Churches are considered to be business concerns, and must, therefore, keep accounts and pay corresponding taxes.*

18. Nationalization, according to law, of real estate held in trusteeship for the Clergy.*

19. Increase in the punishment that the Reform Laws decree for violators of the same.*

20. Elimination of schools run by the Clergy.*

Capital and Labor

21. Establishment of a maximum of eight hours of work a day and a minimum salary* on the following scale: a peso for each part of the country in which the average salary is less than a peso, and more than a peso for those regions in which the cost of living is higher and one peso would not suffice to save the workers from poverty.5

22. Regulation of domestic service and servants in residences.**

23. Adoption of measures preventing employers from evading application of maximum time and minimum salary to piecework.**

24. Prohibition of employment of children under fourteen years of age.**6

25. All owners of mines, factories, shops, etc., must maintain the best hygienic conditions on their properties and must service danger areas in a manner guaranteeing the safety of the lives of workers.*

26. All employers or rural property owners must provide hygienic lodgings for employees when the nature of their work necessitates their receiving shelter from said employers or proprietors.*

27. All employers must pay indemnity for accidents occurring on the job.*7

28. All debts of rural day laborers to their employers are hereby declared null and void.**8

29. Adoption of measures to prevent landowners from abusing sharecroppers.*

30. All landowners and overseers of fields and houses must compensate tenants for necessary improvements which tenants make on their property.**

31. All employers, under pain of severe penalty, must pay employees in cash; fining of workers, deducting from their day wages, delaying payment of set wages for more than one week, and refusing to pay immediately a worker leaving a job his accumulated earnings, are all prohibited and subject to punishment; company stores [*tiendas de raya*] are outlawed.*

32. All enterprises or businesses must hire only a minimum of foreigners. At no time may a Mexican be paid less than a foreigner doing equivalent work in the same establishment, and Mexicans must never be paid in a manner different from the way in which a foreigner is paid.**[9]

33. Sunday is an obligatory day of rest.*

Lands[10]

34. Landowners must make all the land they possess productive; any extension of land that the owner leaves unproductive will be confiscated by the State, and the State will employ it in accordance with the following articles.*

35. For those Mexicans residing abroad who so solicit, the Government will provide repatriation, paying the transportation cost of the trip and allotting them lands that they can cultivate.**

36. The Government will grant land to anyone who solicits it, without any conditions other than that the land be used for agricultural production and not be sold. The maximum amount of land that the Government may allot to one person will be fixed.*

37. In order that the benefits in this section should extend not only to a few who have resources for cultivating land but also to the poor who lack resources, the State will either create or develop an agricultural bank which will lend money to poor farmers at low interest rates, payable in installments.**

Taxes

38. Abolition of the present tax on corporations and on individuals, leaving the Government the task of studying the best means of lowering the stamp tax until it becomes possible to abolish it.**

39. Elimination of tax on capital of under a hundred pesos, exempting from this privilege churches and other businesses considered harmful or unworthy of guarantees granted to useful enterprises.**

40. Increase in the tax rate on usury, luxury items, and vices [e.g., alcohol and tobacco—JDC], and decrease in taxes on basic staples. The rich shall not be permitted to make arrangements with the Government to pay less taxes than those imposed by the law.**

General Points

41. To make practicable the writ of *amparo*, simplifying the procedures.*11

42. Restitution of the free-trade zone.**

43. Establishment of civil equality for all children of the same father, eliminating the differences between legitimate and illegitimate children which the present law now establishes.**

44. Establishment, whenever possible, of reform colonies, instead of the jails and penitentiaries in which offenders suffer punishment today.**

45. Elimination of political bosses [*jefes politicos*].**

46. Reorganization of municipalities [*municipios*] which have been suppressed or weakened, and strengthening of municipal power.*

47. Measures to eliminate or restrict usury, pauperism, and scarcity of basic staples.**

48. Protection of the Indian race.**

49. Establishment of ties of union with Latin American countries.**

50. Upon the triumph of the Liberal Party, properties of public officials who make themselves rich under the present dictatorship will be confiscated, and these properties will be applied toward the fulfillment of the section on Lands—especially to restore to Yaquis, Mayas, and other tribes, communities, or individuals the land of which they have been dispossessed*—and toward amortization of the National Debt.

51. The first National Congress to function after the fall of the dictatorship will annul all reforms of our Constitution made by the Government of Porfirio Díaz; it will reform our Magna Carta, wherever necessary to put into effect this Program; it will create laws

necessary for the same end; it will regulate articles of the Constitution and of other laws that so require, and it will study all those things considered of interest to the Fatherland, whether or not they are enunciated in the present Program, and it will reinforce the points listed herein, especially in the matter of Labor and Land.

Special Clause

52. It remains the duty of the Recruitment Board of the Liberal Party to address itself as quickly as possible to all foreign governments, informing them, in the name of the party, that the Mexican people do not want any more debts burdening the Fatherland and that, therefore, it will not recognize any debts that the dictatorship, under any form or pretext, thrusts upon the Nation, whether by contracting loans, or by recognizing, too late, previous obligations which no longer have legal value.**

Reform, Liberty, and Justice

St. Louis, Missouri, July 1, 1906

President, RICARDO FLORES MAGON
Vice-President, JUAN SARABIA
Secretary, ANTONIO I. VILLARREAL
Treasurer, ENIRIQUE FLORES MAGON
First Committeeman, PROFESSOR LIBRADO RIVERA
Second Committeeman, MANUEL SARABIA
Third Committeeman, ROSALIO BUSTAMANTE

NOTES

1. A single asterisk indicates that the provision called for in the PLM Program was later adopted in the 1917 Constitution; double asterisks indicate that the provision called for in the Program went further in its demands than those incorporated into the 1917 Constitution.

2. The PLM Program left out freedom of travel (Article 2 of the 1917 Constitution). Also, although implicit in Point 5, the Program did not mention freedom of assembly (Article 9 of the Constitution).

3. Article 22 of the Constitution allowed the death penalty for other crimes: "The death penalty for political crimes is likewise prohibited; and for other types of offense, it may be imposed only upon traitors to the Fatherland

in a foreign war, parricides, homicides by treachery, premeditation, or gain, incendiaries, kidnapers, highway robbers, pirates, and offenders who have committed grave crimes of a military character."

4. The Constitution permitted forigners to hold properties if they were granted concessions by the State "provided they agree before the Ministry of Foreign Relations to consider themselves as nationals with respect to said properties and not to invoke the protection of their governments in reference to same; should they fail to respect the agreement, they will be penalized by having to return to the Nation the properties they may have acquired. Under no consideration may foreigners acquire direct ownership over lands and waters within a zone one hundred kilometers wide along the Nation's borders, or fifty kilometers along the coast" (Article 27). Subsoil rights were reserved to the nation (Article 27). Foreigners could be sent out of Mexico on a simple order from the President and were forbidden to participate in the nation's politics (Article 33). PLM Point 15, though briefer, is more restrictive of foreigners in economic matters. The prejudice against Chinese in Point 16 reflected the sentiment of a large number of Mexico's northerners, who viewed Chinese immigrant laborers as unfair competition, or "dirty," or convenient scapegoat for their angers. In the "exposition" of its Program, the PLM explained the ban on Chinese immigration as a step toward eliminating wage competition of Chinese workers, who "accept the lowest wages."

5. The Constitution did not fix the amount of the minimum wage, leaving that to the discretion of municipal and state commissions (Article 123, p. IX). However, the Constitution went beyond the PLM by providing for overtime pay (Article 123, pt. XI) and for profit-sharing, amounts to be determined in the same fashion as the minimum wage (Article 123, pts. VI and IX).

6. The Constitution was much weaker (Article 123, pts. II and III): "Unhealthful or dangerous work is forbidden for women in general and for youth less than sixteen years of age. Industrial night work is also forbidden for these two classes; and they may not work in commercial establishments beyond ten o'clock at night. Young persons more than twelve and less than sixteen years of age shall have six hours as a maximum day's work. The labor of children under twelve years of age is not subject to contract." On the other hand, the Constitution made generous provisions for pregnant women (Article 23, pt. V).

7. The Constitution extended these points slightly, to include provision for housing, medical care, markets, recreation, and municipal services, under certain conditions (Article 123, pts. XII and XIII). Also, social security was encouraged, although not instituted (Article 123, pt. XXIX), and employment agencies were provided for (Article 123, pt. XXV).

8. The PLM Program omitted strictures against monopolies (Article 28 of the Constitution) and said nothing about abolishing slavery and titles of nobility (Articles 2 and 12 of the Constitution), although PLM's Points 28 and 29 served, in part, the latter purpose.

9. The Constitution's Article 32 was much less stringent. Curious omissions from the PLM Program were the right to form labor unions and cooperatives and the right to strike (Article 123, pts. XVI, XVII, and XXX, of the Constitution).

10. The brevity of this section is misleading. The PLM's Point 50 provided for the restitution of *ejidos*, as did the "Exposition" preceding the Program: "The restitution of *ejidos* to those communities that have been dispossessed of them is a matter of clear justice." By not raising the question of indemnity for expropriated lands, the PLM went further than the 1917 Constitution, which provided for indemnity (Article 27). In other agrarian respects, the PLM Program was equal to the later Constitution, or went beyond it, as indicated by double asterisks.

11. There is no exact translation of *juicio de amparo*, which in Mexico is roughly equivalent to a writ of appeal.

MADERO'S MANIFESTO AND
THE PLAN de SAN LUIS POTOSÍ

In 1906, the same year that the PLM issued its manifesto (see Reading 23), Francisco Madero broke off his association with Ricardo Flores Magón. Madero, a member of a wealthy hacendado family in Monterrey, believed that the PLM under Flores Magón's leadership was becoming too radical, anarchistic, and unrealistic in its demands. As a result, Madero soon inherited the leadership and organization of two more moderate political groups, the Nationalist Democratic party and the National Anti-reelectionist party. In June 1910, he was sent to prison in San Luis Potosí for opposing the election of Díaz. Escaping on October 6, he fled to San Antonio, Texas, where he issued his manifesto "To the American People" and his plan for a new government. The manifesto, predated October 5, was directed as much against Vice-President Ramón Corral as President Díaz. It declared the recent elections illegal and called for a November uprising. Although Article 3 of the Plan de San Luis Potosí promised some vague agrarian reforms, Madero's revolt was primarily a middle-class one which sought modest political reforms rather than social revolution. However, Madero's revolt attracted many agrarians and workers who would not be contented with a simple reformist government and who would continue the struggle of revolution after 1910.

[Extracts—Translation]

OUR BELOVED LAND has come to one of those historic moments when extreme sacrifices must be made for liberty and justice. . . . An intolerable tyranny oppresses us, with no alternative but a shameful peace based on might instead of right. . . . obedient to the single will,

Reprinted from the U.S. Department of State, *Papers Relating to the Foreign Relations of the United States (1911)* (Washington: Government Printing Office, 1918), pp. 351–52.

or caprice of Gen. Porfirio Díaz, who in his long administration has shown his chief aim to be his own continuance in power at whatever cost. . . . The evil of such a government, under which organized expression of opinion is impossible, was greatly aggravated by the determination of Gen. Díaz to name his successor, and by his choice of Señor Ramón Corral as that successor the evil has now become unbearable. Accordingly many Mexicans, with no recognized political standing—for no man during these last 36 years could acquire it—have resolved to regain for the people their sovereignty.

We who have so resolved have organized, among others, the National Anti-reelectionist Party, whose slogan is "An honest ballot and no second term." The two principles comprised by this slogan are the only ones whose application can save the Republic from a dangerous extension of the dictatorship which grows daily more despotic and immoral.

The Mexican people have rallied to the standard of this party, sent their delegates to the national convention, which it shares with the Nationalist Democratic Party, and nominated Dr. Francisco Vázquez Gómez and me for Vice President and President. . . . My campaign was a triumphal march, for the magic words "An honest ballot and no reelection" electrified the people throughout the country and made them resolve to put those two principles into effect. The moment, therefore, came when Gen. Díaz perceived the situation and, realizing that he could not meet me to advantage in a lawful contest, put me in prison before the election, which was fraudulently conducted; violence, even to the filling of the jails with unoffending freemen, being employed to enforce the frauds.

The Mexican people protested against the illegality of that election, and in doing so employed, each in its proper turn, every recourse offered by the law of the land, going finally before Congress, hopeless as it was to do so; for the people well know that that unlawful body obeys implicitly the will of Gen. Díaz. . . . They knew, indeed, that in following me at all outrage awaited them; but nevertheless, for liberty's sake, they went with admirable stoicism to the polls, ready to face any affront.

It was necessary to take those fruitless steps—party organization, appearance at the polls, conduct of the election strictly within the prescribed procedure. By this orderly conduct we expected to show to the world that the Mexican people are able to use the instruments of democracy. They were, however, not allowed to use them; and they clearly show by their present attitude that they know I should have been elected if their electoral rights had been respected, and that they do not recognize the Government of Gen. Díaz.

By virtue of this knowledge and attitude, by virtue of the national will, I hereby declare the recent elections illegal and the Republic, therefore, without a legitimate government. I hereby provisionally assume the Presidency of the Republic until the people shall have nominated, according to law, their governing officials. In order to do so, they will have to remove from power the audacious usurpers, and I should display a dishonorable weakness and a betrayal of them were I to fail to lead those that have trusted me and by force of arms compel Gen. Díaz to respect the will of the nation.

The present Government, although deriving from violence and fraud, will enjoy up to the 30th of November next a certain aspect of legality in the regard of foreign nations, since it has been tolerated by the Mexican people. But it is imperative that the new administration, deriving from the fraud of the old, shall be prevented from usurping and entering into power, or shall, at least, find most of the nation in arms against it.

Therefore I appoint 6 o'clock of Sunday night, the 20th of November next, as the time for an armed uprising, according to the following—

PLAN

1. The elections for President and Vice President of the Republic, Justices of the Federal Supreme Court, and Deputies and Senators, held in June and July of this year, to be declared void.

2. The present Government of Gen. Díaz to be ignored, and likewise ignored all the authorities whose power should derive from the people.

3. To avoid as far as possible the disorder inherent in all revolutionary movements, all laws are to be kept in force except those that manifestly would counteract the principles herein proclaimed; except also the laws and decrees that sanction the fiscal acts of the Díaz administration: *Provided*, That the obligations of that Government contracted with foreign Governments and companies before the 20th of next November are to be respected. . . . Proceedings whereby lands have been unlawfully seized are to be subject to review, and if

found abusive of the law of the lands are to be restored to the rightful owner, together with indemnities for damages suffered: *Provided,* That where, before the date hereof, lands thus seized have passed into the possession of a third party, the former rightful owner will receive indemnity only, to be paid by those for whose benefit the seizure was made.

4. Besides the constitution and existing laws, it is hereby declared that the principle of *no reelection* of President or Vice President of the Republic, governors of States, and presidents of municipalities is a part of the supreme law pending the appropriate amendment of the constitution.

5. I hereby assume the character of Provisional President of the United Mexican States, with the power to make war against the usurping Government of Gen. Díaz. As soon as the national capital and more than half of the States of the Federation are under the control of the people the Provisional President will call nation-wide special elections, to occur 30 days after the call, and will deliver his office to the President-elect as soon as the result of the election is known.

6. The Provisional President before surrendering his office to his duly elected successor will report to the Congress of the Union the use he shall have made thereof.

7. On and after November 20 next, 6 o'clock p.m., all citizens of the Republic will take up arms to oust from power the present authorities. . . .

8. When the authorities make resistance, they are to be compelled by force of arms to respect the popular will, but in such cases the laws of war are to be rigorously observed. Especial attention is directed to the prohibition of the use of expansive bullets and the execution of prisoners. Attention is also called to the duty of every Mexican to respect the persons and property of foreigners.

9. Such authorities as resist the materialization of this Plan will be imprisoned and held for trial before the courts upon the termination of the revolution. . . .

An honest ballot. No second term.

FRANCISCO I. MADERO.

San Luis Potosí, October 5, 1910.

PUBLIC OPINION, THE CIENTÍFICOS, AND DÍAZ IN 1911

José Ives Limantour

José Ives Limantour (1854–1935) was born and educated in Mexico City. In 1893 he became minister of finance, a post he held until Madero's revolt forced his resignation in May 1911. A financial genius, Limantour is usually given credit for much of the economic progress that characterized the Porfiriato. In the 1890s, under Limantour's direction, the Mexican national budget showed a surplus for the first time in modern history. Limantour retired the internal debt, balanced the budget, and established Mexico's national credit and banking system. But as a result of the international financial panic of 1907, Limantour and Mexico found themselves in trouble. By 1910 Mexico was suffering from serious financial instability, reflected in part by a soaring inflation, a decline in export prices, and weaknesses in the central banking system.

Because of these difficulties (and perhaps to get him out of the country during an election year) Limantour was sent on a financial mission to Europe. Purposely by-passing the bankers of New York City (who already had too much influence in Mexico), Limantour attempted to refund Mexico's debts and negotiate new lands in Paris. Upon his return to Mexico in March 1911 he was well aware of the precarious position of Díaz's government and the people's loss of confidence in that government. His discussions with Díaz finally persuaded the president to reform his government, leading to the resignation of all the cabinet members except Limantour and Manuel González Cosío. His own refusal to resign brought him criticism and stirred public anger. Finally, on May 24, 1911, he and Díaz were forced to resign and go into exile in Paris. Díaz died there in 1915. Limantour died twenty years later.

The following selection is Limantour's account of public opinion in March 1911 and of his discussions with Díaz concerning his resignation from the cabinet. Limantour attempted to dissociate himself from the other científicos in the cabinet, especially after they had fallen into disrepute. Note Limantour's awareness of public discontent, an awareness that Díaz did not share. This reading provides valuable insight into the issues of the day, at least from the perspective of one of Díaz's most important "establishment" figures.

Reprinted from José Ives Limantour, *Apuntes sobre mi vida pública* (Mexico: Editorial Porrúa, 1965), pp. 229–39, by permission of the publishers. Translated by Juarez Mazzone.

PUBLIC OPINION IN MEXICO IN MARCH, 1911. Attitude of the President toward the "Científicos." My situation with respect to them. Resignation of the Cabinet.

The government did not gain anything more from the victory of Casas Grandes than a respite of two or three weeks, of which, naturally, it took little or no advantage. The effect on the morale of the seditionists and the sympathizers of the revolution was very small, since in a short time the uprisings and violent demonstrations of the opposition spread to many parts of the country; and furthermore, the general population and the supporters of the Government were very far from recovering their confidence. The latter, upon seeing that the battle had not ended the armed movement, understood the great change that had occurred in the public attitude, that from conservative, which was the general tone of things, it was moving away rapidly in its words and deeds from the Chief-of-State and all those that belonged to the government group; and thus, the uneasiness took root.

From the moment of my arrival in the country, I noticed the great change that had occurred in public opinion during my absence. Generals Don Gerónimo Treviño and Don José María Mier made me aware of the gravity of the situation during the many hours that the train was detained at their command in Monterrey, because of the report that they received that a group of insurgents was lying in wait for me a little beyond Saltillo. The attitude of my aforementioned friends, who always had my confidence because of their loyalty, experience and calm, profoundly impressed me. But I was even more impressed by the stories of various Cabinet colleagues and personal friends, who came out to greet me, concerning the policy of the President, the state of the country and the enormous agitation that there was everywhere. But what surpassed anything I might have imagined regarding surprises, was the spectacle of the enthusiastic demonstrations of sympathy, and at the same time anguish and hope, with which thousands of people of all social and political groups received me on the morning of March 20th in the Mexico City train station. Everyone wanted to talk to me, as if a favorable solution for the situation depended on me, to tell me what they thought about the aspirations of the country and how to attain them. One didn't have to be very observant to note the immense confusion and the great feeling of deception that reigned then in all Mexico, even among most loyal supporters of the Government; and in the midst of such great confusion only two things could be clearly made out: a great uneasiness and the loss of confidence in the Government.

As I went about talking to all types of people, in my home as well as in public places, in the Ministry and even in the Presidential palace, my first impressions were more and more confirmed; and despite the alarm that the super-excitement of some and demoralization of others produced in me, I must confess that what was about to cloud completely my judgement and make me lose my calm, was the great diversity of opinions, demands and desires with which I found myself faced and which made completely impossible the formation of a plan that might be based on the judgement or the aspirations of a large enough group of well intentioned and well known people. It pains me to say it, but if one desideratum stood apart from the ideas expressed by the people I spoke to, it was only that of a total change in policy and people, including the President of the Republic himself. They only thought about tearing down and not rebuilding; everyone talked about removing officials from their posts, but when it came time to propose their substitutes, discord reigned. Nevertheless, in spite of their preferences, they put before all other considerations the desire for change of any sort, be what it may, good or bad, it made no difference, and this almost sick super-excitation existed, sometimes disguised, other times frank and open, even among people who visited the President and his family in their own home. On more than one occasion I had to intervene very rudely to stop the scandalous talk of some people who passed themselves off as friends of the family and declared themselves openly in favor of the retirement of General Díaz.

(It would be appropriate here to describe with greater detail and more vividly the state of exhaltation and restlessness that reigned in Mexico toward the end of March, and principally the great loss of popularity and prestige that had been suffered by the President, whose resignation was being asked for every day by a growing number of people.)

All the other reports and arguments about the situation were, of course, surpassed in pessimism by those of the members of the Cabinet and other friends who came out to meet my train near San Luis Potosí. They saw the advent of the revolution as formidable and irresistible and severely criticized the policies of General Díaz. They told that the President had no choice but to gradually remove from the government the most well-known men of the "Científicos," who in a special way, were a target for the opposition, and this would show the entire Nation that these men didn't have the slightest influence on him. To back up their statements they recounted a long series of events that had happened during my absence, many of which I did not know about, and they attributed them to the passive attitude of General Díaz who didn't want to make any changes in his policies until my arrival in Mexico City, fearing that the "Científicos," finding themselves out of the Government, might begin to attack it, in this way increasing the general discontent.

These friends were entirely convinced that any kind of collective collaboration with the Government was already impossible, not only because of the aforementioned reason, but also because of the lack of a firm, well defined policy which, utilizing the healthy elements of the Nation, might have a chance to end the crisis. Summing up, the impressions they communicated to me were the following: The country was moving toward an abyss without any possibility of stopping, given the chaotic situation to which we had come, in great part, because of the ambivalent policies of the President; and there was no other choice open to the "Científicos,"—since it no longer was up to them to change the situation and they would never oppose General Díaz—than to withdraw completely from politics, regaining, each of them, his own freedom of action, a resolution that we all made on the very train that took us toward the Capital and that one of us summed up in the word, "disperse," which we repeated several times as we took leave of each other.

While under the influence of these impressions, I had my first interview with the President, in whom I did not take long in detecting the firm intention of removing the "Científicos" from public life. Since this idea fit so well in my scheme of thought and that of my friends, I didn't object in the slightest; and in order not to offend any of his Ministers, he requested that I be the one to inform the Cabinet of the need for them to present their resignations, which they did immediately and willingly. But there was great disagreement when I told him of my intention of also leaving the Government. With a tenacity and energy which because of the apparent wear and tear of age he didn't seem capable of, General Díaz tried to dissuade me, claiming with thousands of reasons that I do not need to repeat here, that I was not the same case as the others, but rather in entirely different circumstances which, far from disqualifying me, demanded my efforts to end the crisis. For three days, morning, afternoon and night, we discussed this matter, the President using every argument that his singular ability for winning this type of debate could muster up, until, as a last recourse, he concluded, telling me in a manner and tone which I could not be sure were of resentment, concern or the anger which had overtaken him, that it would be for him "like a stab in the back" which he would be getting if I, before the whole world, after finding out in a few days how the situation was going, discarded the portfolio that with general blessing I had kept for eighteen years, especially when everyone knew that I was returning from Europe, recalled by the President, to galvanize the forces of the government (after having taken the pulse of public opinion and the official attitude of the United States and taking into account what awaited me in the Republic with a readiness to straighten out the situation).

As hard as the comparison was for me which the President used in his eagerness to emphasize the damage that my resignation from the Government could cause him at this critical moment which he was going through, I managed to keep my calm, thinking about the consequences which might result from a decision taken by me impulsively, or which was founded only on selfish considerations; and we agreed to postpone the matter for the last time, but only for a few hours. In that interval the few people whom I told what was happening either opposed my giving in to the President's wishes or abstained from giving me advice; no one encouraged me towards an affirmative answer. Despite this, upon reviewing the reasons in favor of and against my resignation, I was very impressed with the candid declaration of the President that by resigning I would adversely affect the situation. A man of character and with the great responsibilities of Chief-of-State, such as General Díaz, never reveals his fears nor allows his political strategy to depend on the whims of another person. By telling me what he had, the President, because of this, did not allow me to have doubts about his absolute sincerity, and even less when some of his judgements on the nature of the crisis coincided very closely with my own. The illusion that I could do something, using the information I had collected as well as the support of a part of the enlightened public which was favorable toward me, and taking advantage of the unique opportunity that had been presented to make some reforms that for many years seemed to me indispensable, and at the same time might contribute towards the pacification of the country, influenced me a great deal, together with other considerations of a general nature to accede to what was being asked of me. But I could not be certain, examining well my own conscience, that the sentiments of affection, gratitude and loyalty toward General Díaz were not the predominant factors in my mind which brought me to assume the most terrible responsibility in my whole life. Let those who give little worth to these sentiments condemn me without mercy! As for the others, I hope that at least they will concede that the circumstances were extenuating.

When the public learned about the fall of the Cabinet and saw that with the exception of this writer all the Ministers reputed to be, correctly or incorrectly, "Científicos" had left the government, there was a great uproar that among not a few persons became real indignation because I had not joined the ministers who were leaving.

To a certain degree it can be explained that many of those who had not had occasion to be close to me and by what they heard or because of a personal fondness, or because of their participation in some government project, or other circumstances also not directly concerned with me, came to consider me as the party leader, and therefore believed that I was obliged to obey all the duties that such a situation would demand. Nevertheless, if they had considered that such a supposition could only be based on doubtful estimates and not on clear and precise facts, or on my own acts or words, some light of understanding might have broken through the cloudy appearances, and today the same people who censured me would understand the injustice of their charges.

In fact, on what was the belief that I was the leader or one of the leaders of the "Científico" party based? Of course, in order not to get into details that lead to a long discussion I will ignore the argument that the oft mentioned political party has never existed except in the imagination of those who wished to give the appearance of a political body to a certain number of individuals to thus fight them more easily before public opinion, making this group the target for every shot; and I simply answer the question saying: this belief is only due to the fact that I had been among the first to sign the Manifesto of the Liberal Union in April, 1892 and we were designated ironically with that name, "Científicos," and that I took part in the Cabinet of General Díaz, thus occupying an outstanding position which, I must say in passing, I did not owe to the circumstance of being one of the signers of the above mentioned manifesto, but rather to considerations of a merely personal nature that preceded the Liberal Union. As hard as they may look, no other explanation will be found for the legend that I am trying to destroy the country. As it is well known concerning all militant politicians, no matter what their philosophy, the center of the activities of the "Científicos" was someplace else and the instructions that in certain circumstances were given to friends that requested them never came from me.

My participation in what one might call the politics of the group was very secondary and almost always accidental. It occurred in simple conversations with some friends that were not always the same and in which what was said or agreed, all very informally, did not have the slightest hint of conferences or resolutions of a group that proposed to follow its own line of conduct. There were not lacking, of course, in those meetings, either initiatives or censures, but matters didn't pass that point, because of our firm and sincere support of the President and the conviction that any sharp discord would be contrary to the interests of the country. This kept us from taking propagandistic or organizational steps that might be interpreted unfavorably by him.

There is a world of difference between the position that I really occupied in the Government in relation to the "Científicos" and the one that the general public supposed. Few, very few, noted that my attitude could be amply explained by my ties, not with politics, but rather of an intellectual order, that joined me for many years with a small number of men who received the same training as I and were educated with the same socio-political doctrines; and the number is even smaller of those who haven't considered that neither by deeds, nor omissions, has my conduct given any reason for a false impression to be spread. Well then, have I ever been seen attending meetings where electoral questions, propaganda, etc. were being discussed, or chairing meetings, attending party rallies, accepting favors of a political nature, attempting to gain popularity, committing acts of real leadership? By chance, does anyone know from a credible source that I invited or employed anyone to work in my favor, or in the exclusive interest of the group; or that I have given money or materials with that objective; or that I have directed or fomented movements of public opinion, guiding them in a direction independent of that of the government? Is there anyone who can prove that the Department of the Treasury, while I was at its head, financed political newspapers, persecuted members of the opposition or directed the Government press in matters outside of its field? Has there been a single case of a Federal authority, or a State Governor or a simple Political Chief who has received letters or recommendations of mine favoring the interests of my supposed political friends? No, evidently no. But there is more, and it is not about abstentions but rather positive deeds. When in the organs of the opposition there was talk of maneuvers of mine to assure the triumph of the much talked about ghost-party, didn't I make the most definitive declarations through the press, denying all the reports about the political role attributed to me?

Applying a calm criteria to the facts and considerations mentioned, I believe that as intimate as my relations have been with several of the most well known "Científicos," and despite the fact that I have always been linked to them in political ideals and tendencies, they cannot justly attribute to me either the merits or mistakes, much less the power or responsibilities of the leadership of the group. I was one of many, but surely the least active, in spite of the fact that our opponents have attempted to see in my person the head of the group with the preconceived objective of attacking me as a member of the Cabinet to nullify more easily everyone.

If I had been only accused of having committed in good faith the error of remaining at the side of General Díaz, instead of resigning with the other Ministers who dropped out of the Cabinet, I would not feel, perhaps, on solid ground to argue; but my conduct on this point has been so severely judged especially by my own friends that for this reason it has seemed convenient not only in my own benefit but also in the interest of history to give at some length all the necessary explanations, so that each person might appear in the role that it was destined for him to play.

Before concluding the matter, I want to add a few words. Everyone knows of the magnitude and sincerity of the affection with which General Díaz honored me and that, naturally, this affection was returned by me with great enthusiasm. These deep sentiments of friendship confirmed by the endless number of honors and demonstrations of confidence that he tendered me, despite our differences of opinion in some matters, surely explain better than the personal merits that the President attributed to me, the tight bonds that joined me to him during so many years in a cooperative effort in which I was associated, perhaps to a greater degree than any other person, in his great work of national reconstruction. This consideration was, as has already been said in another part of this book, one of the most effective in bringing me to decide to join my fate to that of General Díaz in the difficult moments, knowing perfectly that I was going to displease my friends and take on many outside responsibilities without increasing the hope of obtaining the support of the majority of my fellow citizens in the policy of pacification that I was going to begin; and this, when I could have withdrawn tranquilly to my home, with very good reasons, leaving others to continue struggling and controlling the consequences of this struggle against so many agitators that rose up and prospered during my absence.

I know very well that the frank confession that I have just made will not absolve me of the sin of subduing in part, in favor of personal considerations, the most general and respectable considerations of a public nature. I have a clear conscience, nevertheless before such accusations, because besides everything that might be said about the way to serve the public best, whether it is working rigidly in a straight line, or seeking the points of least resistance to achieve one's objective with less difficulty, no one who knows the human heart can judge with impartiality my conduct in the incident of the change of Cabinet without taking into account the exceptional nature of the close relations that I am proud of having had with the greatest public figure in the history of our country, and which had such a strong influence on my determination not to break with him.

THE PORFIRIATO:
LEGEND AND REALITY

Daniel Cosío Villegas

It is fitting that the final selection in this anthology be an excerpt by the dean of Mexican historians, Daniel Cosío Villegas (1898–1976). Professor Cosío Villegas did more than any other contemporary Mexican scholar to promote the study of Mexico's culture, economy, and history. He did this in his capacities as president of El Colegio de México (a research and teaching institute), as founder of the Fondo de Cultura Económica (an outstanding publishing house for economic works), and as director of the Historia Mexicana *(Mexico's finest professional journal of Mexican history). Perhaps he made his most important contribution as general editor and contributor to the massive ten-volume* Historia moderna de México, *the standard reference on Mexico's history between 1867 and 1911.*

In the following passage, Cosío Villegas examines the legend of the Porfiriato as an age of consolidation in which Mexican nationality and political institutions were forged. Cosío Villegas questions the validity of these generalizations, arguing that nationalism had a long history before Díaz and that political institutions were dissolved rather than consolidated during the Porfiriato. Compare this account with preceding ones, especially Smith's argument about the development of economic nationalism during the Porfiriato and Turner's allegation about the origins of land confiscations (see Readings 12 and 18). If Cosío Villegas is correct about the antecedents of nationalism, then perhaps, contrary to Turner's account, many of the "negative" features of the Díaz era (like the plight of the Indian) also had their antecedents during earlier administrations.

THE PORFIRIATO must have been, as the legend has it, an era of consolidation. The tranquility of the period suggests that divisions or differences were neither so violent nor so irreconcilable as to lead to war. It

Reprinted by permission from Lewis Hanke, ed., *History of Latin American Civilization,* vol. 2 (Boston: Little, Brown and Co., 1967), pp. 295–300; originally published as Daniel Cosio Villegas, "El porfiriato, era de consolidación," *Historia Mexicana* 13 (1973): 76–87.

was, moreover, an era in which means of communication improved significantly, thereby increasing opportunities for Mexicans to become acquainted and have contact with one another. Finally, one suspects that consolidation was also furthered by the undeniably authoritarian character of the regime, for extraordinary power makes itself felt on everything and everyone, impressing a uniform cast on the entire society.

Such must have been the Porfiriato. To be certain, however, one would have to ask whether the process of consolidation was general or selective. According to the legend, the regime was notably successful in promoting the consolidation of two areas at least: Mexican nationality and institutions. . . .

The consolidation of the Mexican nation has been the result of a very long process. Perhaps it dates from the incipient imperialism of the Aztecs, which . . . imposed some unity on the political and cultural diversity of the numerous Indian groups of the period. The conquest and domination of the Spaniards, despite the elements of profound disparity which they introduced, gave to the native civilizations elements of community, language, religion, and government which they had hitherto lacked. The consequences did not take long to appear, for the first clear manifestations of a spiritual nationalism were evident in the eighteenth century. But it was above all during that calumniated first half of the nineteenth century that the process of national formation was accelerated, precisely because of the misfortunes that befell the newly born nation. . . . The war with the United States and the very loss of territory helped, like few other events, to consolidate our nationality, first through the sensation of danger and the feeling of hatred for the aggressor—sentiments which constitute a negative force but a tremendously effective one when a weak people is involved. Secondly, no matter how unjust and painful the loss of half of our national territory was, it is undeniable that it drastically reduced the material and spiritual task of forging the nation, as well as the time that would be needed to accomplish this task. Finally, this unhappy war also taught us that when our internal struggles passed certain limits of rancor and persistence, the danger of aggression and the irreparable loss of the nation would become real and substantial.

It does not seem that the country made use of this sad but beneficial lesson, for in a very short time, during the wars of the Reform and Intervention, the two contenders, blinded by immediate partisan interests, appealed for foreign aid. But this occurred for the last time because it became apparent that with the aid came the foreign soldier, that is, the flesh-and-blood enemy of Mexican nationhood. These two wars fought so bitterly that, by way of a reaction, they created a conciliatory climate that bore fruit throughout the entire period of the Restored Republic. . . .

[By 1876], then, Mexico, as a result of so many painful and seemingly sterile struggles, was beginning to gather the positive fruits of its misfortunes; it had gone a long way toward placing general interests before partial interests.

Does all this mean that the Porfiriato did not contribute in any way to the task of consolidating the Mexican nation? By no means. It merely means that the process was lengthy, that it was initiated a long time before 1876, and that the principal direct contributions had been made previously. The contribution of the Porfiriato, while it was very important, seems to me to have had an indirect character. With the railroads, telegraph, and telephone, with the general improvement of communications and transportation, particularly of the press, the circulation of Mexicans, as well as of their wealth, ideas, and sentiments, also improved.

It is less easy to define and very difficult to assess another factor in the consolidation of the nation which appeared in a singularly active manner during the Porfirian age. Mexico had always lived under the thumb of regional caciques; accordingly, federalism had a reality that was political, social, and economic, as well as geographic and ethnic. Only Juárez emerged in 1867 as a great national figure; but the impossibility of preserving the unity of the liberal party and Juárez' need to lead his own faction in order to defend himself and prevail over the factions of Lerdo and Díaz made him lose to a large extent the general and superior character of a national figure. Díaz, on the other hand, less scrupulous in his political practices and born of a revolutionary coup and not of lawful elections, had far more liberty of action. Finding the field already sowed and blessed with better luck, he at length succeeded in putting an end to the regional caudillos and in transforming himself into the sole caudillo, that is, into the national caudillo. To this must be added the popular aura that Díaz always had, the memory of his glorious campaigns against the foreign invader, his very age, his granite-like physical appearance, and his conscious effort to acquire and exhibit the air of a man who was superior to petty and fleeting passion; his was the air of the guardian of the permanent interests of the country, the air of a monarch who receives homage not only from his own subjects but also from the outside world, the civilized world.

But Porfirio Díaz did not become merely a decorative national symbol, like the flag or anthems which evoke and exalt patriotic sentiments upon reaching the eyes or ears, not even in the more intellectual sense of serving as a symbol of national unity, like the English monarch. He was also authority, and in many respects the sole authority; he was power, and in many respects the sole power. Family disputes were laid before him, as well as disputes involving towns, authorities, or interests. All the organs of public power depended on him: legislatures, courts, judges, governors, political and military chiefs. Not only was he seen everywhere, like God, but he also made himself felt everywhere. . . .

There can be no doubt that, as the legend claims, juridical, economic, and social institutions were consolidated to some extent. One merely has to consider the peacefulness, prosperity, and longevity of the regime to admit this; when there is peace, wealth, and time, there are opportunities and resources for the undertaking of projects that in turbulent periods are left for "better times." Unfortunately, history requires more than generalities; it requires analysis and a body of facts.

With respect to juridical institutions, the work had already begun. The first great bodies of law antedated the Porfiriato: the constitution itself, the organic law of public instruction (1867), the law governing juries in criminal cases (1869), the organic law on the recourse of *amparo* (1869), the penal code (1871), the civil code (1871), the code of civil procedure (1872), the code pertaining to aliens (1876), etc. But these were few in number and limited in influence, in part because most of them could be applied only in the Federal District and in part because the conditions of the country were not sufficiently normal for their beneficial influence to be felt. During the Porfiriato, these same codes were revised, made more consistent, and complemented with new ones . . . while important legislation, such as the law on credit institutions, was also enacted. To this body of true juridical creation, there ought to be added the regulatory and administrative achievement. These gains placed the country on the path to a normal, regular existence, which in many respects became ideally impersonal. In addition, the law in general appeared to attain a respectability, a stature, that made it impervious to human negation or threats.

All this is very well, but how can one forget that political institutions are a part of juridical institutions? Can it be sustained that political institutions were consolidated during the Porfiriato? They simply disappeared, and something that does not exist is not susceptible of consolidation or dispersion.

In this matter there is no defense or qualification. No Porfirista—not even the most passionate, nor the most timid, nor the most shameful, nor the most cynical—has ever dared to affirm that Mexico progressed politically during the Díaz regime. This is the explanation of [Rafael de] Zayas Enríquez: the people of Mexico voluntarily ceded their political rights to Porfirio Díaz so that he might return them little by little as the Mexicans learned how to be free. This is the opinion of [Francisco] Bulnes: "it passes the limits of stupidity to assail General Díaz for not having done the impossible—to be a democratic president in a nation of slaves." . . .

According to Emilio Rabasa, one of the few Mexican political writers of true talent, "the dictatorship if Díaz was characterized, *above all,* by respect for *legal forms,* which he always preserved in order to keep alive in the people the sentiment that their laws were respected even though they were not enforced, and that they remained on the books so that they might recover their ascendancy in the not-too-distant future." This is the point that truly deserves investigation, for on it depends the answer to the question of whether political institutions were consolidated during the Porfiriato.

Is it possible to respect a law that is not enforced? Can a law which is not enforced remain in force? Can a law which is not enforced someday recover its ascendancy? To me, it is as clear as daylight that a law which is not enforced provokes mockery, compassion, but never respect; a law which is not enforced is a dead law, and what is dead can never remain in force; a law which is not enforced has no power and in consequence can never recover what it never had. Finally, to describe as the "not-too-distant future" an era which, like that of Díaz, lasted for thirty-five years is to forget that in so long a time a whole generation was born and raised in the delightful atmosphere of the law that is not enforced but is respected. I would say exactly the opposite of Rabasa: that nothing degrades and demoralizes a people so much as the constant, repeated, daily spectacle of the non-enforcement of the law. . . .

It is this attitude toward the law, especially the political laws, that indicates the gulf between Porfirio Díaz and the great liberals of the

Reform. The latter had a blind faith in the law as a pick-axe to strike down old and noxious institutions and in the law as a cherished mould for shaping new ones. For this reason they respected the law, and to preserve or change it, they were capable of risking their lives or their futures. . . .

Porfirio Díaz, who fought for the liberal cause from his boyhood, who once accused Juárez of conservatism, did not have that respect and veneration for the law which was the very essence of Mexican liberalism. For Díaz, the law was a dead letter and consequently lacked spirit. For him, the *fact* was the instrument of change, and the fact, of course, was power and might. Because he despised the law, he did not change it or trouble himself about it; he simply forgot it and sought power in the invincible fact of being stronger than everyone else. . . .

The conclusion of all this seems obvious to me, as well as logical. Some juridical institutions were consolidated during the Porfiriato, and some were not. Those that were consolidated were the secondary ones, while the major ones—the political institutions—simply disappeared.

SUGGESTED READINGS

The items suggested here do not include those already cited in the anthology, and are limited to recent publications. Individuals desiring a more complete list of works should refer to one of the standard histories of Mexico, such as Henry Bamford Parkes's *A History of Mexico* (Boston: Houghton Mifflin Co., 1969) or Charles C. Cumberland's *Mexico: The Struggle for Modernity* (Oxford and New York: Oxford University Press, 1968). The most complete and best-researched general history to date is Michael C. Meyer and William L. Sherman, *The Course of Mexican History* (New York: Oxford University Press, 1979). Each chapter is accompanied by a list of recommended studies in English, and there is a useful bibliography at the end of the text for those who read Spanish. Another excellent work on nineteenth- and early twentieth-century history is Jan Bazant's *A Concise History of Mexico from Hidalgo to Cárdenas, 1805–1940* (Cambridge: At the University Press, 1977).

The reader is also encouraged to use bibliographical aids like Charles C. Griffins, ed., *Latin America: A Guide to the Historical Literature* (Austin: University of Texas Press, 1971), pp. 376–93. Students interested in graduate study in Mexican history should become familiar with Richard E. Greenleaf and Michael C. Meyer, *Research in Mexican History* (Lincoln: University of Nebraska Press, 1973). See also Robert Potash, "The Historiography of Mexico since 1821," *Hispanic American Historical Review*, 40 (August 1966): 383–424. Spanish readers are urged to consult volume 15 of the *Historia Mexicana* for *Veinticinco años de investigación histórica en México*. Interpretative essays relating to nineteenth-century Mexican history can be found in the Oaxaca proceedings, *Investigaciónes contemporáneas sobre historia de México* (Mexico and Austin: UNAM, El Colegio de México, and the University of Texas Press, 1971).

Readers of Spanish will have no problem finding books that deal with aspects of Mexico's nineteenth-century history. Mexico City is a leading publishing center of such works. For example, SepSetentas, subsidized by the Secretaría de Educación Pública, published over three hundred volumes between 1971 and 1976, most of which relate to Mexican culture and history. Works published by SepSetentas on nineteenth-century Mexico include Enrique Florescano, *Estructura y problemas agrarios de México 1500–1821*; Fernando Díaz y Díaz, *Santa Anna y Juan Alvarez frente a frente*; Josefina Váquez de Knauth, *Mexicanos y norteamericanos ante la Guerra del 47*; Moisés González Navarro, *La Reforma y el Imperio*; Rafael de Zayas Enríquez, *Benito Juárez*; Jean Meyer, *Problemas campesinos y revueltas agrarias (1821– 1910)*; T. G. Powell, *El liberalismo y el campesinado en el centro de México (1850 a 1876)*; John M. Hart, *Los anarquistas mexicanos, 1860–1900*; and Abelardo Villegas, *Positivismo y Porfirismo*. For the Díaz period, the Fondo de Cultura Económica has published Ralph Roeder's two-volume *Hacia el México Moderno: Porfirio Díaz* (1973). For diplomatic relations during the early years of the Revolution, see Berta Ulloa's *La Revolución intervenida* (El Colegio de Mexico, 1971).

Recommended works in English include Karl M. Schmitt's study of United States–Mexican relations, *Mexico and the United States, 1821–1973: Conflict and Coexistence* (New York: John Wiley & Sons, 1974). Life in Santa Anna's Mexico is described by Fanny Calderón de la Barca in *Life in Mexico: The Letters of Fanny Calderón de la Barca*, edited by Howard T. Fisher and Marion Hall Fisher (1843; reprint ed., Garden City, N.Y.: Doubleday and Co., 1970). Students interested in the ideological struggle between liberals and conservatives should refer to Unit III of Joseph S. Tulchin, ed., *Problems in Latin American History: The Modern Period* (New York: Harper & Row, 1973). There one can find many primary documents, collected and edited by Charles A. Hale. Suggested readings for the Porfiriato include the following: Carlos B. Gill, ed., *The Age of Porfirio Díaz: Selected Readings* (Albuquerque: University of New Mexico Press, 1977); Anthony Bryan, *The Politics of the Porfiriato: A Research Review* (Bloomington: Latin American Studies Program, Indiana University, 1973); Barry Carr, *The Peculiarities of the Mexican North, 1880–1928*, Occasional Papers no. 4 (Institute of Latin-American Studies, University of Glasgow, 1971); Leopoldo Zea, *Positivism in Mexico* (Austin: University of Texas Press, 1974); Juan Gomez-Quiñones, *Sembradores Ricardo Flores Magón y El Partido Liberal Mexicano: A Eulogy and Critique* (Los

Angeles: UCLA, Aztlan Publications, 1973); and, for one of the better accounts of the Cananea strike, see C. L. Sonnichsen, *Colonel Greene and the Copper Skyrocket* (Tucson: University of Arizona Press, 1974).

All students of Mexican history should be aware of the wealth of material in periodical literature. Of special importance for Mexican history are the *Hispanic American Historical Review (HAHR), The Americas,* and *Historia Mexicana.* The names of other significant journals can be found in the *Academic Writer's Guide to Periodicals, I. Latin American Studies,* compiled and edited by Alexander S. Birkos and Lewis A. Tambs (Kent, Ohio: Kent State University Press, 1971). A selective sample of articles recently published in these journals include Hugh M. Hamill, Jr., "Royalist counterinsurgency in the Mexican War for Independence: The Lessons of 1811," *HAHR* 53 (August 1973): 470–89; Thomas Schoonover, "Mexican Cotton and the American Civil War," *Americas* 30 (April 1974): 429–47; John M. Hart, "Nineteenth Century Urban Labor Precursors of the Mexican Revolution: The Development of an Ideology," *Americas* 30 (January 1974): 297–318; William D. Raat, "Ideas and Society in Don Porfirio's Mexico," *Americas* 30 (July 1973): 32–53. In some instances an entire volume is devoted to a particular historical theme or era; for example, volume 54 (February 1974) of the *Hispanic American Historical Review* treats the role of labor and economic development during the Porfiriato, and volume 23 (April–June 1974) of the *Historia Mexicana* emphasizes the development and structure of the Mexican state. The importance of Cosío Villegas for Mexican historiography (see Reading 26) is reflected in Charles A. Hale's article, "The Liberal Impulse: Daniel Cosío Villegas and the *Historia moderna de México,*" *HAHR* 54 (August 1974): 477–98.

Because of current interests in audio visual materials, a few words about films and teaching are in order. The best guide to Latin American instructional and feature films is Jane M. Loy's *Latin America: Sights and Sounds, A Guide to Motion Pictures and Music for College Courses,* Consortium of Latin American Studies Program Publication no. 5 (Gainesville, Fla., 1973). See also the two reports by E. Bradford Burns printed by the Latin American Center at UCLA entitled *The Visual Dimension of Latin American Social History: Student Critiques of Eight Major Latin American Films* and *The Use of Film for the Study of Latin American Social History.* Two of the better-known periodicals in this area are *Film and History* and the *Film Quarterly.* See also J. A. S. Grenville, *Film as History: The Nature of Film Evidence* (Birmingham:

University of Birmingham, 1970). Films available for classroom use include *Juárez* (Distributor: Indiana University; accompanying the film is a book of readings, *Benito Juárez and the French Intervention in Mexico*, edited by Lewis Hanke), *The Forgotten Village* (Brandon Films, Hollywood), *North from Mexico* (Mass Communications, Inc.), and, at ten North American universities (Amherst, Buffalo, Connecticut, Iowa, Nebraska, Princeton, SUNY, Texas–Austin, Texas–El Paso, Tulane, and UCLA), the documentary of the Revolution, *Memorias de un Mexicano*.

Two volumes which discuss the teaching of Latin American history and studies are the *History Teacher* 2 (March 1969) and *New Directions in the Teaching and Research of Latin American Area Studies* (vol. 2 of the *Proceedings* of the Pacific Coast Council on Latin American Studies, 1972). For public school teachers, *Teaching about Latin America* (Albany: State Education Department, 1972) is especially recommended. An earlier and still valuable essay is Lewis Hanke's "Unthinkable Thoughts," in his edition of *History of Latin American Civilization: The Modern Age* (Boston: Little, Brown & Co., 1967), pp. 510–15; a critical response by Gunnar Mendoza appears in the same volume, pp. 516–23.

Index